D1468783

The Inner World of Money

The Inner World of Money

Taking Control of Your Financial Decisions and Behaviors

Marty Martin

 PRAEGER

AN IMPRINT OF ABC-CLIO, LLC
Santa Barbara, California • Denver, Colorado • Oxford, England

Copyright 2012 by ABC-CLIO, LLC

All rights reserved. No part of this publication may be reproduced, stored in a retrieval system, or transmitted, in any form or by any means, electronic, mechanical, photocopying, recording, or otherwise, except for the inclusion of brief quotations in a review, without prior permission in writing from the publisher.

Library of Congress Cataloging-in-Publication Data

Martin, William F., 1960–
    The inner world of money : taking control of your financial decisions and behaviors / Marty Martin.
        p. cm.
    Includes index.
    ISBN 978-0-313-39824-7 (hbk. : alk. paper) — ISBN 978-0-313-39825-4
(ebook)   1. Finance, Personal—Psychological aspects.   2. Money—Psychological aspects.   I. Title.
    HG179.M3134   2012
    332.024—dc23   2011052100

ISBN: 978-0-313-39824-7
EISBN: 978-0-313-39825-4

16 15 14 13 12   1 2 3 4 5

This book is also available on the World Wide Web as an eBook.
Visit www.abc-clio.com for details.

Praeger
An Imprint of ABC-CLIO, LLC

ABC-CLIO, LLC
130 Cremona Drive, P.O. Box 1911
Santa Barbara, California 93116-1911

This book is printed on acid-free paper ∞

Manufactured in the United States of America

This book is dedicated to my loving family beginning with my wife, Geral, and son, Armand, as well as my parents, Bill and Jean Martin, and sister, Pat. Not only is this book dedicated to the living but my maternal and paternal grandparents who raised me as a child, teen, and young adult providing me with many life and financial lessons that I shall share with you in *The Inner World of Money: Taking Control of Your Financial Decisions and Behavior*.

Invictus

Out of the night that covers me,
Black as the Pit from pole to pole,
I thank whatever gods may be
For my unconquerable soul.

In the fell clutch of circumstance
I have not winced nor cried aloud.
Under the bludgeonings of chance
My head is bloody, but unbowed.
Beyond this place of wrath and tears
Looms but the Horror of the shade,
And yet the menace of the years
Finds, and shall find, me unafraid.

It matters not how strait the gate,
How charged with punishments the scroll,
I am the master of my fate:
I am the captain of my soul.

—William Ernest Henley (1849–1903)

Contents

Preface

Stunned by huge wealth losses in stocks and real estate, Americans saved more and spent less for a while. Then, in 2010, Americans went on a spending spree, once again demonstrating that old habits are difficult to change. The summer of 2011 appeared looking a lot like the dreaded financial debacle of 2008/2009. Economists were analyzing what went wrong and making forecasts about what looms ahead. Media pundits were broadcasting stories of hype and fear, stoking anxiety and even a sense of profound emotional loss as tens of millions of Americans watched their financial futures drain down the sink of the global financial marketplace.

As a psychologist specializing in financial psychology and working in two worlds, academia and practice, I could no longer afford to sit on the sidelines. Nor could I simply look in my rearview mirror and comment on what should have happened. Nor could I simply look out the front window and make forecasts of what likely happen knowing that many forecasts today are a little more than magical thinking. I was called to share with you, the reader, my experience, insight, and perspective, and in this book, I have drawn upon my own experience as well as the literature of psychology, behavioral finance, neuroeconomics, and managerial decision-making. Making better financial decisions and engaging in more constructive financial behaviors are two concrete actions that you can and should control.

As I scanned the popular literature and the academic literature searching for a single text or article that addressed financial decision-making and financial behavior wrapped together in a way that reflects the reality of how we live our financial lives, I was disappointed that there was nothing that really pulled these two factors together in a holistic way. In the backdrop of my life, I was approaching 50 and beginning to understand in a heartfelt way—not a detached, intellectual way—about "leaving the world better off." This book, *The Inner World of Money: Taking Control of Your Financial Decisions and Behavior*, is my humble attempt to "leave the world better off" by equipping you with the knowledge, skills, tools, and confidence to make better financial decisions and engage in more constructive behaviors.

In summary, *The Inner World of Money* is about unlearning, learning, and re-learning. That's the essence of this book. My hope for you is that you live a higher quality financial life and, as a result, your piece of the world is better off.

Acknowledgments

To acknowledge is to do more than simply recognize but to honor and embrace. There are five individuals who quickly come to my mind and heart to be acknowledged, honored, and embraced.

First and foremost, without the unconditional loving support of my wife, Geral Martin, throughout this entire process, this book would not have been possible. Her gentle and sometimes not-so-gentle nudges and reminders enabled me to focus upon *The Inner World of Money: Taking Control of Your Financial Decisions and Behaviors* without having to concentrate on some of the more mundane aspects of life such as mowing the grass every weekend and shoveling snow during the cold months in Chicago.

Second, upon reflection, I assembled a virtual team of advisors, coaches, and mentors who not only provided critical feedback along the way but also challenged me to uncover the creative part of myself buried by years of formal academic training and writing academic articles in peer review journals. Specifically, Herta Feely of Chrysalis Editorial Services taught me to keep it short and sweet but interesting as she edited my manuscript for style, grammar, and punctuation as well as spelling every now and then. Christy Heady, published author and owner of *Where Art Means Business,* inspired me to bring out my own voice, to experience life as a prompt for sharing my experience, perspective, and caring with others in my writing.

Cicily Maton, CFP, founder and owner of Aequus Wealth Management Resources in Chicago, Illinois, has served as a caring mentor as I have created in collaboration with her and her daughter, Michelle Maton, CFP, EA, an integrated, collaborative financial planning practice that focuses on the inner and outer world of money for our clients—individuals, couples, and families. In our work with family businesses, physicians, health care executives, and health care entrepreneurs, we noticed the importance of making financial decisions and how this has an impact on their work and quality of life.

Introduction

Has the mix of economic trauma and aging made us more frugal, more prudent—or merely fearful? Markets crashing . . . shrinking portfolios . . . disappearing jobs . . . increasing financial stress . . . the world seems out of control. This does not mean that one's finances have to be out of control. This book explores how readers can get their finances under control and enjoy a more stable relationship with money. *The Inner World of Money: Taking Control of Your Financial Decisions and Behaviors* shows you how. This easy-to-understand book includes information on many of the more important concepts you need to know about managing your finances using self-assessments, checklists, exercises, tip sheets, real-life examples, and a lot more.

Earning, saving, spending, and investing involve two worlds—the outer and inner; this book guides you in gaining control of your financial decisions and behaviors over the course of your life. This book goes beyond helping the reader understand the differences between bonds, stocks, CDs (certificates of deposit), mutual funds, and ETFs (exchange-traded funds), it also presents the techniques of behavioral finance, an emerging science combining the best of finance and psychology. *The Inner World of Money* brings cutting-edge research from the laboratory to the reader with special attention to the latest advances in not only behavioral finance but also neuroeconomics, evolutionary psychology, positive psychology, sustainability, socially responsible investing, and happiness studies.

You will find that *The Inner World of Money* includes time-tested strategies, such as how to avoid the traps of compulsive spending and overcoming poor money habits for those who fritter away their money. You will gain practical, proven approaches to develop the skills necessary to be in greater control of what you earn, how you save, why you spend, and how to invest by not only reading this book but also completing all of the exercises and self-assessment tools. By reading *The Inner World of Money*, you will acquire the skills necessary to keep track of your bills; tame your debt; reign in your splurging; and create a spending plan that works.

Adults throughout the world are searching for psychological comfort and practical ways to make healthier financial decisions and to engage in financial behaviors, which helps to weather the economic downturns by learning how to protect years of hard work and to live life fully for years to come. *The Inner World of Money* is the right book for these turbulent times as well as for the better times to come.

The benefits of reading *The Inner World of Money* are many. This book:

- Shows you how to break down the complexities of making, saving, and investing money by following five simple rules.
- Shows you how to take personal responsibility for your financial life and well-being by taking control by influencing what you can and letting go of the rest.
- Refute your old money-scripts by building sound money management strategies.
- Provides you with practical strategies to confront under-earning, inertia, and procrastination.
- Gives you the tools to make powerful financial decisions for today and tomorrow.
- Gives you the tools to challenge and re-wire your unhealthy money habits and even addictions, compulsions, and impulses.
- Equips you with skills to talk about money like an adult.
- Equips you with a way to talk with children about money and prepare them for financial independence and well-being.
- Challenges you to live more fully now by experiencing flow, connectedness, and contribution to the planet and the well-being of others.
- Challenges you to design a new routine to manage your finances in a way that is aligned with your values.

Each chapter of *The Inner World of Money* applies cutting edge research in psychology, behavioral finance, neurosciences, and managerial decision-making along with real life illustrations from the front lines of working as a financial psychologist in a private practice, a wealth management firm, and as a speaker and trainer. This book challenges you to be an active and engaged reader by holding yourself accountable to answer the many questions interlaced throughout each chapter and to complete the exercises. Reading passively may provide you with a level of enjoyment but to improve your financial decision and financial behaviors, then I challenge you to be a more engaged reader. This means actually doing the exercises not just in your mind but by actually writing your responses, reflecting on what you have written, and then making a commitment to yourself to do something different. This book is for you and about you. As you turn to the first chapter, you will discover that the world of money, finance, and economics is not as complex as you may think. Your first step in taking control of your financial decisions and behavior is to increase your competence in how money works.

1

Money Makes the World Go 'Round

The legendary mutual fund giant John Bogle, the founder of the Vanguard Group, gave the commencement address at Georgetown University's Mc-Donough School of Business in 2007 and began with this story:

> Here's how I recall the wonderful story that sets the theme for my remarks today: At a party given by a billionaire on Shelter Island, the late Kurt Vonnegut informs his pal, the author Joseph Heller, that their host, a hedge fund manager, had made more money in a single day than Heller had earned from his wildly popular novel *Catch 22* over its whole history. Heller responds, "Yes, but I have something he will never have . . . Enough." (Bogle, 2007)

The measure of success should be more than the accumulation of money in whatever account you may have. At what point do you say to yourself . . . enough. All the money in the world will not make you 100 percent safe and secure. This is one of the reasons why we buy insurance to make us feel safer and to secure what we have built up over time, whether it is our home, our car, our income-earning ability, or our possessions.

Although money makes the world go 'round, money alone is never enough. After reading this chapter, you will understand how money works and how money can work for you. You will also be more financially literate as you turn the last page of this chapter. Financial literacy is possible for all of us regardless of our current circumstances, our previous experiences, and our backgrounds. To be financially literate is the first step in taking control of your financial decisions and behaviors. It's time to begin our journey toward becoming more financially literate.

MONEY MAKES THE WORLD GO 'ROUND, OR SO THEY SAY

Singers from Liza Minnelli to R. Kelly have sung a song with the lyrics "money makes the world go 'round." Money makes the world go 'round from Wall Street to Main Street. Money is valuable. The value of money is both tangible and intangible. The tangible value of money is based upon what we can exchange money to buy in terms of goods and services. The intangible value of money is what money symbolizes to us and others. The history of money is important to know to increase your appreciation of the lyric "money makes the world go 'round."

Paper money is relatively new. Before we used paper bills, we used coins. Before we used coins, we bartered, using a whole host of objects from wheat to cattle, from spices to silk, from whiskey to beads and fur. Money has different meanings in different cultures, including in social, psychological, religious, political, and economic contexts. Money is primarily an instrument for conducting transactions and for measuring how much economic value a particular good or service is worth compared to another good or service. Not only does money have exchange value, but it also has symbolic value. Money is a double-edged sword.

IS MONEY A MEANS TO AN END OR AN END IN ITSELF?

The response to this question is not straightforward. Your orientation toward money will largely determine your relationship with money and how you earn money as well as how you use money. Do you use money to purchase goods, services, and experiences that you need or want? Or do you use money to signify that you have achieved a certain level of status or to determine your own self-esteem? It is indeed possible that money is both a means to an end and an end in itself.

Money as a Means to an End

Money as a means to an end represents the exchange value of money. In our current economic system, we need money to meet our most basic daily needs from housing to eating. We also need money to meet higher-level needs like protection from hazards through the purchase of insurance and investing in our own skills and development to earn more income through paying for higher education. The end is not the money itself but what the money can buy to meet other needs.

Even politicians view money as a means to end. You may remember that former President George W. Bush encouraged Americans to go shopping after the tragic terrorist events that took place on 9–11. But what may be good for the health of the U.S. economy may not be good for you. Think about people that you know who spent their way into debt. The economy benefited in the short run, but these people and maybe you got stuck with the bill. There was no financial bailout for everyday consumers spending more money than they had in their bank accounts. But there was a financial bailout for the bankers, insurers, and even car manufacturers. Since President Ronald Reagan, a shift has taken place in the United States based upon our love for rugged individualism. The name for that shift is individual responsibility. Others refer to that shift as the "trickle down economy." A few, including myself, call that shift "You're on your own." In other words, you need money to make ends meet. If you come up short, then too bad. If you come up with a little bit extra this week or this month, you better tuck it away to smooth out the next financial pothole or air pocket.

Money as an End in Itself

Money as an end itself borders on accumulating more and more money for the sake of having more rather than for the aim of using money for some specific purpose. For example, most Americans believe that money is both necessary and sufficient to be happy, according to happiness researchers in an article entitled, "The Pursuit of Happiness: Time, Money, and Social Connection" (Moligner, 2010).

What about you—do you believe that all you need to make you happy is money? Or suppose that your income and wealth was cut by half—would your happiness be cut by half? Or imagine that your income and wealth doubled—would your happiness double? Happiness researchers tell us that more money buys happiness up to a point. Furthermore, the real question may not be how much money you have but how much attention you spend on the acquisition and accumulation of money in your life. Charles Dickens's *A Christmas Carol*, written in 1843, tells the story of Ebenezer Scrooge. One of the major lessons of this legendary tale is how greed is bad. Greed seemingly has no end.

MONEY AND PURPOSE

Rick Warren's highly acclaimed book, *The Purpose Driven Life*, was a national bestseller in part because of the focus placed on identifying the purpose of your life and then living your life according to that purpose. Money serves a purpose. The purpose of money is to use money as means to an end or as an end in itself. Be clear about your purpose regarding your money.

Even if you use money for a purpose, it can be dangerous if the purpose is solely to collect stuff. In extreme cases, individuals collect so much stuff that others may wonder if they are hoarders or pack rats. Madonna sang about the reality of our materialistic world in her top-selling song "Material Girl." This hit song of the 1980s celebrated "the consumer power that women exercise in today's material world" (Linder, n.d.).

You know that we are living in a material world. The key discovery and challenge for many, given the fact that we are living in a material world and many of us have claimed ourselves to be a "material girl" or "material boy," is to recognize that acquiring stuff, even really nice and expensive stuff, does not equal happiness. You also know that materialism is not the path to fulfillment, contentment, and happiness.

Materialism can be like a wild horse on the prairie that needs to be tamed and reined in. For money to serve a useful purpose, that untamed part of ourselves about spending money wildly needs to be reined in to control us and align our behaviors with our purpose. Those bitten by the highly contagious conspicuous consumption bug have to be protected from themselves and the marketing parasites sucking money and savings out of their lives in exchange for more stuff. Materialism focuses on stuff that temporarily satisfies but leaves you longing for something more or different or unique. In the end, if your purpose is fulfillment, happiness, or contentment, money does not automatically and instantly bear these fruits. However, money can certainly help. Or it may be more appropriate to point out that the lack of money to meet basic needs can clearly get in the way.

Beyond Materialism: Using Money with Purpose

You earn, save, and invest for various purposes: first to meet the basic necessities of life (clothing, food, and shelter), then perhaps to own a home, pay for your children's education, and then for retirement, vacations, and finally for other luxury purchases. Some of these purchases are costly while others are less significant. Some of these are long term and others are short term. The single biggest long-term objective is usually retirement.

Before you can begin using money with purpose, you have to discover and align your decisions and actions with your purpose. Ways to discover your purpose for using money include asking yourself these questions:

- If I only had one year to live, how would I use my money?
- If I won a $10,000,000 lottery, how would I use my money?

- If my income remained the same for the rest of my life, how would I use my money?
- If I were diagnosed with a terminal illness with no cure or treatment in sight in my lifetime, how would I use my money?

The answers to these questions are powerful. These questions stretch you in ways that may make you feel slightly uncomfortable. In my experience as a financial psychologist over the years asking my clients questions of this sort, I have found that to identify purpose, stretch questions are essential.

The answers to these questions will also shape your money identity and define your relationship with money. Some individuals view money as a tool to make more money. This is the view of investors. Others view money as a resource that can be directly sourced through earnings, through increases in value by investing, or through using the money of others by borrowing money in exchange for paying interest. What is your money identity? Are you an investor, a safe saver, or a borrower?

I Am a Safe Saver or Investor

Investors use money to grow more money. Investors search for value and opportunity. Investors accept risk but also expect a rate of return that is greater than the risk. This is known as the risk premium. An easy example is to compare two individuals. The risk-adverse individual or the safe saver walks into the bank with $100,000 and puts in into a FDIC insured bank account paying a guaranteed 1 percent interest rate. At the end of the year, this individual now has $101,000. The other individual walks into a brokerage office or goes online and invests $100,000 in some basket of stocks, bonds, and mutual funds. This individual does not know for sure what the rate of return will be. This individual also accepts the risk that at the end of a year that they could lose some of the $100,000. In return for taking on this risk, the individual expects, based in part upon historical performance, that the rate of return will be 4 percent. Assuming that the rate of return in a year was 4 percent, and then this individual has $104,000. The risk premium is the difference between the sure return in the bank ($1,000) and the invested rate of return ($4,000). In our example, the risk premium is $3,000. A natural question is as follows: Is this worth the risk? This depends upon the individual and, in part, their identity as an investor or safe saver.

I Am a Borrower

Unlike the safe saver or investor, an individual with $100,000 will walk into a bank and seek to borrow money perhaps using the $100,000 as collateral. In short, they put their $100,000 at risk in case they default on the terms and conditions of the loan. Borrowing is appropriate in specific situations. However, borrowing has a cost. The cost is the interest that you pay to the bank or credit card company. A key consideration is to find out the difference between the cost of money to borrow versus the cost of money to save and invest. If you are saving money at a bank, you get a guaranteed amount back in terms of interest. If you are investing, you get an expected, although unknown amount, back in some period of time. If borrowing, you pay a fixed interest rate or even worse, a variable interest rate for some period of time.

Some borrowers even use other people's money at very high interest rates to purchase goods and services that do not retain their value for a long period of time like food, toiletries, and utilities rather than borrowing to increase your skills to earn more income. Borrowing itself is neither good nor bad. Clarify the purpose of borrowing. Also, be sure that you are not too highly leveraged. What does that mean? This means that the cash coming into all of your accounts is largely being used to pay off the interest and principal on your debts.

Now you know the difference between using money as a means to an end and using money as an end itself as well as the purpose of money in your life not to mention your identity as a safe saver, investor, or borrower. By sitting down and really defining for yourself your relationship with money, you are now ready to understand the five pillars of personal financial planning.

THE FIVE PILLARS OF PERSONAL FINANCIAL PLANNING

Personal financial planning is the process of planning one's earning, spending, financing, and investing so as to optimize one's financial situation. A personal financial plan specifies one's aims and objectives. It also describes the saving, financing, and investing that are used to achieve these goals.

A financial plan should contain the personal finance decisions related to the following components referred to from here on as the five pillars of personal financial planning.

1. Budgeting
2. Managing liquidity
3. Financing large purchases
4. Long-term investing
5. Insurance

Budgeting

The first of the five pillars of personal financial planning is budgeting. Budgeting is simple to understand but difficult to do. Budgeting is knowing how much money is coming into your household and how much money is going out of your household. You can develop a budget on a daily basis, a weekly basis, a monthly basis, a quarterly basis, or an annual basis. A daily basis alone and an annual basis alone are not enough. Not only do you want to set up a budget, but you want to use your budget to monitor if your spending is in line with your income.

Smart budgeters adopt tools from big business. Chief financial officers set up systems in organizations for managers to know whether they have a positive or negative budget variance. This is fancy language for knowing if you have spent more than you have (negative variance) or if you have spent less than you have (positive variance). You should have a positive variance (spend less than you have). What do you do with the extra? You use that amount for savings and investing.

Some folks are resistant to budgeting because it increases accountability. I agree. The increase in accountability is an increase in accountability to yourself and, in certain circumstances, your loved ones. Effective budgeting is based upon the well-established principles of self-monitoring in psychology. Self-monitoring is associated with positive changes in behavior such as smoking cessation, weight reduction, and exercise. There are a variety of tools to help you budget ranging from software programs to web-based programs. Like any tool, it is only as good as the skill employed in using the tool appropriately.

Budgets change as life circumstances change. If you get a raise, then your budget may change. If you get fired, then your budget may change. If your children leave the nest, then your budget may change. Budgets are dynamic, not static. The next of the five pillars of personal financial planning is managing liquidity or cash.

Managing Liquidity

Liquidity is readily available cash, or other means of making purchases. Liquidity is needed for purchasing items, such as groceries, and meeting unexpected expenses, such as repair bills. Money management involves decisions regarding how much money to hold in liquid form and the precise forms in which the money is to be held. Generally, the more liquid an asset is, the lower the return to be expected from it. The most liquid assets are currency. Money is currency. These assets provide little or no interest. Slightly less liquid assets, such as deposit accounts in banks, provide more interest but are slightly less accessible. Generally speaking, you should not hold all of your wealth in liquid form since assets that are less liquid (such as bonds and stocks) generally offer much higher expected rates of return. Your money may be more secure under your mattress or in a bank but inflation will slowly eat away the spending power of your money.

What happens if you don't have enough cash to pay for something? If you are like most of us you grab your credit card. For others, you have the cash money (liquidity) but you prefer to use your credit card for a variety of reasons such as to get points, cash back, or miles with your favorite airlines. Just as you have to manage your money, you must also manage your credit. Credit management is concerned with decisions as to how and what sources of credit to use. While the credit is a source of additional liquidity, it has the disadvantage that interest has to be paid—often at a high rate. Do not be fooled by the term "credit" when referring to a credit card.

Credit cards are a misnomer. They are truly debt cards or borrow cards or loan cards. The issuer of the credit card is not crediting your account or giving you money or even allowing you to withdraw money that is your money free and clear. A debit card, on the other hand, is your money in your account. As such, each time you use your debit card, you are withdrawing money from your account. This distinction between credit, debt, and debit is so important that I shall say it again. *Credit cards are debt instruments like loans at high interest rates.*

Picture yourself walking into one of your favorite stores to buy a pair of shoes. First, you walk into a store to buy shoes worth $100 and you whip out your credit card to buy the shoes. Second, you buy the same pair of shoes for the same amount but this time you pay cash. When you purchase the shoes with $100 in cash, then there is nothing to worry about at all. When you buy the shoes with your debit card, there is not much to worry about other than being charged an overdraft fee if you withdraw more from your account than what your current balance happens to be. In contrast, if you pay with a credit card at 20 percent annual interest, then you have taken out a loan to pay for the shoes. Of course, you did not walk into a bank, wait in line, fill out a loan application along with a current pay stub and copies of IRS 1040 for the past two years, and then give all that information for the loan officer to declare, "Congratulations! You have been granted the $100 loan to pay for your shoes." This begs the question: What does happen if I buy shoes with a credit card for $100 at 20 percent annual compound interest?

Let's do the math. If you catch yourself saying, "I'm not good at math" or "I don't understand math" or "I hate math," do not put the book down. You cannot become financially competent and money smart unless you do the math. I am not talking about algebra or calculus. I am talking about adding, subtracting, dividing, and percentages. Let's return to our example. You have purchased shoes for $100 using your credit card at 20 percent annual compound interest. If you intend to pay off the shoes in one year paying $10 per month on average, then you will have paid a total of $120.00 for the shoes—$100 for the shoes and $20.00 for borrowing the money by using your credit card. If you take two years to pay off the credit card principal of $100, then you will have paid $245.32 total giving the credit card company $145.32 dollars for loaning you the money. Managing liquidity both cash and credit effectively and wisely prepares you for the next pillar of personal financial planning—financing large purchases.

Financing Large Purchases

The financing of large purchases may be generated by saving or by borrowing. When you are paying for a service or object within the two years, it is best to tap into your savings account or better yet, a designated savings account with the name of the object you want or need, such as vacation account, tuition account, or washing machine account.

The single largest purchase for Americans is buying their home. For the vast majority of us, this has to be financed. Why? Most of us simply don't have the money and the interest rate on a credit card is dangerously high for such a large purchase and length of time (15 to 30 years) to pay off the balance. Most of us also finance our cars, whether new or used. You know the drill, even if you have only bought one car, you negotiate the price of the car with the sales representative who ultimately says, "I have to check with my sales manager to see if I can give you such a great deal." The sales representative returns smiling and says, "I would love to give you this deal but my sales managers I can only take off this much." At this point, you know you have been played. But buying a car is a game, so you say, "OK, I'll take it." Then, the discussion turns to how you will pay for the car—cash money or finance the car. Like most of us, you need a loan to pay for the car. Now, you get sent to the financing representative in the back office sitting behind a desk with a large computer monitor. You give the representative your license and social security number and you wait wondering to yourself, "Will I be approved or not? Will something come up that I don't know about?" When the finance representative says, "You've been approved," you feel a sense of relief knowing that you will take your brand new car home with you that day. The price for taking the bank's car home today is that you get to pay interest on the money that you borrowed to finance this relatively large purchase. A question to ask yourself before you even walk into the dealership is this question, "Who am I buying this car for?" For myself because I love the aesethics and mechanics of the car? For myself as a reward to achieving a long-term goal?

For myself so that I can get to work without being late? For strangers to look at me say, "Wow, they've got it made"? For many of us, we choose to finance cars because our Chevy wallet wants a BMW. We could pay for the Chevy with cash money but the BMW we have to finance, which always means paying interest. Do you factor the interest that you will pay when you are negotiating the price of the car? You should.

Returning to home ownership as a cornerstone of the American Dream is under attack since the mortgage meltdown beginning in 2008 with evaporating home values, vanishing new construction, disappearing mortgages, and escalating foreclosures. Not so long ago, parents would say to their now adult children, "It is important that you set aside enough money to get a down payment on a home that you own. Also, this home will be the biggest investment you will ever make in your life. If you buy right, then you can make a lot of money when you sell the house." Not so long ago, you were a fool if you questioned this sound advice. Now, who is the fool? The parents, the children for listening, the bankers for making the mortgage, or our society for promoting not the American Dream but the American Nightmare for millions of Americans who faced homelessness when the Sheriff evicted them from their homes (I mean the bank's home) or millions more Americans who pay more on their mortgage than their house is worth (underwater).

Our parents have guided their children to buy a $250,000 home from a reputable builder in a great location with a highly ranked school district, plenty of parks, and a first-rate local government. Not only is the house wonderful, but this is one of the fastest growing areas in the city. The children are approved for a 5.7 percent, 30-year mortgage. If they decide not to pay off the mortgage early, then they would have paid more for borrowing the money to purchase the home (interest) than the cost of the home. In short, interest paid over 30 years is $272,361, which is $22,361 more than the purchase price of the house at $250,000. Combining the two, the children will pay a grand total of more than half a million dollars ($522,361). This illustration begs to ask several questions:

- What could they have bought for half a million dollars ($522,361)?
- Are the children in the wrong job . . . should they be mortgage bankers to get $272,361 for loaning $250,000?
- If the children had paid for the house in cash ($250,000), what could they have done with $272,361?
- Will I save $272,361 in taxes by having a 5.7 percent, 30-year mortgage?

The skeptics or realists reading this example may be thinking, "Give me a break, who has $250,000 stashed away to buy anything." There is another way.

Let's assume that the children pay $100 more a month to their mortgage payment for the entire 30 years. Will this make a difference? Yes. In fact, the difference amounts to almost $50,000, or $47,488 to be precise. Over 30 years, the children would have paid a grand total of $474,873.91 instead of $522,361. The lesson is obvious. Pay more than the minimum. Be sure to find out if the mortgage company will penalize you for paying more. Why would they do such a thing? Because you are taking money out of their pocket and putting money in your pocket.

There is another way to avoid paying a half a million dollars for a quarter of a million dollar house. I know what some of you may be thinking as you read that last sentence, "houses are great investments . . . they always go up in value . . . in 30 years, my house will be worth $750,000 so when I sell my home, then I will make a profit of $250,000 even if I paid a half a million dollars in total to the mortgage company." Do not assume that this is the case in the 21st century. This is not your parents' or grandparents' economy. Things seemingly have changed in substantial ways challenging long-held assumptions and wisdom. Moreover, common sense has to be reframed even about practical things like buying a home. What's the other way? Get a 15-year instead of a 30-year mortgage.

A 15-year mortgage at 5.7 percent over 30 years will cost you a grand total of $372,480.62 rather than $522,361—a savings of $149,880.38. What could you do with $150,000? Do you feel any guilt about depriving the mortgage industry of $150,000 in profit? This savings is not free. If you elect to pay off your mortgage in 15 years instead of 30 years, then your monthly payment will increase. Your monthly payment will be $2,069.34 for a 15-year mortgage versus $1,451.00 for a 30-year mortgage. This amounts to $618.34 per month or $7,420.08 per year. This reality is that you must have more liquid cash available every month to dedicate to your mortgage to save you $150,000. These illustrations are not summed up by the cliché' "pay me now or pay me later."

To some extent, there is some truth to "pay me now or pay me later," but you are paying much less by paying cash for a house, paying more than the minimum each month over the entire length of your mortgage schedule, or obtaining a 15- versus a 30-year mortgage. Before you outright say, "This is not what I have been told growing up," pause and think about this for a while and then decide.

Financing large purchases goes beyond paying for a home, which is the single largest purchase for the overwhelming majority of Americans but also includes financing college and financing cars. The same principles apply to other large purchases. Even before you decide how to finance such a large purchase, ask yourself if you really need or want or can afford that purchase. Also, stop and ask yourself if you were to save or invest and use that money to purchase a home, a college education, or a car, then you would not have to finance the purchase. Now that you have a better understanding of financing large purchases, it is time to look at long-term investing, which is the fourth pillar of personal financial planning.

Long-Term Investing

Investing is placing money at risk in the expectation that the money will increase in value. Typically, investing today involves allocating money in stocks, bonds, mutual funds, commodities (such as gold), and exchange-traded funds (ETFs). Investing involves balancing risk and return. In general, the more risk you take, the greater the expected return. The key lesson to be learned with investing is that there are *no guarantees*. None. Nada.

Investments in stocks can benefit from time diversification. Over long periods of time, good periods can balance out bad periods. Also, from a long-term perspective, the accumulated income from investments becomes more important in determining the final sum accumulated. For example, $1,000 invested at 4 percent over 30 years will grow to $3,331.49 compounded monthly whereas at 8 percent it would grow to $10,935.72 compounded monthly. If you were to put $1,000 into a bank at 1 percent for 30 years, then you would have $1,349.69 compounded monthly at the end of three decades. What's the difference between 1 percent and 4 percent over 30 years? ($1,981.80). And what's the difference between 1 percent and 8 percent over 30 years? ($9,586.03). So, you can see that if you take more risk (aiming for 8 percent return on your $1,000), then the reward is greater. On the other hand, if you take less risk (aiming for preservation of $1,000 at a 1 percent return), then your financial reward is lower but your need for security may be higher. Later, we shall use this same example but look at what happens with inflation. Inflation is an increase in prices. My father always remarked, "I remember getting an allowance of 25 cents and I'd go to the movies, get popcorn, and a pop." This is not the case today because of an increase in the price of movie tickets, popcorn, and soda. This is inflation. If your income goes up at the same rate as inflation, then you break even. But if your income falls behind inflation, then you are losing your spending power. And if your income races past inflation, then you come out ahead.

For most people, the most important reason to invest is not to save for retirement. The most important result of long-term investing is not to achieve the greatest return. The most important source of motivation is not to send your children to college without strapping them with tiresome debt or to fully pay off your home—free and clear—not owing the bank anything. What is the most important reason for long-term investing? To fund your life's aspirations, dreams, and plans. Clearly, these aspirations, dreams, and plans may involve retirement, college, and home ownership. Are these means to an end or an end in itself?

If you are finding this difficult to digest, then pause and reflect on whether you are seeking to fill your storehouse with the most money . . . to accumulate more and more. Will you ever be satisfied? Psychologists would bet their money that if your goal is to have more of anything that you will never achieve that goal. How come? One word—greed. Is long-term investing an end (more money, more money, and more money) or is it a means to an end (linked to some life aspiration, dream, or plan)?

An emerging specialty within financial planning is life planning. Life planners emphasize using money to fund your life's aspirations, dreams, and plans. Traditional financial planners emphasize chasing the highest return possible even if you invest your money in unconscionable activities like financing the development of bombs killing hundreds of innocent children, the development of consumable products with known links to increasing the risk of cancer, or supporting companies that bonus executives while at the same time lay off hard-working employees to fight for their life in this increasingly economic jungle. Returns are aspects of long-term investing.

Depending upon your spiritual tradition, the purpose of long-term investing may go beyond seeking to fulfill your personal and familial aspirations, dreams, and plans. Your purpose may not be discovered by turning inward and engaging in self-reflection but turning outward and upward asking the following questions:

- Why did my creator put me here at this moment in history?
- What does the world require of me based upon my unique gifts and talents?
- What can I leave for this world to benefit from when I leave this world?

These questions may not be for you. That's OK. But please give them a chance. Sit down or stand up . . . pause . . . reflect . . . ask these questions of yourself out loud. Listen to your answers out loud. If you need money to fund the answers to these questions, then you have now found the motivation for long-term investing for you.

Can you have it all—good returns, more money, personal and familiar fulfillment, and deep fulfillment by leaving the world a better place and living out your purpose as defined by the creator? *Yes.* Is this greed? Who really knows? If you want it all, if you need it all, then realize that it may not come all at one time like going to a big box store and being able to pick up anything you need at one time and simply drop it in your shopping basket. Investing is easier if you know that you have a solid cushion to absorb money shocks and other life shocks. Insurance is the fifth and final pillar of personal financial planning.

RETIREMENT PLANNING

There are two types of retirement plans: defined benefit (DB) and defined contribution (DC). A DB plan is a traditional retirement plan. Your employer sets aside money for you until you are vested. "Vested" means that you own the money your employer saved for you and are eligible to make decisions about that money. Before you are vested, you are not eligible to make decisions about the money because it is not "your money" until you become vested. On retirement day, you walk down to human resources, and they will inform you how much money you will receive every month until your natural death or they will tell you how much money you have in total that you can take in a single check. If you have a DB plan, a very important decision is whether you want to receive your retirement income monthly until your natural death (this is like an annuity), or you can opt to get a big, fat check. This requires you to invest the money wisely because there is no guarantee of a monthly income if you opt for the single check.

The other major type of retirement plan is the DC plan. Pauline Skypala, a reporter from the *Financial Times*, commented on the increase in DC plans. Your employer sponsors a DC plan on your behalf as an employee. In a DC plan, you "own" the money from the very beginning as soon as you are eligible to participate in the DC plan. You contribute money from your wages on a pre-tax basis up to an amount allowed by the U.S. government, and your employer can elect to contribute money to your DC plan too. If your employer adds money to your DC plan, then your employer is providing a match. You want a match from your employer.

The higher the match, the better the situation for you. On retirement day, you walk down to human resources and instead of getting a definitive number, you may be asked, "What's your balance in your retirement account?" or you may be asked, "Do you have the web address or phone number to customer service to where you held your retirement accounts?" This conversation is very different. The end of the story with DC plans is that it is your responsibility to first set aside money, with or without an employer match, and second to manage your retirement plan yourself or in consultation with a financial advisor.

In short, the difference between a DB plan and a DC plan is as follows. A DB plan is a "we've got your back plan," and a DC plan is a "you're on your own" plan. The fundamental difference between these two retirement plans is who bears the risk—you or your employer. In a

DB plan, your employer bears the risk. Your employer tucks away money, your employer invests the money, and your employer guarantees you a defined, fixed amount of retirement income for life. In a DC plan, you bear the risk. You set aside money, you invest the money based upon the investment options available to you, and there is no guarantee at all.

Insurance

Insurance entails making payments to an insurer for financial protection. There is property insurance, which provides compensation in the event of damage to, or loss of, property such as houses and cars. Life insurance pays money to dependents in the event of one's death. A range of other eventualities can be insured against. For example, it is possible to take out insurance to cover health care expenses or loss of income.

Sometimes insurance is combined with a savings scheme. This is the case with life insurance products such as whole life policies. Someone considering such policies should give thought to the question of whether it might be advantageous to keep insurance policies and savings schemes separate.

Insurance prepares you for the dreaded what-ifs, which are part and parcel of living, working, and playing. What if you are employed and you slip on ice and break your arm that you need to drive and type? What if you forget to check the oven before you leave to run a quick errand and come back to a smoky house with the fire department in front of your home? What if you have a routine colonoscopy and the gastroenterologist perforates your intestines? What if you are eating caramel popcorn and crack your tooth and while driving to the dentist you notice that you cannot see at a distance? What if you become very, very sad and anxious about not being able to work after breaking your arm and wondering if you can pay all of your bills even with your disability coverage? What if you are driving on a beautiful sunny day and you are swept up with the weather and hit the car in front of you totaling the car and sending the driver off to the emergency room and rehabilitation for the next three months? The big what-if is this—what if you don't have enough money to pay for any of these unforeseen events? Who will pay? Will you be taken to court? Will your wages be garnered by the court? If you're not feeling a bit more anxious after all of these what-ifs, then either you need to re-read this section or wake up and smell the coffee.

Now to relieve some of the anxiety that I purposefully created to wake you up to the realities of accidents and mistakes. Let's take each one of these questions and review what type of insurance may protect you in part or in full from the financial consequences of these events, which are largely although not completely out of your control.

- What if you are employed and you slip on ice and break your arm that you need to drive and type thereby not being to work until you recover?

If this happens and you have health insurance, then you are set for most purposes. However, you need to check your deductible. A deductible is the amount you have to pay before your health insurance kicks in. If your deductible is $500, then you have to pay $500 before your health insurance pays anything. Upon going to the urgent care center or emergency department, you will be greeted by a smiling staff member asking, "Do you have insurance? Your co-pay is $20." You respond, "Yes, I have insurance and here is your $20." It's not quite over yet because you probably also have co-insurance. Co-insurance is the proportion of the total bill that you have to pay after being sent an EOB (explanation of benefits) in the mail by your health insurance company and receiving one if not numerous bills from the center, the physician, x-ray technician, and maybe the lab. Your health insurance policy may pay for 80 percent and you have to pay the remaining 20 percent. The 20 percent is co-insurance.

You are discharged from the hospital with a cast, but you cannot work due to your broken arm. You discover after contacting human resources that your company offers short-term disability insurance, which will pay you a certain percentage of your salary for a period of time. Once short-term disability is exhausted, then you can apply for long-term disability insurance, which will pay you a lesser amount than short-term disability insurance. The good news is that your employer picks up the tab for disability insurance. The bad news is that if you leave that organization, then you are no longer covered. It is smart to get disability insurance separate from your employer just in case you are a victim of downsizing or you decide to leave.

- What if you forget to check the oven before you leave to run a quick errand and come back to a smoky house with the fire department in front of your home?

Don't laugh . . . this example comes from personal experience when I was living in New Orleans when I left something on the stove to go to the washeteria (as they day down South, also known as the Laundromat) and came back home greeted by the New Orleans Fire Department, who had put out the kitchen fire but looked at me in a not-so-friendly manner. My excuse was that I was a young college student.

Fortunately, I had renters insurance, which covered the property. However, there was a clause in the renters' insurance policy that stated that damage or harm resulting from negligence was not covered. I must admit I was negligent. If I were a homeowner and had homeowner's insurance, I would imagine that I would not have been covered due to negligence.

If I was not negligent, then more than likely I would be covered by renters' insurance or homeowner's insurance or even property and casualty insurance. Accidents do happen. Get coverage to protect yourself against the financial consequences of accidents.

- What if you have a routine colonoscopy and the gastroenterologist perforates your intestines?

This type of insurance protection takes us back to the discussion on how health insurance works. In this case, you really want to make sure that your health insurance policy covers preventive services (e.g., colonoscopy, mammograms, etc.). You also want to find out if they cover these preventive services at 100 percent or are you expected to pay some of the bill too (i.e., co-insurance). Also, find out if you have co-pays, because some health insurance policies do not require a co-pay for preventive services. Since the passage of the Patient Protection and Affordable Care Act on March 23, 2010 and signed by President Barack Obama, many preventive services are provided without any co-pay but check with your insurance company or employer.

- What if you are eating caramel popcorn and crack your tooth and while driving to the dentist you notice that you cannot see at a distance?

Popcorn kernels are as hard as a rock and can be dangerous to your oral health. You feel the pain and decide you need to visit a dentist. Fortunately, your dentist can fit you in on the same day. You check your dental insurance policy that you get from work and are glad to know that you have $1,200 a year in benefits. Will the dentist charge you more than $1,200? What if somebody else in the family needs dental care within the year? You arrive at the dentist and while you are being checked in by the smiling receptionist, you cannot help but notice the fact that your dentist accepts all major credit cards. If the bill is over $1,200, then you can pull out your credit card. Knowing what you now know about not credit cards but debt cards, you should find out if you can finance the amount that is not covered with 0 percent interest or even negotiate a discount.

The dentist fixes your cracked tooth and now you are pain free, but your mouth feels like it is huge. As the anesthesia wears off, you are getting closer

to the optometrist. After waiting for about 30 minutes, the optometrist invites you back to the examination room to undergo a comprehensive visual
examination. While having your eyes examined, you wonder how much all of
this will cost because you do not have vision insurance and the examination
is "free" if you decide to purchase eye wear from that optician. If you had vision insurance, then you would not feel so uneasy or if your health insurance
included an annual eye exam as one of the preventive examinations, then
you would not feel so uneasy. Like your dentist, your optometrist and the optician accept all the major credit cards . . . debt cards.

- What if you become very, very sad and anxious about not being able to
  work after breaking your arm and wondering if you can pay all of your
  bills even with your disability coverage?

Depression is the common cold of mental illness. Anxiety is an internal signal that danger is near. Occasional depression and anxiety are normal. Chronic
depression and anxiety is not normal. Depression and anxiety that are so
debilitating that you cannot function at home, work, or school are not
normal.

You realize that you need to talk to a mental health professional about your
concerns. You do not believe in taking medication unnecessarily. You check
your health insurance plan and find out that the deductible still applies, the
co-pay still applies, and co-insurance still applies, but even with the passage
of the Mental Health Parity Act on September 26, 1996, some mental health
services may be higher than if you were seeking care for a physical illness.
Like your dentist and optometrist, your mental health professional will take
all major credit cards, checks, cash, and debit card payments.

- What if you are driving on a beautiful sunny day and you are swept up
  with the weather and hit the car in front of you totaling the car and
  sending the driver off to the emergency room and rehabilitation for the
  next three months?

To make matters worse, let's imagine that you have accumulated $300,000
in a saving account and $100,000 in an investment account. The driver that
you hit contacts an attorney who hires a private investigator who finds out
that you have access to $400,000 in cash. The attorney is now interested in
pursuing legal action on behalf of the driver, who has now visited the emergency department, a chiropractor, a massage therapist, and a mental health
professional for post-traumatic stress disorder (PTSD). The consulting ortho-
pedic surgeon at the hospital recommends three months of painful physical
therapy.

The insurance claims representative of the driver investigates the damages and decides the car is totaled. This car was worth $15,000. The driver is now out $15,000 for the car, out $5,000 in medical bills not covered by health insurance, and out $4,000 in mental health bills not covered by health insurance. The attorney recommends that the driver sue you for $150,000 for all damages including pain and suffering. At this point, you remember a television show about umbrella liability insurance, which covers you for events like this and pays what your car insurance will not cover. You wish that you had signed up for this policy because you discover that your car insurance company will only pay $50,000 resulting in you having to pay the other $100,000 out of your savings. If you had bought umbrella liability insurance, then you would file a claim and risk an increase in premiums but you would still have protected all of your savings and investments.

HOW DO I EVALUATE THE PERFORMANCE OF MY FINANCIAL LIFE?

The five pillars of personal financial planning are key to living a life in which you use money wisely. The wise use of hard-earned money is a skill that you can develop by reading about finances, attending financial seminars, talking with individuals who know more than you do about finances but are not selling you something, and practicing your newly acquired knowledge and skills. Do not be afraid to ask questions of your financial service providers from your insurance agent to the benefits specialist at work responsible for retirement plans. The five pillars of personal financial planning set the stage for you to evaluate the performance of your financial life.

The evaluation of your financial life is bigger, broader, and bolder than returns on your investment and retirement portfolios. This is not to minimize the importance of maximizing returns on your savings, investments, and job, but in the end there ought to be more to keeping score than chasing a percentage increase in economic value. One tool that is widely used is the Financial Satisfaction Survey developed by Money Quotient which is the tool we use at Aequus Wealth Management in working with our clients.

It is now time to build upon the foundation of what you have been reading about for the past several pages. You now know considerably more about saving and investing. In the next chapter, without having to pay a lot of money in tuition, you will have the opportunity to be exposed to the time-tested, research-driven concepts taught in graduate psychology and MBA programs. The classroom will be brought to you in the next chapter as you learn how to set goals that not only exist on paper but also happen in real life . . . your life. Setting goals is one of the cornerstones of taking responsibility for your financial life.

REFERENCES

Bogle, J. C. (2007, May 18). Commencement Address to MBA Graduates of the McDonough School of Business, Georgetown University. http://johncbogle.com/wordpress/wp-content/uploads/2007/05/Georgetown_2007.pdf.

Damato, K. (2010, December 5). Retiring in 10 years? Uh-oh. *Wall Street Journal*, R1.

Lindner, C. (n.d.). Trollope's Material Girl. http://www.christophlindner.nl/sites/default/files/trollope's%20material%20girl.pdf

Moligner, C. (2010). The pursuit of happiness: Time, money, and social connection. *Psychological Science, 21*(9), 1348–1354.

Skypala, P. (2010, December 6). Rethinking UK's pension provision. *Financial Times*, 6.

Warren, R. (2011). *The Purpose Driven Life*. Grand Rapids, MI: Zondervan.

2

Are You Taking Responsibility for Your Financial Life?

Are you taking responsibility for your financial life? You may be asking yourself, "What does he mean by responsible?" or "I didn't even know I had a 'financial life.'" Your actions demonstrate whether you are financially responsible or not. And your actions reflect the decisions you have made.

RESPONSIBILITY: IT'S MORE THAN YOU THINK

To begin with, to act responsibly boils down to knowing what you have to do or want to do and doing it. Two phrases that capture the essence of responsibility that we are hearing more frequently are to "man up" or "put on your big girl or big boy pants." An example of financial responsibility is saving. Imagine a washerwoman in Mississippi saving $150,000 and donating that money to her employer—The University of Southern Mississippi. This is the story of Miss McCarty, who bequeathed $150,000 to her employer by acting in a financially responsible way over many years. This story reminds me of what my grandfather used to say to me as a child in his gentle, yet sturdy voice, "Marty, it's not what you make. It's what you save."

How did a washerwoman who earned a meager income save $150,000 over her working life and then donate that to her employer? It is told that she divided her paycheck into tenths and invested her money in certificates of deposit (CDs), and with the "magic of compounding," she saved enough to money to bequeath $150,000 to the University of Southern Mississippi.

Responsibility. Breaking down the word responsibility, you get *response + ability*. When I reflect on the word *response*, what comes to mind is reacting to a stimulus—either internal (in your head) or external (outside of you) or both. As for *ability*, what surfaces is the capacity to use energy to do work. Financial responsibility is work. Acting in a financially responsible way is reacting to internal and external stimuli or triggers to achieve a financial goal or objective, such as saving. Not only must you react to internal or external stimuli or triggers, but then you must align your energy and do the work necessary to achieve that financial goal or objective. I am pretty confident that Miss McCarty at the University of Southern Mississippi knew this intuitively. And it worked for her and for others who benefited from her generous $150,000 gift. There are four cornerstones to acting financially responsible. Her story reminds me of the four cornerstones of acting financially responsible.

FOUR CORNERSTONES OF ACTING FINANCIALLY RESPONSIBLE

To act responsibly requires these four cornerstones:

1. Be attentive and present.
2. Be honest with what you sense.
3. Be purposeful.
4. Be accountable.

Be Attentive and Present

To be attentive and present, you first have to make sure that you are mentally alert. Second, you must focus on what is going on in the here and now, which may include fighting off internal and external distractions. To act financially responsible, shift your focus away from the big decisions and focus a bit more on the small, daily decisions such as deciding whether to buy a small coffee from Dunkin' Donuts or a grande latte from Starbucks. The price difference for one day is meaningless, but the price difference for a month, six months, or a year adds up to bigger bucks. Farmers often remark, "Small foxes spoil the vine." To act with financial responsibility is to be attentive and present to the day-to-day financial decisions.

Be Honest with What You Sense

Now that you are attentive and present, you can focus on what's going on around you that requires you to act. Make sure you're honest with yourself. Some psychologists say that we construct our realities. I agree. Construct your reality (perception) on what is real and not imagined. For instance, certificate of deposit (CD) rates are stubbornly low hovering around 0.5–1.5 percent for one-year, two-year, and five-year CDs. Yet, inflation is bouncing around 2–3 percent. If you do the math, you come up short because of the difference between how much prices are rising versus what you can save. Be "real" with yourself. Don't fool yourself by imagining that CDs will cushion you against inflation and that CDs are a sound investment to "grow" your money.

Be Purposeful

We, as humans, are both purposeful and instinctual. Fundamentally, to be purposeful is to think. Daniel Pink (2009) in his widely heralded book *Drive*, writes about how we are designed as humans to be purposeful. Purpose is natural. Others have written about the importance of purpose in our life, including Rick Warren in his book *The Purpose Driven Life*. The key is to know and remember that we are self-directed. This means that you have the power within you to set sail to a place that is meaningful for you, travel in a boat that works for you, and navigate a route that makes you feel safe and comfortable yet gets you to your destination. Begin responding with purpose. Purpose is not measured by speed or efficiency, but by effectiveness and meaning. You are more than a bundle of animalistic instincts.

Yet our instincts can get in the way of our purpose and acting responsibly. You make a firm decision to only spend $500 on holiday gifts. You take out $500 cash committed to spending the money on holiday gifts only. After shopping for about two to three hours and spending $200 on gifts as planned, you feel hungry and notice a wonderful, alluring aroma of food from the food court. You quickly walk to the counter and order a delicious slice of pizza, a soft drink, and a cookie for $10. You did not plan to spend your holiday gift money on food and you did not bring any food money with you on this shopping trip. What's the big deal, you're probably thinking. What's $10? The big deal is that instinct tripped you up. Now, you have $10 less for gifts. No big deal but picture yourself shopping for a sweater for a relative and as you are walking up to the counter to pay for the sweater you notice a brightly colored scarf for only $29.99 marked down 50 percent with an additional 10 percent at the cash register. Without even thinking, what do you do? You buy the sweater and the scarf. Were you attentive and present? No. This is not a big deal because you still have most of your money for holiday gift shopping but you spent $10 on food that was almost instinctual if not impulsive and nearly $30 on a scarf totaling $40. These two purchases were not aligned with your purpose, and you have to hold yourself accountable for your choices and actions.

Be Accountable

Time is not a renewable resource. There are three basic types of people in the world today: the accountable, the victim, and the slider. The first group, the accountable, willingly accepts responsibility. The second group, the victims, is truly getting the short end of the stick and is at the mercy of others. The third group, the sliders, find anyway possible not to accept responsibility by making excuses and blaming others and situations for their fate in life. Sliders shift responsibility to others.

Our focus in this chapter will be on the accountable group. What is accountability? It is making and following through on your commitments to self and others. More simply, it is doing what you know you must do and when you should do it. Another way of knowing whether you are demonstrating accountability in your financial life is to "walk your talk." Psychologists call this "congruence."

The four cornerstones of financial responsibility are pillars upon which the stability of your financial life may rest upon, assuming that you truly resonate with these four cornerstones. In short, how do you feel about embracing responsibility in your financial life? To answer this question, take the time to assess your attitude toward embracing responsibility in your financial life by responding in writing to the following statement

1. It is important to always take responsibility for my financial behaviors no matter what the situation or circumstance.

I agree/disagree because:

This question about taking responsibility regardless of the situation or circumstances seeks to assess to which one of these three groups you most belong: the accountable, the victims, or the sliders. If you wrote about how you agree with that statement, then this suggests that you embrace financial responsibility. This means that you are a member of the accountable group. On the other hand, if you wrote that you are only a victim of life's situations and circumstances and you do not have any control or influence, then you are failing to embrace financial responsibility in your life. This means that you are a member of the victim group. As such, if you are not responsible for your financial life, who is in charge? Does that person or institution or system have your best interest and financial well-being at heart? And finally, if you wrote that you don't have time or energy or the ability to be in charge of your financial life, then you are abdicating your financial fate to others. This means that you are a member of the slider group. Financial responsibility slides off your back like a fast moving car slithers off the road right after it rains.

GETTING BACK TO YOUR FINANCIAL LIFE

You have a financial life. It may not be the financial life you dreamed of, but you've got one. The good news is that you can change your financial life. The other part of the story is that you are responsible for your present financial life and your future financial life. You may not be completely responsible for your past financial life, but you are completely responsible for your present and future financial life.

Sitting in a New York City outdoor café on a tree-lined street, drinking a latte and eating an organic salad, I was re-reading George S. Clason's best-selling book *The Richest Man in Babylon*. I was captured by the following passage, which illustrates the simplicity and power of the story about financial responsibility:

> From early dawn until darkness stopped me, I have labored to build the finest chariots any man could make, soft-heartedly hoping some day the Gods would recognize my worthy deeds and bestow upon me great prosperity . . . I wish to be a man of means. I wish to own lands and cattle, to have fine robes and coins in my purse. I am willing to work for these things with all the strength in my back. (page 6)

Right after reading the very last word, I heard the word "DePaul" from two young ladies who sat at a table about four feet away—one slender and white and the other African American and a bit more full-figured. I continued to read *The Richest Man in Babylon*, but in a distracted way, because I was really eavesdropping on their conversation about their first couple of weeks in a graduate MFA degree program in costume design, which went something like this:

MFA Student One:	"I know they say we are not supposed to focus on money but love what we do. But I want a good life."
MFA Student Two:	"You're right. Money is almost a taboo subject. Yet some of our professors are very well known and do quite well. I really want to be a designer."
MFA Student One:	"I would like to be a designer, but I really want to write for Vogue. I also want to pay my bills."
MFA Student Two:	"I know. I had a good job for the past five years. But no benefits."

At this point, after going back and forth in my head with "Should I say something?" or "I should let them know I teach at DePaul," or even "I don't want them to think that I'm nosey." After all that self-talk, I quietly whispered, "I'm sorry but I overhead you say DePaul. I teach at DePaul." Without any eye rolling or teeth sucking, both of them welcomed me with smiles and we proceeded to talk about goals and how in this economy you cannot afford not to have a financial game plan with concrete goals even if you are an artist.

In a capitalistic society, such as ours in the United States, the collective belief is that you are raised largely by your parents in a nuclear family, you are educated in a public or private school, you attain some post–high school skill, trade, or credential, like a bachelor's postgraduate degree, and then you enter the workforce, where you work until you retire. Unlike birds, who gain independence from their parents quite early, it can take 18–25 years before our children are launched from their nests and required to survive on their own. Our collective psyche includes the idea that you must make it on your own. The societal expectation that your success is dependent upon you, and you alone, takes no pity on anybody who does not succeed. In fact, we react with contempt and at times anger toward those in our society who "free load" off the government or "cannot pull their weight." In short, if you succeed, congratulations. If you fail, it's your damn fault and you need to ask yourself, "What did I do to screw up my life?"

To be frank, there is another way of viewing your financial life beyond the laws of Darwinian capitalism, where only the strong survive. This new view also does not embrace "trickle-down" economics, in which a small percentage of the population or a small percentage of companies benefit from financial largesse and you wait for them to share the wealth with you. How long have you been waiting, and how long will you wait? Remember, it is your financial life.

FIND THE RUDDER FOR YOUR FINANCIAL LIFE

A rudder is what you use to stay on course when navigating your boat through lakes, rivers, seas, and oceans. Without a rudder, you are likely to go adrift, run aground, and get miserably lost. With a rudder and a map, you know where you are headed and you can steer your boat to take you to your destination. Based upon my experience working with clients, those clients that own their financial life and act in a financially responsible way have a rudder.

Below are three financial rudders for your financial life. Some individuals have only one rudder, and some have more than one rudder to prepare them for whatever may be thrown their way. The first two rudders are based upon the work of psychologist, sociologist, and philosopher Erich Fromm, who wrote *To Have or To Be* (1976). He named two life orientations:

1. Consumer or "having" orientation.
2. Experiential or "being" orientation.

There is a third orientation he did not mention and that is the:

3. Producer or "doing" orientation.

Each of these orientations or rudders will be described now.

Consumer or "Having" Orientation

Growing up in America, you are all too familiar with the "having" orientation. This rudder steers you to places to shop and spend not only money but time and energy. If you add up all of the time you have spent "shopping till you drop" or engaging in "retail therapy," then you have paid a high price, or what economists call "opportunity cost." Kulananda and Dominic Houlder (2002) remind us the cost and price of money: "A person's relationship with money—earning and spending it—takes up more time and energy than any other activity; it's the biggest relationship we have" (page 5).

The key is to be aware of the price and the cost.

Opportunity cost occurs when you do one thing, which means that you cannot do something else even if you are a multitasker. For example, you decide to spend your evenings, weekends, and vacations shopping either alone or with family and friends. This means that you cannot spend your evenings, weekends, and vacations gardening, exercising, learning, or volunteering, because the human reality is that you can only be in one place at a time. So what?

Your financial life is dependent upon opportunity cost. Time is the great equalizer in our society, assuming you are living beyond the level of physical survival. You have 168 hours in a week like everybody else. Assuming that you sleep 6–8 hours per night, as recommended by the National Sleep Foundation, and then you have 112–126 hours remaining each week. What you do with this time is driven largely by one of these three rudders or orientations.

Imagine the cost of a consumer orientation and spending a lot of your discretionary time acquiring all sorts of stuff. One of my former clients, a 40-something, divorced office manager steered her way to retail outlets, such as T. J. Maxx and HomeGoods, nearly every day after work, and then on weekends, she would often return the items she'd bought, which soaked up another 4–5 hours each weekend day. Adding up all of the hours, this very nice, warm, and intelligent, not to mention hard-working, loving mother of two teenage children, spent a minimum of 14 hours a week consuming and acquiring. To put this into perspective, she worked 35 hours a week as an office manager. She spent nearly two full work days not producing or earning additional income but consuming, spending, and acquiring. Her opportunity cost was not only wasting time and energy, but also developing back pain from walking on those hard-tiled floors sitting on concrete slabs that adorn strip malls. Her family suffered as well because while she was shopping they were not able to connect and enjoy one another. Take a moment to write down your opportunity cost for being engrossed in a "having orientation."

What is my opportunity cost for being engrossed in a "having orientation"? More simply, what am I giving up by steering my life toward acquiring, consuming, and spending?

Experiential or "Being" Orientation

Growing up in America, a "being" orientation may be seen as passive, weak, and a waste of time. Our society is an action-oriented society. We are increasingly about speed. Our society is focusing more and more on "doing more with less" and "getting the greatest bang for your buck." In short, we are competitive. We are taught to win. We are taught to go for the win-win at times, but also to admire heroes and superheroes. Heroes who are victorious at the expense and pain of others, that is, the win-lose and even the win-destroy.

There is another way. This way is also American. Yet, many of us associate this way with the Eastern spiritual philosophy. This Eastern way places "being" at the center of the design of a life rudder and financial rudder. Money allows you to look beyond survival, safety, and to look within as well as to connect with others. To "be" is to be present . . . to notice while not fighting against internal thoughts and feelings, pleasant or unpleasant.

Do you need money to be gripped in a "being" orientation? This is a great philosophical debate that will not be solved here. For the purpose of your financial life, the answer is "yes," and this will be further explored in chapter 9. For now, "to be" is to be open to experiences that you both design and find yourself in throughout your life. "To experience" is to get involved with your internal and external world and find joy in the simple things.

On a recent, somewhat crushing busy trip that began in La Jolla, California, on a Monday, then took me through Nashville, Detroit, Toledo, and

Dearborn in four days to arrive back home in Chicago on Friday night, my "rudder" steered me to walk along the beach in La Jolla, California, on that first day, and then to savor the tantalizing tastes and smells in "Greektown" Detroit and enjoy a walk around the Dearborn Inn surrounded by Ford buildings, serving as reminders of the responsible imagination of Henry Ford. None of these experiences cost me any money other than dinner at a Greek restaurant. I will no doubt forget what I ate and even the name of Greek restaurant, but I shall always remember these experiences and recall the good feeling associated with them.

The beauty of experiences is that they can be relived again and again. In fact, they often grow better with time, like a fine aged wine or cheese.

Producer or "Doing" Orientation

Sitting in the Sam S. Shubert Theatre, constructed in 1913, and waiting for the curtains to rise for the play *Memphis*, I was reminded of all that was produced to put this play together. The film and theater industries, unlike any other industries that I am aware of, actually have a job title to match the action verb "produce"—the producer. There are also production houses, where films are produced before they are made in the studios or sets.

What is a producer? They usually raise money to produce a production—be it a play or a film. They oversee the finances of productions. If the producer fails to do his or her job, then the film or the play will never be made. Producers must be financially responsible before the show appears. Are you acting as the producer of your life film or life play? If you fail to act with responsibility as the producer, your life goals and dreams may never be realized.

Using a play as an analogy for overall personal production, you are the director, or so I hope, because if you are not in charge of your life, then you'd better be able to trust where someone else is leading you. As the director, you have a goal or a picture of what the final product looks like, but you need to engage a choreographer (this is you too) to assist you with all the hundreds of details and steps to go from here to there. Prior to any production, there should be a design or blueprint. A growing number in the financial planning and financial psychology community call this blueprint a "financial life plan." As the writer of your own financial life plan, it is up to you and a cast of actors (or supportive others with and without professional training and experience) to help you bring your design to life.

In the end, it is in the "doing" not simply the "planning" that you produce. Imagination alone is not production. Inspiration alone is not production. Planning alone is not production. Modeling alone is not production. Forecasting alone is not production. Financing alone is not production. Purposeful doing is production. Clearly, you do not have to make something tangible to produce.

Producing and doing have value. Philosophers have written about the value of work. Erich Fromm (1973) has something to add regarding the meaning of work when he wrote, "I am because I effect" (page 235), in his book *The Anatomy of Human Destructiveness*. The manifestation of being productive or doing is an effect. Work is the cause. Essentially, work is purposeful activity. Maria Ros, Shalom H. Schwartz, and Shoshana Surkiss, a team of researchers, have described the meaning of work as exploring "the significance of work as a vehicle for reaching cherished goals" (1999, page 50). To produce is to learn how to set goals. To produce is to offer objects and experiences for others to consume, use, or learn. For instance, if you produce tapes on mindfulness meditation, then you are seeking to assist others in learning how to be still, present, and in the moment. Not only are you helping others but you can see the fruits of your labor. Being productive is powerful because you realize that what you do has an effect. In other words, you matter and your work matters.

To complete this section of the chapter (on finding the rudder of your financial life), please complete the following quick self-assessment to determine which of the three financial life rudders is the most prevalent for you and which one needs additional focus with or without the support and expertise of others.

Before taking this self-assessment (Table 2.1), realize that it is not my place to regard one of these three financial life rudders as more worthy than another. This is your decision because it is your life. Take responsibility for your life. Then hold yourself accountable for the experience and results of your life. Some of you may find it helpful to look again at the three financial life rudders or orientations—"having," "being," and "doing"—before taking this self-assessment.

After completing this assessment, take a look at the Financial Life Rudder Quick Self-Assessment Score Box (Table 2.2) to make sense out of your Financial Life Rudder Quick Self-Assessment. You will notice that Question #10 is missing from the assessment. Question #10 does not directly focus on the three financial life rudders but is a brief way of discovering if you have cultivated the habit of setting goals, which is the focus of this chapter and will be further discussed for the rest of the chapter.

Look at your three total scores on the last row of your scoring sheet and find the orientation with the highest number in the total score box. The orientation with the highest number in the total score box is your primary orientation. It could be that your total scores are the same for all three orientations. If that is the case, then you do not have a primary orientation. This suggests that you are well balanced. And this is OK.

Table 2.1
Financial Life Rudder Quick Self-Assessment

1. I prefer a having orientation.	1	2	3
2. I prefer a being orientation.	1	2	3
3. I prefer a doing orientation.	1	2	3
4. At this point, I need to consume more.	1	2	3
5. At this point, I need to experience more.	1	2	3
6. At this point, I need to produce more.	1	2	3
7. Others tell me to consume more.	1	2	3
8. Others tell me to experience more.	1	2	3
9. Others tell me to produce more.	1	2	3
10. Setting goals is a habit for me.	1	2	3

1 = Least like me
2 = Somewhat like me
3 = Most like me

Table 2.2
Financial Life Rudder Quick Self-Assessment Score Box

Having orientation	My score (1, 2, or 3)	Being orientation	My score (1, 2, or 3)	Doing orientation	My score (1, 2, or 3)
Question #1		Question #2		Question #3	
Question #4		Question #5		Question #6	
Question #7		Question #8		Question #9	
Total score (add up your scores for questions #1, #4, and #7).		Total score (add up your scores for questions #2, #5, and #8).		Total score (add up your scores for questions #3, #6, and #9).	

The purpose of this quick self-assessment is to reveal to you what your primary orientation happens to be as you spend your time, energy, and talent. You can always change your primary orientation if you want to or need to or you trust the observations of others, particularly those who have your best interest at heart.

MOVING BEYOND THINKING AND TALKING:
IT'S ALL ABOUT ACTING

This chapter is about putting yourself in the driver seat of your financial life. Now, you have to know where you are going. But only knowing where you are going without filling up your gas tank and actually doing the drive will get you nowhere and you will have nobody to blame but yourself.

Acting financially responsible is not easy anymore with economic uncertainty, employment insecurity, and rocky stock markets, not to mention rising prices for many daily goods and services, such as food, and stagnant wages and declining home values. Before the passing of my grandmother, she used to always say with a smile, "Getting old ain't for sissies." I would agree with this statement and add, "Taking financial responsible ain't for sissies."

REFERENCES

Clason, G. S. (1998). *The Richest Man in Babylon*. New York: Signet.

Fromm, E. (1973). *The Anatomy of Human Destructiveness*. New York: Holt: Rinehart and Winston.

Fromm, E. (1976). *To Have or To Be?* New York: Harper & Row.

Gladwell, M. (2008). *Outliers: The Story of Success*. New York: Little Brown and Company.

Kulananda & Houlder, D. (2002). *Mindfulness and Money: The Buddhist Path of Abundance*. New York. Broadway Books.

Ozmete, E., & Hira, T. (2011). Conceptual analysis of behavioral theories/models: Application to financial behavior. *European Journal of Social Sciences, 18*(3), 386–404.

Pink, D. H. 2009. *Drive: The Surprising Truth of What Motivates Us*. New York: Riverhead.

Prochaska, J., & DiClemente, C. (1983). Stages and processes of self-change of smoking: Toward an integrative model of change. *Journal of Consulting and Clinical Psychology, 51*(3), 390–395.

Prochaska, J., & Velicer, W. (1997). The transtheoretical model of health behavior change. *American Journal of Health Promotion, 12*(1), 38–48.

Ros, M., Schwartz, S., & Surkiss, S. (1999). Basic individual values, work values, and the meaning of work. *Applied Psychology. An International Review, 48*(1), 49–71

Ryan, R. M., & Kasser, T. (1993). A dark side of the American Dream: Correlates of financial success as a central life aspiration. *Journal of Personality and Social Psychology, 65*(2), 410–422.

Tills, T. S., D. J. Stach, G. N., Cross-Poline, D. B., Astroth, & P. Wolfe. (2003). The transtheoretical model applied to an oral self-care behavioral change: Development and testing of instruments for stages of change and decisional balance. *Journal of Dentist Hygiene, 77*(1):16–25.

Warren, R. (2002). *Purpose Driven Life*. Grand Rapids, MI: Zondervan

3

Financial Scripts

You walk into a store for the very first time to buy laundry detergent as an independent adult. And what do you do without even thinking about it? You buy what your mother bought and perhaps even what her mother bought. Whether it is Tide or Clorox is not important, although it is central to marketers, who want to establish brand loyalty and write a script in your head. What is vital for you is to face the human fact that even if you think you are an independent thinker . . . you aren't.

This does not mean that you are not smart or that you are lacking somehow. But it does mean that you develop schemas or scripts at an early age. Moreover, you largely live with those schemas or scripts until death. You, like others, have schemas or scripts about almost every facet of life, from relationships to money. Money schemas or scripts are the focus here. Before going any further into exploring your money schemas or scripts, a very quick review of the history of schemas or scripts is in order to get some key concepts straight.

HISTORY OF SCHEMAS OR SCRIPTS

Pierre Janet developed the concept of schemas to explain how we organize a lot of information—we do more than memorize. Later, Aaron Beck, the father of cognitive therapy at the University of Pennsylvania, defined a schema as "a structure for screening, coding, and evaluating the stimuli that impinge upon an organism . . . On the basis of the matrix of schemas, the individual is able to orient himself in relation to time and space and to categorize and interpret experiences in a meaningful way" (1967, page 419).

Dr. Beck's definition of a schema needs to be delicately unpacked because there are key concepts that you must understand. As an example, we will apply this definition to the schema "I will never be a saver." Dr. Beck means that if presented with the option to save for retirement or your children's college education, for example, you will first *screen* out information you regard as relevant or irrelevant based upon the schema "I will never be a saver." If you hear a commercial about a 529 college savings plan with this schema, you will more than likely not remember even hearing the commercial. Or if a notice at work invites you to attend a retirement planning seminar with lunch provided, you might deny or not recall ever receiving such a notice. In short, you tune out that which does not fit into your existing schemas.

What does Dr. Beck mean by "coding" the stimuli? Coding is a fancy term for memorizing and cataloging information. Returning to the option of saving for retirement or saving for your children's college education, Dr. Beck would predict that you may not even store this information. Why? Because we tend to see and hear what we want to see and hear. This is selective attention, perception, and memory in action. Or we may store the information, but put it into the irrelevant file folder because of the schema "I will never be a saver." In this case, you remember seeing the 529 college savings plan commercial and also receiving the retirement planning seminar notice, but you quickly forget or could not recall exactly what you saw, where it happened to be, or even when it happened to be. You just have this foggy recollection of "something about saving for college or some program about something somewhere about retirement."

Lastly, in Dr. Beck's definition of a schema, the phrase "evaluating the stimuli" refers to the way we place a cognitive judgment on the opportunity to save as fitting or not fitting our schema *"I will never be a saver."* For most of us, we engage in actions that support our existing schemas. For instance, even after actually tuning in to the 529 college savings commercial and remembering the essential facts about the commercial, you conclude "This isn't for me because I can't save. I don't do that." Why rock the boat? More specifically, why rock your boat?

Going back to Dr. Beck's definition of a schema, if you decide to rock your boat by shifting your schema from "I will never be a saver" to "I can put away money for retirement or save up for college. That's me," then you will find yourself being more aware of opportunities to save and saving will fit in with your internal self-talk. With this alignment taking place between your thoughts and the outside environment, you will save more because it matches your self-talk.

But if you hold on to the "I will never be a saver" schema, like superglue bonding together two pieces of wood, then you will probably not save or do so with considerable discomfort. The danger in this type of schema characterized by absolutes like *"never"* is that it is self-reinforcing. In short, you stay in a loop, or a vicious cycle. Each and every time you say "yes" to a dysfunctional schema, you strengthen it like warm currents fuel winds into a ravaging hurricane.

Following in the footsteps of Dr. Beck, a psychologist by the name of Michael Mahoney introduced the term "automatic thoughts." Dr. Mahoney defined automatic thoughts as "a surface level of cognition that can be brought into awareness fairly readily" (Mahoney, 1995, page 42). Others have called automatic thoughts "self-talk," which we shall spend considerable time talking about in this chapter. Why? Think about it: We talk to ourselves all the time. We talk ourselves into and out of messes. We talk ourselves into great experiences and everyday, mundane experiences. Let's return to the previous story about why you buy the type of detergent that you buy. This is based upon a schema that you probably developed at an early age and thoughts or cognitions that you have about the pros and cons of Tide or Clorox.

YOUR HISTORY WITH MONEY

We just reviewed very quickly the history of schemas. You too have a history with money, or what we will call a "money history." It is critical that you delve into your own money history to find the source of your current money self-talk. Like an archaeologist digging in the ruins of the cradle of civilization, you will need to unearth relics of the past, dust them off, examine them, and decide whether they are treasures worth keeping and preserving or simply trash to be thrown out forever.

After identifying what self-talk needs to be preserved and what self-talk needs to be trashed, you will be equipped with ways of increasing self-talk that elevates you financially and also how to modify self-talk that devalues you financially. In essence, you will learn how to change your money self-talk that is not serving you well and learn how to replace it with more positive money self-talk.

Let's get out our archaeological tools and put on some rugged clothes that will get dirty, dusty, and stained, because we're going to dig up some skeletons in the closet along with some very old baggage by writing a money autobiography.

WHY WRITE A MONEY AUTOBIOGRAPHY?

Writing your money autobiography based upon unearthing your personal and family history with money is challenging. In a nutshell, you will tell a story about your life with money at the center of that story.

The benefits are many and include increasing your understanding of what drives your money behaviors and what feelings money evokes in your life. The ultimate benefit is to become more conscious and intentional about your financial decisions and behaviors. Remember, the title of this book is The Inner World of Money: *Taking Control of Your Financial Decisions and Behaviors*.

You will begin by writing your money autobiography after reflecting on what you learned from the key people in your life about how to earn, invest, spend, give, and even waste money, and how these early money lessons shaped your own self-talk about money. As you write your money autobiography, don't worry about being a good writer, just focus on the facts and the feelings you're experiencing. Clients and workshop participants who report truly benefiting from writing a money autobiography often find that after digging deep, they liked some of what they saw and other things they didn't like, but regardless, it was their money history.

Many people find this a sobering experience that brings to surface once-distant pleasant and painful feelings that can be looked at more objectively. Many of my clients and workshop participants have shared that they feel more empowered, more mindful, and simply more in control of their financial thoughts and behaviors. When spouses or partners read or share their money autobiographies with each other, you will often hear them say, "Now this really makes sense" or "I had no idea and that helps me to know you better and understand you better."

How do I begin? Read each question and give yourself time to respond to each one. You can do this either on paper or on your PC or iPad.

1. What is your first memory of money?
2. What is your happiest memory of money? Your unhappiest?
3. What attitudes and behaviors about money did you learn from your mother, father, or grandparents?
4. How did your family communicate about money?
5. As a child growing up, did your feel rich or poor? Or in between? Why?
6. What role did money play in your life as a young adult?
7. Which of your parents' or relatives' money decisions or behaviors continue to affect you today? Describe.
8. How did your relationship with money change when you became a parent (if applicable)?
9. How do you feel about your present financial status compared to the past?
10. What will do you with your money as you approach the end of your life?

11. Will you inherit money? How does that make you feel?
12. Reflecting back on your life, what is one of the best lessons that you learned about money? Describe.

Write about your memories, relative to the facts and feelings you had about money, as a child, adolescent, young adult, and even mature adult, depending upon your age. For some, it is easier to draw a timeline and then write, or you may want to organize by topic, such as saving, spending, and so forth. I recommend limiting how much time you spend on this in one sitting. You might consider focusing on just one question each day to maximize how deep you dig. Responses may be a few sentences or a few pages. As you answer these questions, it is important to focus both on feelings as well as on factual accounts.

Your responses are your responses. You will not be graded, evaluated, or judged. Write as honestly and freely as possible. Be as specific as you can be. Obviously, time affects our ability to remember, but what counts in this exercise are your impressions and recollections.

Why am I writing this money autobiography? Good question. Beyond the benefits described above, writing your money autobiography gives you the opportunity to reflect on the development of your current financial thoughts and behaviors. For many, the benefit emerges not from digging up dirty laundry or old wounds, but in making connections between the past and the present and recognizing that some connections should be preserved and others cut. Clarity about the past allows you to live in the present with greater objectivity. Living in the present with greater objectively enables you to design the financial life you want and to plan ahead with a more solid foundation based on both facts and feelings.

After answering all 12 of the money autobiography questions, a critical question must be answered. The question is: *What lessons have I learned about my current financial decisions and financial behavior?* In the space provided, jot down your answer. Be honest with yourself.

Regardless of your answer, your money memories are not permanent. You may have responded that overall your money memories are like a giant rubber band tied around your waist and though you try to move forward, you find yourself getting pulled back by the painful past. Or you may have written that your money memories are like rocket fuel propelling you to move forward after you set a new course. Or you may have responded that, at times, predictably or unpredictably so, your money memories are both like the giant, powerful rubber band and the rocket fuel, but you feel like a child, dizzy after too much spinning around. Your money autobiography is no doubt different from others, as it should be, because you are unique in ways that go beyond your fingerprints.

Remember, you are making new memories every day. If you are not satisfied with your answers from the money autobiography, then identify three changes you can commit to making, realizing that you cannot re-write history but you can write your future.

Change #1: _____
Change #2: _____
Change #3: _____

Before you push submit or enter, review your three changes and ask the following:

- Am I trying to re-write history or am I changing today and tomorrow?

I hope you answered that you are trying to change today and tomorrow. Yesterday is history. Yesterday may be good or bad, but yesterday is in the past. Focus on today and tomorrow.

For some of you, it may be challenging to make these three changes a reality in your life, particularly if you have a rubber band tied around your waist pulling you back to the past. If this is the case for you, then continue reading this chapter because very shortly you will learn how to use the three approaches to these change.

- Switch channels.
- Fire the internal critic.
- Stay in the here and now.

These three approaches work not only for the changes based upon your money autobiography but also other changes in your life that require a shift in the way you think.

Even if your negative money memories seem insurmountable, like trying to climb over a 30-foot high wet stone wall, then remember that all of the memories are more than likely not negative. In fact, some are good not in an absolute way but in a relative way. What do I mean by relative? By "in a relative way," I mean as compared to events over your entire life. As with all memories, your memories about money will be better or worse during certain time periods.

For instance, when I was an undergraduate at Xavier University of Louisiana in the Big Easy, life seemed very difficult, even with an academic scholarship. The scholarship simply didn't cover all my expenses—rent, food, books and transportation—during one of the worst recessions prior to the 2000 dot.com bust and the recent Great Recession. I had to find work and developed a reputation as the "walking and jogging guy," because students and faculty often saw me trekking across New Orleans. My feet were my primary form of public transportation, whether on balmy days in the winter or sweltering, suffocating days in the humid summer of south Louisiana. Looking back at my college days in the Big Easy, I do not have fond memories about money, but in my thirties and forties, my memories about money became relatively better . . . a whole lot better to be honest. And to be honest, I know what I think and do today will shape my memories when I look back on my fifties. And, of course, I want those money memories to be good ones.

Returning to the three approaches to changing your cognitions, or reframing your negative money memories, are quite simple. Do not think for a moment that simplicity is not effective and powerful. Again, as a review, below are the three approaches, and each one will be described in greater detail to enable you to use all or any one of these three approaches as you seek to change a money memory or cognition that is based upon the past:

- Switch channels.
- Fire the internal critic.
- Stay in the here and now.

SWITCH CHANNELS

Some of us go through life watching the same television station, listening to the same radio programs, reading the same blog, or, almost obsessively, watching the same YouTube channel. Mix it up. When you turn one channel off and another on, it is like entering a sunlit room from a dark one. Initially, your eyes are blinded by the light, but then they adapt. And then you can actually see and experience things that you've never experienced before. Not only do you have to switch television stations but also change your thoughts, scripts, and tapes about money. Some of you have been watching the same old shows about money scarcity or get rich now or unrestrained greed for too long. To change your financial behaviors, you may have to switch to another channel with different messages such as a station that showcases money abundance or getting happy or balancing greed with giving. Are you ready to switch channels?

FIRE YOUR INTERNAL CRITIC

A couple of years ago in sunny Marina Del Ray, cradled along the Pacific Ocean, I attended an improvisational boot camp for public speakers, a few of whom were easily pulling in six figures. The coach, a long-time improvisational comedian and radio personality, asked each of us, after several warm-up exercises designed to stretch our minds and bodies, to give an impromptu speech in front of the other budding (and accomplished) public speakers. Nora, a very attractive and smart young woman of Asian descent, dragged her tiny yet elegant body up to the front of the warm, second-floor room overlooking the harbor and froze. Like an ice sculpture in freezing New England temperatures in February, she stood elegantly, silently, and absolutely motionless. Not a single word came out. The only expression was one of raw fear . . . quiet terror. Sitting near the front, I turned back to see the expression of others. To my surprise, the expressions of others were warm, embracing, friendly, and encouraging. I wondered to myself, "Who is she reacting to, because her expression and the expression of the audience do not match."

The public speaking coach, a somewhat burly but loveable guy, eased up to her like a firefighter talking a frightened citizen into jumping to safety from a building that's in flames. The public speaking coach, calmly yet with convincing authority, commanded, "I want you to look at your shoulder and accept that internal critic sitting on your shoulder telling you that you can't do this and that you shouldn't do this." Nora nodded, yet remained wordless, and nearly motionless. The public speaking coach, raising his voice, said, "I need you to talk to the internal critic. Do not fight, but accept, the internal critic." Nora's face began to soften, just like the features of an ice sculpture in the warmth of the midday sun. This went on for about five or six minutes and then Nora began to speak. Nora fired her internal critic. Some of us have internal critic about money that says, "You're stupid with money"; "Money is too complex"; "You are no good with money"; or even, "Only men are good with money." Are you ready to give your internal critic a pink slip?

STAY IN THE HERE AND NOW

It almost goes without saying that money memories are past focused not present focused. One of my clients told the painful story of how her father's emotions would rise and fall with his commission checks. As she recalled, his checks would quite literally take the family from a shopping spree at Lord &

Taylor's to a scavenger hunt for the basics at the Dollar General. The relent-less, non-stop tune in her head rang ever louder and stronger, "Feast or fam-ine . . . feast or famine." My client yearned for stability. "I must have a stable predictable paycheck always," she said. For her, a steady paycheck was an anchor against unpredictable waters.

This client lived a life filled with memories of sailing in calm blue waters one day, then suddenly capsizing, but never knowing which would occur on any given day. Can you imagine the confusion and loss she experienced from having to shop in such vastly different stores, and also the embarrassment of crossing social classes? There were times when she even had to sell some of her finer clothes and possessions at consignment shops and second-hand stores to get cash for food and other basics. If you can imagine this scenario, then you may be feeling a sense of loss, sadness, or even mild depression. Our past can drag us down and back to the past if we fail to look at what is going on now and what the future holds.

Many of you, like me, have had the experience of feeling very stressed out about a situation one day and then feeling much calmer a day or two later. For instance, during the market downturn of the summer of 2011, with fresh memories of the financial crisis of 2008, many investors looked fearfully at retirement portfolios, which were down by 15 percent, 20 percent, or higher. This triggered anger, panic, anxiety, and even mild depression. However, quite often when individuals examined their statements the very next day, their emotional reaction was not as raw as the day before, despite the fact that the portfolio had not changed even a single percentage point. What hap-pened? Assuming that the situation remains the same and this was you, the only thing that changed was your perspective. Are you ready to change your perspective and stay in the here and now?

Once you have reframed your money memories based upon your Money Autobiography, then it is time to focus on your current self-talk . . . your money self-talk. This will be the focus now in this chapter.

SELF-TALK, DECISION, AND BEHAVIOR: IS THERE A CONNECTION THAT MATTERS?

One of the first steps in modifying your self-talk is to realize what you can and cannot control. Your self-talk and your behaviors, such as spending, sav-ing, and investing, are all within your control, for the most part.

Recognizing Money Self-Talk

Self-talk is relatively easy to spot. One of the reasons that self-talk is easy to spot is that we have about 70,000 thoughts a day and up to 75 percent are negative. Robert M. Schwartz, a clinical researcher, wrote in the journal *Cognitive Therapy and Research* that healthy individuals have a ratio of 1.7–1 positive to negative thoughts. In short, those individuals who are higher functioning think nearly twice as many positive thoughts as negative thoughts. Have you ever caught yourself thinking, "You can't take it with you" or "Money doesn't grow on trees." Self-talk comes in two flavors: positive self-talk and negative self-talk. Some have called these rational and irrational beliefs. In general, positive self-talk is based upon evidence. In contrast, negative self-talk is based upon illusions and delusions—not psychotic delusions but the type of delusions in which we fool ourselves. Remember, you have control over your self-talk and your beliefs.

Positive Self-Talk

Negative self-talk is going to occur; the key is to focus on the positives, not the negatives. This should not be confused with positive thinking alone. Positive self-talk occurs when you create and have thoughts that are factually accurate, reflect multiple rather than single possibilities, and are supportive without sacrificing honesty.

When I was working on my master's thesis in psychology at Catholic University of America, I studied the self-talk of basketball players at the free line. I found that basketball players who engaged in more positive self-talk than negative self-talk hit the baskets more often, even after a series of misses. A research team at Saint Louis University, in a review of the literature published in the *Journal of Sport Science and Medicine*, argued that "athletes who incorporate self-talk imagery will ultimately benefit from increased levels of awareness, concentration, and performance enhancement" (Peluso et al., 2005, page 544).

A lesson that I learned after successfully defending my master's project in cognitive sports psychology is that positive self-talk can easily be distinguished from negative self-talk. Table 3.1 outlines the differences between

Table 3.1
Positive and Negative Self-Talk: The Differences

Attributes	Positive self-talk	Negative self-talk
Reality based	Based upon facts and data	Based upon perceptions only
Time orientation	Present and future	Present and past
Results orientation	Performance focus	Results focus
Locus of control	Internal locus of control	External locus of control
Sense of agency	I and me	You, them, and us

positive and negative self-talk. Distinguishing between the two is a skill I have applied throughout my career, including in my current role as a financial psychologist in academic and applied settings.

Now that you have a better sense of positive self-talk and how it compares and contrasts to negative self-talk, it is time to dig deeper into negative self-talk and how to both prevent such talk and address it when it occurs.

Negative Self-Talk

There are some telltale signs of negative self-talk or irrational beliefs. Watch out for any of these words because they are indicators of negative self-talk:

- ✓ Should
- ✓ Always
- ✓ Must
- ✓ Ought
- ✓ Never

Cognitive behavior therapists call these "absolutes." It is rare that absolutes are factually based. Dr. Albert Ellis, a legendary psychiatrist and one of the pioneers of cognitive behavior therapy, is famous for saying, "Shouldhood is shithood." This may seem crass and even vulgar; however, the point is that when you impose absolutes on your thinking, you fail to give yourself a break or cut yourself some slack. Be gentle and kind, yet honest, to yourself.

Negative self-talk comes in different flavors. The major flavors of negative self-talk are the following: (a) past-centered negative self-talk; (b) uncontrollable-centered negative self-talk; and (b) perfection-driven negative self-talk. Each of these three negative self-talk flavors will be explained, using the idea of asking for a raise as an example.

First, past-centered negative self-talk might sound like this: "I asked for a raise seven years ago and damn near got fired . . . it's too risky." Not "letting go" of past stuff and old baggage focuses you away from the future, where you have the most control and influence, and keeps you trapped in the past.

Second, uncontrollable-centered negative self-talk sounds like this: "The economy is bad. The housing market has not picked up. Inflation is relatively low. Now is a bad time to ask for a raise." All of these macroeconomic factors, while arguably true, are beyond the control and even influence of the person asking for the raise, unless perhaps you are Federal Reserve Chairman Ben Bernanke.

Third, in perfection-driven negative self-talk the individual might think to himself or herself, "There is a right way and a wrong way to ask and get a raise. I need to buy some more books and attend a couple more salary negotiation workshops to make sure that I ask in just the right way at the right time." Such a person may never actually get around to asking for a raise because they keep rehearsing about the optimal way to ask, they keep researching to learn how to ask in the best way possible, and they keep wondering what mistakes they may make if they do not ask for the raise in the right way. Embracing standards is a noble pursuit but embracing perfection is paralyzing.

After you have identified your version of negative self-talk among the three mentioned above, it is time to change your self-talk. Let's begin by listing self-talk that you are willing to consider altering. To begin, write down your answers to Self-Talk to Potentially Change, Free Association exercise below.

For each of the seven categories, write out the first thought that comes to mind. This is called free association.

SELF-TALK TO POTENTIALLY CHANGE, FREE ASSOCIATION

1. How I feel about my job/career . . .

2. How I feel about my financial advisor/broker/accountant . . .

3. How I feel about the people I depend on financially . . .

4. How I feel about the people who depend on me financially . . .

5. How I feel about me as a saver . . .

6. How I feel about me as an investor . . .

7. How I feel about me as an earner of income . . .

After writing the very first thought that came to mind, it is now time to identify whether the first thought was positive or negative. If you discover that more of your first thoughts or self-talk are more negative than you desire, the good news is that you are probably not alone. And the really great news is that you have the power within you to change your self-talk. In the next section, there are seven techniques you can use to modify your self-talk.

Modifying Money Self-Talk

At this point, after knowing the difference between positive and negative self-talk, you may be asking yourself this very important question: *How do I know which self-talk or beliefs need to be changed?* After decades of research in goal-setting and goal-achievement, one thing is crystal clear to me: set two to three goals at a time if you wish to accomplish those goals.

The heart of modifying your negative self-talk is to remember that you are developing a new habit or a new way of thinking. This is not easy, but the good news is that you were basically taught to think so you can learn how to think differently.

To stop negative self-talk, you must remember that it is a skill. Cognitive behavior therapists call this skill "thought stopping." One of the powerful techniques to stop negative self-talk takes me back to when I had a private practice in clinical psychology and I had a colleague make a bright red stop sign with a yellow handle that I held up in front of my clients who engaged in negative self-talk. This usually prompted them to screech to a verbal halt, as if caught speeding, and look at me in a very curious almost embarrassed way as if to say, "What . . . what did I say?" I would smile back and repeat the negative self-talk that they just recited. And then I would ask, "What evidence or facts do you have to back up that thought?" This is the second skill for modifying your negative self-talk. The typical response was, "I don't know" or "That's the way I've always looked at it" or "I just feel that way" or "What's wrong with that because that's the way it is and has been . . . always." All of these responses fail to acknowledge the power of the individual to identify evidence or facts to back up their automatic, negative thoughts, because in most cases there is no evidence or facts to back up: These negative thoughts are based on beliefs not data. Beliefs are subjective and emotional. Data is objective and often factual. Then, I would typically say, "These are beliefs, opinions, and points of view that are important, but they are not facts or evidence. Let's try replacing your negative self-talk with something a bit more positive. What else could you have thought in that situation that is more factually based, even if you don't believe it now?" This focus on the objective world not the inner world or evidence is a second powerful technique to stop negative self-talk.

To sum up these first two techniques: (1) first you can either imagine a stop sign every time you catch yourself engaging in negative self-talk, or you can get a family member, friend, or colleague to flash a bright red stop sign each time they hear you verbalize negative self-talk. (2) you can search for evidence. Get in the habit of proving that your thoughts are reality based by demanding the evidence. In addition to these two techniques, there are five

other techniques that have benefited many individuals committed to changing their negative self-talk.

1. Paper-clip technique
2. Self-talk log
3. Visualization
4. Using more precise language
5. Repeating positive self-talk

All in all there are a total of seven techniques you can use as a resources to
modify your negative self-talk. Two of these techniques, the paper-clip technique and the self-talk log, should be done first and are used frequently by
high-performing golfers, basketball players, and other athletes.

The Paper Clip Technique: The purpose of this technique is to become
more mindful of how much you engage in negative versus positive self-talk
or how much you engage in one specific type of negative self-talk. Visit the
local office supply store and purchase paper clips, preferably the ones that
come in a variety of colors. Put all the paper clips in either your left or right
pocket (assuming you have two pockets). Every time you experience negative self-talk, reach into the pocket with paper clips, take one out, and put
it in the other pocket. After you finish your day, count how many paper clips
moved from one pocket to the other. This will give you some data about the
frequency of negative self-talk. Obviously, a sign of progress is that you are
moving fewer and fewer paper clips from one pocket to the other.

This next technique, money self-talk log, will add color to the paper clip
technique. Color? In other words, the paper clip technique only measures
the frequency of your negative self-talk but provides no feedback on the content of your thinking. This is the reason why you need to keep a self-talk log
to complement the paper clip technique.

Money Self-Talk Log: The purpose of the self-talk log is to describe or
add some color to your negative self-talk and even positive self-talk. Using a
piece of paper or an electronic spreadsheet, make six columns with the head-
ings: Date/Time, Situation, Thoughts, Emotional Response, Positive, and
Negative (see Table 3.2). Under the Thoughts column, record each thought
as soon as possible after you think it. Do not censor, block out, or edit the
thought. Next, describe how you are feeling while or shortly after recognizing your thoughts. Finally, put an "X" in either the positive or negative column, whichever one accurately describes the thoughts and feelings.

You will no doubt discover patterns to your self-talk. My negative self-talk
is like a night owl and loves it when I am sleep-deprived or feeling pressure
from an external deadline. The self-talk log is similar to journaling but more
structured. The next technique is visualization.

Table 3.2
Money Self-Talk Log

Date/Time	Situation (Who was present, what were you doing, where were you?)	Thoughts	Emotional response	Positive	Negative
July 1 11 A.M.	Sitting down in the dining room paying bills by myself.	I'll never be able to save any money.	Disappointment, frustration, anger		X

Visualization: The purpose of visualization is to engage your inner, natural ability to imagine. We are able to imagine at any age and under any condition. Paint a picture of yourself engaging in positive self-talk or even imagine writing the words of negative self-talk in your mind and then taking a GIANT eraser and ERASING the negative self-talk only to be replaced by positive self-talk. Some of my clients have even imagined their negative self-talk as marble or granite and then pulling out a sledge hammer and crushing the marbleized negative self-talk into tiny pieces only to reveal positive self-talk emerging from the rubble. In addition to using the paper-clip technique, the self-talk log and visualization, it is important to pay attention to your choice of words.

Using More Precise Language: The purpose of being more exact in your thoughts is to catch yourself from making over-generalizations and other cognitive distortions, which we shall review in the following pages. A good way to be more precise in your thoughts is to cultivate the discipline of thinking with the following points in mind.

- *Time:* Specify the time frame or time horizon.
- *Place:* Specify the location.
- *Person:* Specify who is involved.
- *Probability:* Specify whether the thought only applies to a unique, low probability situation or to a more general, high probability situation.
- *Perception:* Specify the data behind the thought, rather than solely relying upon the feelings behind the thought.
- *Perspective:* Specify how someone else might think about the situation, event, or circumstance.

These six points to increasing how to think in a disciplined way will aid you in challenging your negative self-talk and thinking in a more objective fashion. To learn how to think in a more specific and disciplined way, let's return to the thought (I'll never be able to save any money) that was used as the example in the money self-talk table (Table 3.2). Reframe that thought as: "I will not be able to save more than $50 per pay period in my bank account for the next six months, although I realize that others who have it much worse are able to save maybe as little as $25 per pay period or each month." Although this thought is still framed in the negative (I'll not be able to . . .), it meets the following criteria upon closer inspection:

Time: (for the next six months)
Place: (in my bank account)
Person: (I)
Probability: (there are no hedge words such as perhaps, maybe, or possibly)
Perception: ($50)
Perspective: (although I realize that others who have it much worse are able to save maybe as little as $25 per pay period or each month)

Disciplined, deliberate thinking is an art. You will get better with practice. By using more specific language, you are developing a habit of the mind that will benefit you, your family, and your financial life.

The last of the five techniques to modify negative self-talk is similar to a positive affirmation or what is simply called here as "repeating positive self-talk."

Repeating Positive Self-Talk: The purpose of this technique is to rely upon a tried and true method of establishing habits . . . practice. Practice can be boring, as my 15-year-old son often reminds me when I am drilling him on French verbs or the periodic table in chemistry, but beyond the boredom is mastery. Malcolm Gladwell, the noted author of *Outliers*, found that masters of any skill are not necessarily more talented, but they have devoted at least 10,000 hours (the equivalent of five years of full-time work) practicing a relatively narrow skill, such as shooting baskets or trading stocks. Imagine that you have spent 10,000 hours practicing negative self-talk, you will become a master of . . . oh no . . . negative self-talk. Flip this to positive self-talk and you will become a master of positive self-talk. When you first begin this, you will say to yourself, "I don't believe this crap. I'm lying to myself." Keep thinking positive self-talk and gradually you will find that positive self-talk is as natural as negative self-talk.

In reviewing these five techniques to modify your negative self-talk, it is clear that you have choices. With choices, if one technique does not work or feels awkward, then move on to another technique. If you discover after two to three months that none of these techniques work, then don't blame me, but really look within yourself and ask this question: Am I gaining something of value by holding onto my negative self-talk? If you answer "Yes," then psychologists call this "secondary gain." Remember when you were a little boy or girl and you got a cold or flu and your mom or grandmother peppered you with affection, made your favorite foods, relieved you of chores, and cuddled you. Do you remember how good this felt? So good that it was worth getting sick or playing sick. What are you gaining from tightly gripping your negative self-talk?

Another way of looking at negative self-talk is to identify the cognitive distortions that we make, not just about money but other things in our life. The focus here will be money. Understanding and identifying your cognitive distortions, or what Alcoholics Anonymous (AA) calls "stinkin' thinkin'," will assist you in dissolving your negative self-talk while building up your positive self-talk. Similar to rehabilitation, you have to build up new muscles, and this is often quite painful and frustrating, but the pain is worth it if you have greater flexibility, greater speed, and clearer thinking to make better financial decisions, which will drive more constructive financial behaviors.

MONEY COGNITIVE DISTORTIONS

Imagine a dialogue between you and your boss about your annual performance review. These types of discussions can be emotionally charged because the stakes are high. A salary increase may depend upon the review. Your job may depend on the review. Your promotion may depend on the review.

Boss: Well, to summarize, you got a 3 percent increase this year based upon your performance. Any questions? The increase should hit your next paycheck.
You: Thank you. I'm looking forward to the increase.
Boss: Great. I'll see you later today at the 3 P.M. meeting.
You: I'll be there.

As you walk out of your boss's office feeling proud and deserving of the 3 percent increase, you begin to have a few thoughts about the raise.

- "I'm going to save it all or spend it all." [All-or-none thinking]
- "This means that I will get an increase every year." [Over-generalization and jumping to conclusions]
- "Because of this increase, my performance is near perfect." [Mental filter]
- "I must get a raise every year from now." [Should statements]

Cognitive distortions are part of our negative self-talk. There has been a lot of research on cognitive distortions. It is very important that you learn first how to recognize these distortions, catch them early if they arise, and modify them if you failed to catch the distortion. Ultimately you want to prevent these cognitive distortions; this will take time and practice. This too is a mental habit similar to using precise language.

To begin to challenge your money cognitive distortions, carefully review the following list. The 10 items on this list are based upon the work of David M. Burns, MD, the author of the national bestseller *Feeling Good: The New Mood Therapy*. He writes about the connection, not between mind and body, but between thoughts and feelings:

> The first principle of cognitive therapy is that all of your moods are created by your "cognitions" or thoughts—your perceptions, mental attitudes and beliefs. It includes the way you interpret things—what you say about something or someone to yourself. You feel the way you do right now because of *the thoughts you are thinking at this moment.* (Burns, 1980, page 12)

I counsel my clients and workshop participants to first recognize these distortions in others and then yourself. However, be careful when recognizing these distortions in others, because your family and friends may not take kindly to you pointing them out.

ALL-OR-NONE THINKING: You see things as black-and-white or either-or, but not both-and. For example, if your investments fall short of perfect, you see your life as an investor as a total failure.

OVERGENERALIZATION: You see a single negative event such as a market downturn or reversal as a never-ending pattern.

MENTAL FILTER: You select a single negative detail, such as one declining mutual fund, in your portfolio of 10 mutual funds.

JUMPING TO CONCLUSIONS: You make a negative interpretation without specific facts to support your conclusion, such as great companies make great investments.

MIND READING: You conclude one of your advisors (e.g., financial, legal, accounting) is responding negatively to you and you don't bother to verify this.

THE FORTUNE TELLER ERROR: You are convinced that your prediction is an already-established fact. For example, you believe that the stock market, which has been in the doldrums all summer, will remain so in the fall and even winter.

MAGNIFICATION (CATASTROPHIZING) OR MINIMIZATION: You overstate the importance of things, such as quarterly returns, or you inappropriately minimize things until they seem insignificant.

EMOTIONAL REASONING: You assume that your negative emotions necessarily reflect the way things really are: "I feel like I've got to flee the market because the Dow is down."

SHOULD STATEMENTS: You try to motivate yourself with should and shouldn't: "I should pay myself first, no matter what."

LABELING AND MISLABELING: Instead of describing your error, you attach a negative label to yourself: "I'm a terrible investor." When someone else's behavior rubs you the wrong way, you attach a negative label to them: "She's really stupid as an advisor for not knowing when to get me back into the market." Mislabeling involves describing an event with highly colored and emotionally loaded language.

PERSONALIZATION: You see yourself as the cause of some negative external event, which in fact you were not responsible for, such as your portfolio tanking just like the overall market.

Now that you understand the 10 cognitive distortions, it is time to assess your own thinking to see what you have to work on to decrease these cognitive distortions in your financial life and maybe other parts of your life.

Cognitive Distortion Self-Assessment

As you read over each of the 10 cognitive distortions in Table 3.3, rate on a scale from 0–2 if that description is "like me" (2), "somewhat like me" (1), or "not at all like me" (0).

This is not a scientifically validated assessment so do not stress over the responses, but use your score as a quick way to determine how much you are distorting what is really happening with you and your money. Regardless of your starting point as reflected by your score, make a pledge to yourself to challenge your cognitive distortions and to rid yourself of what they call in AA as "stinkin' thinkin'."

Now, for your score, the best score is 0 and the worst score is 20. If you scored between 0–5, then you are doing a great job at seeing reality for what it is. If you scored between 6–10, you are doing a pretty good job at seeing the world objectively. If you scored between 11–15, then you are fooling yourself more often than is ideal. If you scored between 16–20, then you may not be able to accurately process the fact that you are living in your own world—your own bubble.

Table 3.3
Cognitive Distortions Quick Self-Check

Cognitive distortion	Like me	Somewhat like me	Not at all like me
All-or-none thinking	2	1	0
Overgeneralization	2	1	0
Mental filter	2	1	0
Jumping to conclusions	2	1	0
Mind reading	2	1	0
The fortune teller error	2	1	0
Magnification (catastrophizing) or minimization	2	1	0
Emotional reasoning	2	1	0
Should statements	2	1	0
Labeling and mislabeling	2	1	0
Personalization	2	1	0
Total up your score			

Challenging Your Money Cognitive Distortions

Do not confuse challenging your cognitive distortions with replacing your negative thoughts with positive thoughts. This is not a new version of the power of positive thinking. In other words, this is not old wine in new skin. A fair question that you may be asking is the following: If I'm not replacing negative thoughts with positive thoughts, what am I doing? You are being challenged to replace incorrect (unrealistic) thoughts with more correct (realistic) thoughts based upon the facts or evidence. For example, if your thought is as follows, "You should never buy another home because home values will always fall," then replacing this thought with "You should always buy another home because home values will always rise" is the opposite of the original thought but equally incorrect and unrealistic, although for different reasons. A more correct or realistic thought may be as follows, "Home prices may fall, rise, or stay flat, so buying a home depends upon what price you can get for the home and other factors." This thought is more correct and realistic because it is relative, not absolute, and it focuses on more than one criteria.

The benefits of challenging your cognitive distortions are pretty obvious, but they are also too important not to mention. So, here we go. The benefits are two-fold:

- To become more in control of your internal thoughts and belief systems, so that you can alter them to make better financial decisions and engage in healthier financial behaviors.
- To become a steward of your financial life by taking ownership of your thoughts and corresponding behaviors, rather than blaming others and being a victim to others and situations.

Beyond Positive Thinking

Simply replacing an incorrect or unrealistic thought with a more correct or realistic one is not a panacea. However, it does take the edge off of the thought and this influences your mood in a positive way. If you are thinking in a less emotionally charged way, then you are less likely to trigger your fight-or-flight response. The immediate benefit of not triggering your instinctual urge to fight or flee is that you can think more clearly and more objectively.

You may have noted that I used the words "facts" and "evidence" a couple of times. Going back to the original thought, "You should never buy another home because home values will always fall," you will note that it does not stand on its own in the absence of data, facts, or evidence. If you can find several examples where this is not true, then the thought is factually incorrect based upon the data or evidence. A quick way to challenge your cognitive distortion is to phrase the statement as a question. In this case, the question would be as follows: "Is it true that all home values are falling all over the country, or just in a region of interest?" By framing this as a question rather than a conclusion, you have some homework or research to do to find out the answer. Based upon your research, you may find that home values in certain neighborhoods are declining, but home values in other neighborhoods are increasing, so this thought is not accurate. As a review, to begin to challenge your cognitive distortions follow this three-step plan:

1. Identify your cognitive distortions out of the 10 listed in this chapter.
2. Phrase your conclusion or thoughts into a question.
3. Answer the question after you've done your homework and research.

FINAL EXAMINATION

School is a good memory for some and a nightmare for others. Even if you have bad memories of school and negative self-talk about school, you will be given a final examination in this chapter. Why? Knowing about money memories, self-talk, cognitive distortions, and how to challenge cognitive distortions is important, but actually applying them in real life is what counts.

By taking your final examination you can finish this chapter having the confidence and competence to begin changing your self-talk, not today, but right now. Right now!

Before we get to the exam, you need some information about George, a man you will coach in identifying his self-talk and cognitive distortions, and then you'll make recommendations on how George can change for the better and enjoy a more productive and healthier financial life as evidenced by smarter financial decisions and wiser financial behaviors.

George, a 35-year-old sales manager at a local electronics store, is extremely frustrated. He has the smarts and money to save for retirement, while still being able to pay his car loan, mortgage, and other household bills, including utilities, cable, internet, and so on. His employer matches 401(k) contributions up to 5 percent of his salary, which George is not taking advantage of. He makes $50,000 per year, which means that he is giving up $2,500 per year in free (tax-deductible) money from his employer. When probed further about this by the benefits coordinator at work, George thinks to himself, "The stock market is too risky. I better stay in cash." When asked about it, he usually replies to the benefits coordinator, "Not now, maybe later." He has been telling the benefits supervisor this for the past four years. As his salary increases, then he is giving up more and more money. George is anticipating that he will be promoted to district sales manager. This pays $75,000 per year. In thinking about this promotion and the 401K, George says to himself, "I could lose it all in the stock market. This way I am not losing anything." Trying to reason with himself one day, George thought, "If I were to begin putting my hard, earned money into a 401(k), I know the market would tank, and I would be wiped out like millions of others."

Now that you have read this vignette about George, you may be thinking to yourself that you know George. George is like a lot of folks, and unfortunately his thoughts are similar to far too many people. As I said before, George is smart, but he has some room to grow and develop to think more clearly and to get his financial house in order and prepare for retirement.

To begin the final examination, please take out a pen or pencil and a piece of paper, or open your laptop or tablet and answer these questions now. Feel free to reread certain parts of the chapter to get the correct answer.

1. On balance, does George exhibit more positive or negative self-talk?
2. What specific cognitive distortions does George hold onto with his self-talk?
3. Based upon the information provided in the final examination case, what concrete evidence or facts does George have to support these thoughts and beliefs:

a. "The stock market is too risky. I better stay in cash."
b. "I could lose it all in the stock market. This way I am not losing anything."
c. "If I were to begin putting my hard, earned money into a 401(k), I know the market would tank and I would be wiped out like millions of others."

4. What recommendations do you have for George in terms of contributing to his 401(k)?

Please visit www.drmartymartin.com for the answers to this case study and engage in an online dialogue with other readers about George and how to modify your own negative money self-talk while promoting your own positive money self-talk.

REFERENCES

Burns, D. M. (1980). *Feeling Good: The New Mood Therapy*. New York: Harper.
Gladwell, M. (2008). *Outliers: The Story of Success*. New York: Little Brown and Company.
Peluso, E., Ross, M., Gfeller, J., & LaVoie, D. (2005). A comparison of mental strategies during athletic skills performance. *Journal of Sports Science and Medicine, 4*, 543–549.
Schwartz, R. (1986). The internal dialogue: On the asymmetry between positive and negative coping thoughts. *Cognitive Therapy and Research, 10*(6), 591–605.

4

Why Do I Feel Stuck in This Financial Rut?: Confronting Inertia, Procrastination, and Underearning

Have you ever felt stuck like you are in a rut? This is a common question, but what is a rut actually? Being in a rut means that you are habitually in a routine that no longer excites or moves you forward; maybe the routine even saps energy and wastes time. For many of my clients and workshop participants, a rut is made up of two factors: inertia and procrastination. Another rut that is emerging and is gaining some attention is underearning, which is different from under-employment. This difference will be the focus of this chapter. The good news is that you can get out of a rut in your financial life once you learn more about inertia and how to overcome inertia and procrastination. This does not mean that your life or your financial life will be free of all inertia and procrastination. To be honest with you, although this is chapter 4 in the book, I wrote this chapter last because of inertia and procrastination. However, my commitment to completing the book on time was stronger than the inertia, and I did not violate my social contract and internal contract to send all 10 chapters to the editor on time. If you're like me, there are some temporary advantages to inertia and procrastination such as not having to deal with stuff and enjoy more pleasant activities but there are few long-term advantages to inertia and procrastination. If inertia and procrastination had overruled my drive and commitment to finish this book by a specific date, then I would have experienced regret and disappointment, and my word would be of little value to the editorial team and my support system, including my wife and my son, not to mention colleagues, coworkers, family, and friends. To dig deeper into what makes up a rut in your financial life and how to get out of that rut to make better financial decisions and actually engage in financial behaviors designed to support your financial life, we will begin with inertia, then procrastination, and lastly underearning.

INERTIA

There are some valuable lessons to be learned from physics and physicists. The famous physicist Sir Isaac Newton stated: "An object at rest stays at rest and an object in motion stays in motion with the same speed and in the same direction unless acted upon by an unbalanced force" (Newton, 1686). This powerful statement recited and memorized in science and physics classes throughout the world is referred to as Newton's First Law of Motion. This if often referred to as "inertia." This law also applies to human and behavior change.

In fact, an important insight from behavioral finance is the tendency for most of us not to make any changes, or what cognitive psychologist calls the "status quo bias." The status quo bias is inertia or what your parents may call "laziness." Status quo bias suggests that people are much more likely to stick with the status quo even if presented with better options. In studies of retirement savings, for example, researchers have found that status quo bias plays a significant role in determining whether employees participate in a 401(k) plan. Until recently, the default option for most 401(k) plans was nonparticipation, meaning that employees had to actively choose to participate. The conventional wisdom is changing such that the default option should be automatic enrollment. In the language of *Nudge: Improving Decisions about Health, Wealth and Happiness* by Richard C. Thaler and Cass R. Sunstein, automatically enrolling employees into 401(k) plans is an example of a nudge. Nudges move resting bodies. Nudges interrupt the status quo. Nudges are critical to overcoming inertia.

David Gal, a researcher at the Graduate School of Business at Stanford University, wrote an article in *Judgment and Decision Making* entitled "A Psychological Law of Inertia and the Illusion of Loss Aversion," in which he defines the Psychological Law of Inertia and its Corollary as follows:

> **Psychological Law of Inertia:** A person will tend to maintain the status quo unless impelled to alter the status quo by a psychological motive to do so. **Corollary:** The possibility of becoming better off—but not equally as well off—can provide the necessary motive to impel a person to alter the status quo.

Based upon these two definitions, it appears that you have to be psychologically motivated to overcome inertia or the status quo bias. Not only do individuals have to be psychologically motivated but there picture of the future must also be elicited because this how they will experience whether they will be better off by altering the status quo. In essence, images of the future influence our present decisions and behaviors. If you were to imagine that the future is less desirable than the present, then you would prefer the status quo and vice versa. Besides imagining the future, which can have both positive and negative frames, the key area to explore regarding the Psychological Law of Inertia is based upon this question: What do we know about the psychological motivation of saving as one key financial behavior?

Daniel Pink wrote a book titled *Drive* in which he talks about motivation. Similar to Daniel Pink, two academics named Kirstan A. Neukam and Douglas A. Hershey developed a scale called Planning Drive, which is part of their Financial Activation Scale. This scale has five items that seek to capture whether an individual has the drive or motivation to overcome psychological inertia, which is a predictor of intent to plan and save.

1. When it comes to financial planning for retirement, I use a "no holds barred" approach.
2. When doing financial planning for retirement, I feel excited and energized.
3. I go out of my way when it comes to financial planning for retirement.
4. I am highly active in my pursuits toward financial planning for retirement.
5. When I see the chance to further my retirement investments, I move on it right away.

You can tell by reading over each one of these five Planning Drive questions that they are the opposite of inertia and the status quo bias. To discover the intensity of your Planning Drive, respond "yes" or "no" to each of these five items above. If you have more "yes" answers than "no" answers, congratulations! On the other hand, if you have more "no" responses than "yes" responses you have some work to do. Get going and don't allow inertia to set in or fear to paralyze you from planning.

Another interesting fact about human inertia in comparison to physical inertia is that fear can "stop us in our place." Fear is natural, instinctual, and adaptive under many circumstances. Fear warns us of dangers and hazards. But for some of us, fear can take over our ability to make decisions and engage in behaviors that benefit us today and tomorrow. Fear is akin to inertia. Why? Fear saps us of our energy and vitality while at the same time robbing us of peace and harmony. Fear is illusory; it cannot live. Planning drive and fear interact for most of us when thinking about saving, investing, retiring, or any other financial decisions and behaviors. In fact, in an academic study by Kirstan A. Neukam and Douglas A. Hershey in *Financial Services Review*, they concluded that "individuals who are saving the most are those who have the strongest financial goals and the lowest level of fear" (page 34). Cultivating drive or the psychological motivation to overcome inertia is tempered by the intensity of your fear, which is more than likely based upon some rational concerns and others that are imagined or fall backs from your childhood, adolescence, or early adulthood that no longer apply today because times have changed and you have changed.

You may be asking, "How do I develop that level of drive to plan for retirement or another financial goal?" The legendary economist John Maynard Keynes, who in 1936 wrote the now famous book *The General Theory of Employment, Interest and Money,* identified eight saving motives:

1. To build up a reserve against unforeseen contingencies (precautionary motive).
2. To provide for an anticipated future relationship between the income and the needs of the individual (life-cycle motive).
3. To earn interest and appreciation (the inter-temporal substitution motive).
4. To enjoy gradually increasing expenditure (the improvement motive).
5. To enjoy a sense of independence and the power to do things, though without a clear idea or intention of a specific action (the independence motive).
6. To invest money in various projects when moved to do so (the enterprise motive).
7. To bequeath a fortune (the bequest motive).
8. To satisfy pure miserliness, that is, unreasonable but insistent inhibitions against acts of expenditures (the avarice motive).

Although these were written nearly 80 years ago, they are still relevant today. To make practical use of these eight saving motives developed by Keynes, please take the following self-assessment in Table 4.1: What Motivates Me to Save Survey

If you are like most folks, the first question after completing any survey is to wonder how did I do? This self-assessment, like many others in the book, are not designed to give you a grade or to judge you but to serve as a tool to offer some insight into your financial decisions and habits. If you count up your X's under the "Strongly agree" column and if you have more than five, then you are demonstrating a drive to save for retirement, which means that you can probably overcome any inertia assuming that you are not experiencing too much fear. If on the other hand, if you have more than five X's under the "Strongly disagree" column, then you are demonstrating inertia with regard to saving for retirement and now must explore what is the cause of your inertia or status quo bias. Are you realistically imagining the future and seeing the benefits of saving for retirement rather than only sensing the benefits of "leaving well enough alone" or thinking "if it ain't broke don't fix it"? This self-talk may help you in the short run but not the long run because changing

Table 4.1
What Motivates Me to Save Survey

Savings behavior	Strongly agree	Agree	Disagree	Strongly disagree
To build up a reserve against unforeseen contingencies				
To provide for an anticipated future relationship between income and my needs				
To enjoy interest and appreciation				
To enjoy gradually increasing expenditure				
To enjoy a sense of independence and the power to do things, though without a clear idea or intention of a specific action				
To secure enough money to carry out speculative or business projects				
To bequeath a fortune				
To satisfy pure miserliness, that is, unreasonable but insistent inhibitions against acts of expenditures				

a financial behavior such as saving for retirement should not be framed as fixing something that is broken but improving and achieving a long-term goal where the picture of the future has more benefits than the picture of staying the same.

Another way to view Newton's First Law of Motion is to recognize that folks will continue to do what is working for them unless there is a good reason in their mind to drive change. Furthermore, a lot of very successful sales professionals try to identify the "pain" or "pleasure" point in potential clients based upon the following premise: If most of us are in enough pain, enough to want to experience less pain, then we shall embrace any change that relieves our pain. For instance, one my clients was so painfully burdened by hefty debt that she stopped spending impulsively to rid herself of that tortuous pain. If sales professionals cannot drive change through the pain point, then the next option is to find the pleasure point. If you deeply want something so bad that you nearly spend the better part of the day yearning and striving for this desired object, experience, state, person, or good, then you will embrace any change that brings you closer to that point of desire-pleasure fulfillment. For example, one of my clients, at the age of 60, truly desired to be a teacher and made substantial changes in many aspects of her life to achieve that goal including selling her home, moving into a dorm, and dropping some of her more negative friends. Putting on the sales professional mindset, ask yourself the following questions to see whether you are a good prospect for change in your financial life:

What is happening in my financial life that is causing me so much pain, discomfort, and distress?

Use the space below to write your answer here.

What can happen in my financial life that will lift me up in the mornings and keep me engaged in my life throughout the day because I love my financial life?

Use the space below to write your answer here.

Once you finish answering these two pain-and-pleasure drivers of financial behavior change, then step back and determine whether the pain and pleasure is enough to put you into action. The greater the pain and the more intense the desired state that you are seeking, then the greater the magnitude for financial behavior change. Returning to Newton's First Law of Motion, an object will continue to do whatever it is doing unless there is a drive (pain or pleasure) to change. So an object like a coffee mug is going to stay that way unless you apply a force to it by pulling it, pushing it, or picking it up. At times, the inertia is so great or so frequent that what results is procrastination or putting off those things that in the long run benefit us but choosing those things that in the short run provide us with greater satisfaction or relief. Procrastination is a form of avoidance.

PROCRASTINATION

As humans, we are constantly torn between rewarding ourselves right now and waiting for the potential of a reward in the future. Experimental psychologists have asked people, "Do you want chocolate right now or fruit right now?" Most people say, "Chocolate." Yet, if you ask, "Do you want chocolate or fruit one week from now?" Most people say, "Fruit." What would you say if asked that question?

Also, as humans, we tend to procrastinate on those things that have a future payoff, such as exercising and saving for college or retirement. Psychologists describe the tendency to prefer instant gratification over delayed gratification as "hyperbolic discounting." In more basic terms, you "undervalue" future rewards of paying for college and "overvalue" the immediate gratification of going out to expensive restaurants, buying luxury goods, and traveling to Europe. In short, you would rather enjoy the small reward now than wait for the larger payoff in the future.

Are we hardwired to discount the future and go for the gusto with the present? Based upon cutting-edge research in neuroeconomics, the answer appears to be yes. Our limbic system, the more primitive part of our brain, in contrast to our frontal cortex, a more developed part of our brain responsible for well-thought out decisions and problem solving, triggers us to "get all you can right now because you may not be here in the future or the desired object may not be available in the future."

Cost of Procrastination in Your Financial Life

Time is your friend when investing due to the positive impact of compounding. Compounding is your "money making money." By reinvesting your interest, dividends, and capital gains over time, your savings will grow and grow. The longer you allow your "money to make money," the more money you will have at the end.

Procrastination is the enemy of compounding because you do not give your money enough time to make more money. If your money is not making money and you want money, then you have got to make more money with "sweat equity," or in other words, working. Do you feel tired, burned out, or pressured to play office politics when your "money is making money"? No. But how do you feel when you are at your job?

One academic study found that individuals overpay in taxes due to procrastinating and rushing to get their taxes done at the very last minute. Are you like these folks who put off and put off having to rush and pay more later? If you are, then you probably say to yourself, "I'll never do that again." But our memories tend to be short for moderate discomfort, which is usually the price that we pay for procrastination. If the price were higher, then it would be more memorable and we would procrastinate far less.

To fight procrastination, have two deadlines: the real deadline and your deadline. Your deadline should always be before the real deadline so that you are pushing the deadline instead of being pulled by the deadline. How does the work actually? When I get up in the morning, I know that the e-mail inbox is calling my name, "Marty, open us up and see all the emails to read and respond to right now." I typically wait and do the task or tasks that I find the most boring or the most challenging so that I can hit them at my peak in terms of energy, concentration, and focus. While I am doing these unpleasant tasks, such as paying bills or filling out administrative forms, I do not necessarily like these tasks, but I sure do feel good and relieved after I finish. To be honest, without that nagging feeling of having unfinished business to attend to, I feel more energized and confident for the rest of the day. How many of you pay late fees on credit cards and other bills because you put off paying your bills? Stop giving credit card companies and banks your hard-earned money especially since they are robbing us all with high interest rates.

TWO REALITIES: WORK MAKING MONEY VERSUS MONEY MAKING MONEY

To illustrate the "magic of compounding" by your "money making money," picture two individuals, both 30 years old. Both graduated from college. Both earn $100,000 per year. Both have equal living expenses and are taxed the same. They are essentially financial twins except for one reality. Bob has put off saving for his retirement. Instead, Bob spends his money having a good time. Maria enjoys a good time too but recognizes that she needs enough money to have a good time throughout her life after she retires, which she plans to do at age 60, or 30 years from now.

Maria: By deciding to save $5,000 per year now, she will save a total of $245,013.39 by the time she reaches 60, assuming her retirement has an interest rate of 3 percent.

Bob: By putting off saving $5,000 for 15 years, or until he is 45, Bob will save a total of $95,784.41 by the time he reaches 60, assuming his retirement has an interest rate of 3 percent.

Maria @ $245,013.39 – Bob @ $95,784.41 = **$149,228.98**

The cost of Bob procrastinating is almost $150,000. What did Bob get in return for putting off saving for retirement? Are you more like Bob or Maria? How much is procrastination costing you?

How Do We Overcome Procrastination?

Psychologists recommend that you precommit, which means that you take the option away to make a tradeoff decision between now and later.

Dr. Richard Thaler created the Save More Tomorrow (SMT) program to get individuals to save in advance toward their retirement. This saving program is automatic. You make a decision once a year to enroll in the program, and if you get a raise, then your raise is automatically placed into the retirement program. Dr. Thaler knows that automatic decisions enable you to procrastinate less and accomplish more. Not all decisions can be automated, such as the decision to accept less in pay due to scarcity thinking, a low occupational self-esteem, or poor negotiation skills. Far too many people are settling for jobs that do not allow them to reach their full potential or pay their bills. It is time to overcome the inertia of settling and stop procrastinating looking for or creating a job that is aligned with your inner gifts and talents and that pays all of your bills with money left over to invest in your future. The last section of this chapter will help you understand underearning and how to overcome underearning.

UNDEREARNING

If we did all things we're capable of doing, we would literally astonish ourselves.

—Thomas Edison

How can it be possible that in the richest nation in the world with a tradition of innovation and individual ruggedness that tens of millions struggle financially? Even those who are fully employed and lucky enough to have decent benefits still struggle because their income is not keeping up with the cost of goods and services. For some, the wages are simply not enough through no fault of their own. For others, the wages could have been more, but they are not because of something deep within that says, "I'm not worthy of more," or a simple lack in skills about how to negotiate for more and in some cases demand more by communicating your value. The focus of this question here will be on earnings, or what most people refer to as "salary." There is an economic answer to this question, and there is a psychological answer to this question. The emphasis here is on the psychological aspects of underearning, yet the economic aspects will be lightly touched upon.

Economic Perspective

There is a linear relationship between years in school and earnings. The more education you attain, then the higher your income. There are individual exceptions. You can recall a story told to you by one of your pessimistic or cynical associates about a highly educated attorney, doctor, or PhD who is driving a cab or waiting table to argue that education does not matter in terms of salary, but this idea is not validated by economic facts. This is dead wrong at the aggregate level but is true for some individuals. Here are some facts from the College Board's *Education Pays: The Benefits of Higher Education for Individuals and Society*:

- In 2005, the typical four-year college graduate working full time all year made $50,900 compared to a high school graduate working full time all year who earned $31,500. In other words, the college graduate earned 62 percent more than the high school graduate.
- Individuals with master's degrees make nearly twice as much as high school graduates, and those with professional degrees such as medicine and law make nearly three times as much per year as high school graduates.

The lesson is to invest in your education and that of your children because it pays off financially for the vast majority who make this investment. Pursuing higher education does not only mean earning a four-year college degree but also acquiring knowledge and skills in demand by employers. In a joint report published by Deloitte Consulting, LLP and the Manufacturing Institute entitled "Boiling Point? The Skills Gap in U.S. Manufacturing," the demand for talent is more than a simple inconvenience, as illustrated by an excerpt from the report.

> Shortages in skilled production jobs—machinists, operators, craft workers, distributors, technicians, and more—are taking their toll on manufacturers' ability to expand operations, drive innovation, and improve productivity. . . . Unfortunately, these jobs require the most training, and are traditionally the hardest manufacturing jobs to find existing talent to fill. (page 1)

According to the U.S. Department of Labor's Bureau of Labor Statistics, the median hourly wage of a machinist, as an example of a career not requiring a four-year college degree, was $17.41 in May 2008. The education and training required is not a four-year college degree but mastery of trigonometry and geometry is required in addition to reading a blueprint, metalworking, and drafting. For machinists wanting to work in the aerospace manufacturing industry, applied calculus and physics are critical areas of knowledge. Institutions of higher learning such as Belmont Technical College offer two-year degrees in high-demand fields such as power plant technology. The point is that if all you have is a high school degree in this new world of work, then you are going to have a challenging financial life. You don't need the extra stress in your life but this still begs the question: Will a college degree pay off?

Should I Invest in a College Degree or Buy Lottery Tickets to Become a Millionaire?

Imagine that you walk down the street and ask this question: "Should I invest in a college degree or buy lottery tickets to become a millionaire?" The average person on Main Street will probably answer like this: "It depends on what you're going to do with the college degree, or if you can find a job requiring a college degree." According to the Bureau of Labor Statistics, college graduates with a bachelor's degree earned 65 percent more than those with a high school degree and a whopping 130 percent more than those without a high school degree. This is called the "college premium."

As you can see, there is a big difference between a high school diploma and a four-year college degree. One of the most important financial decisions that you can make for yourself and children in your life is to get at a minimum of a four-year college degree. For the more cynical readers, you may have questions:

- Does a four-year college degree guarantee that you will get a job?
- Does a four-year college degree guarantee that you will secure a full-time job with benefits?
- Does a four-year college degree guarantee that you will earn a salary equivalent to their education?
- Does a four-year college degree guarantee that you will not get temporarily laid off?

Does a four-year college degree guarantee that you will get a job? No, particularly in a tough economy like the one we have painfully experienced since 2001. However, the unemployment rate is not as bad for those with more education. So, not only do you make more money but you are also less likely to be unemployed as you obtain more education.

Does a four-year college degree guarantee that you will secure a full-time job with benefits? No, particularly as the cost of benefits rise and employers of all sizes decide not to offer benefits. Employers, large and small, may not have enough consumer demand for the goods and services to invest in employing workers full time, so they offer part-time employment. Part-time employment obviously decreases your total earnings. And whether you are full time or part time and without benefits, then either you have to pay for those benefits out of pocket, which is a lot more expensive than when those benefits are provided by your employer. For instance, if you pay for health care on your own at retail, individually underwritten prices, then will be a big bill compared to if you get health insurance from your employer and your employer picks up 80 percent of the total premium and you pay 20 percent of the premium. According to the American Health Insurance Program, annual premiums averaged $2,985 for single coverage and $6,328 for family coverage in mid-2009.

Does a four-year college degree guarantee that you will earn a salary equivalent to their education? No, particularly as the supply of talent with higher education increases while the demand for talent decreases or fails to grow because of slack consumer demand for goods and services and the lack of investment in companies employing workers. It is clearly a buyer's market for talent for the most part with the exception of a few occupations in high demand, such as nursing and some engineering jobs. This last question moves us closer to the focus of this section—underearning. Unlike unemployment and under-employment, underearning assumes that an individual has the opportunity to earn secure a full-time job aligned with their educational level and earn an income aligned with their educational level but decides to do otherwise. In short, this phenomenon cannot be explained by economic formulas but more so by examining the psychology behind underearning. This in no way minimizes the vicious reality of those who "played by the rules"—the old rules—and earned a college degree but cannot find a job that is aligned with their newly acquired knowledge and skills. Yet, there is more to the story of underearning than simply a bad economy.

Psychological Perspective

Don't blame the floor if you can't dance.

—Source unknown

The book, Overcoming Underearning, by Barbara Stanny, brought underearning out of the dim closet and to center stage in the theatre of work and making money—good money. Here's a brief summary what an underearner looks like according to Stanny:

- ✓ Underearners feel as if they're ensnared.
- ✓ Underearners wait to be rescued by merciful employers, politicians, or charities.
- ✓ Underearners underrate their value at work giving away their talent and time for far less than market value.
- ✓ Underearners need security—they seek the familiar even it keeps them treading water financially.
- ✓ Underearners engage in negative self-talk and self-limiting behaviors.

✓ Underearners happily take what is left over rather than standing first in line.

✓ Underearners live in financial fear—they live from paycheck to paycheck.

✓ Underearners are imprecise about financial and career progress—they don't know how to regulate their financial life.

✓ Underearners are closet wealth haters—they are down or uncertain about the wealthy and even the financially comfortable.

✓ Underearners are controlled by scarcity thinking—they do not see abundance and prosperity only deprivation and failure.

Take the Underearner Self-Assessment (Table 4.2) to see whether you demonstrate some of these characteristics. Circle whether this characteristic is present or absent for you. After making this assessment, add up the total number of characteristics that you circled as present. There is no right or wrong answer. Do not judge yourself as your respond to each question. Be honest with yourself. You can only develop a realistic plan to improve

Table 4.2
Underearner Self-Assessment

Characteristic	Present	Absent
Underearners feel as if they're ensnared.	1	0
Underearners wait to be rescued by merciful employers, politicians, or charities.	1	0
Underearners underrate their value at work giving away their talent and time for far less than market value.	1	0
Underearners need security—they seek the familiar even it keeps them treading water financially.	1	0
Underearners engage in negative self-talk and self-limiting behaviors.	1	0
Underearners happily take what is left over rather than standing first in line.	1	0
Underearners live in financial fear—they live from paycheck to paycheck.	1	0
Underearners are imprecise about financial and career progress—they don't know how to regulate their financial life.	1	0
Underearners are closet wealth haters—they are down or uncertain about the wealthy and even the financially comfortable.	1	0
Underearners are controlled by scarcity thinking—they do not see abundance and prosperity only deprivation and failure.	1	0
Grand total (Add up all "1s")	Total =	

yourself if you are first honest with yourself about your strengths and areas of improvement.

Congratulations! If you scored 3 or less, then you are living out of a spirit of truly valuing your talents, thinking abundantly, and having enough financially to do more than make "ends meet." *Keep Up the Good Work!* If you scored between 6 and 4, then you are headed in the right direction to get paid what you are worth in the labor market, to think more about abundance, and to feel good when you have money left over from your bills. *Proceed with Caution?* If you score 7 or more, then, first, thank yourself for being honest, and second, for each of the items that you circled, come up with a plan to eliminate or decrease that underearner characteristic. For example, if you circled "Underearners happily take what is left over rather than standing first in line," then write down two times in the past when you have done that.

1. _____

2. _____

You may have written something like, "I am lucky to have a job so I didn't toot my own horn when I exceeded the expectation or performance standard" or "I don't need a raise or promotion as bad as my co-worker who is really suffering financially after their divorce or illness." After writing down two examples from your own life for each of these underearner characteristics, then identify whether these examples reflect scarcity or abundant thinking. Returning to the first example, "I am lucky to have a job so I didn't toot my own horn when I exceeded the expectation or performance standard"; this is obviously scarcity thinking because it suggests that jobs are scarce. As for the second example, "I don't need a raise or promotion as bad as my co-worker who is really suffering financially after their divorce or illness," this too is scarcity thinking because it suggests that there is only enough money for one raise or one promotion. This is often referred to as the zero-sum game. If you get the raise or promotion, then that means that your co-worker cannot get the raise or promotion, which may not be true, but if you believe it is true and you suffer from this underearner characteristic, then you will give up this raise or promotion.

What would happen if you switched your thinking from scarcity to abundance? In both examples, you would more than likely ask for more not because you are egotistical, self-centered, greedy, and ruthless but because you recognize and accept that in this economic environment, you have got to advocate for yourself and all those who depend upon you. Knowing the difference between scarcity and abundant thinking is so important to beating underearning that the two will be contrasted in the pages that follow.

Scarcity Thinking

Many of us not only believe or have been told that there is not enough to go around even for you and your loved ones but we also have been told by others and ourselves that we are not deserving of anything more than the scraps. There are three drivers of scarcity thinking: (a) there is not enough; (b) there is only enough for the deserving; and (c) there is enough but only if one person's gain is another person's loss. Each one of these drivers will be explained as a way of getting you to recognize these drivers and rid yourself of these drivers of scarcity thinking.

There Is Not Enough

A focus on lack triggers your survival instincts. You will either dig in or protect yourself or you will go on the attack searching for prey. Underearners usually seek safety and comfort. They accept the current circumstance out of fear that if they push for more that they will end up with absolutely nothing. As the saying goes, "Something is better than nothing." This is true under certain situations and at certain times, but it is also false under other circumstances and other times.

There Is Only Enough for the Deserving

Do you deserve to have more? Do you deserve to be compensated for your gifts, talents, performance, and productivity? Far too many have been told that they don't amount to much at work. Don't believe the hype. Challenge this assumption that others hold of you and conduct an experiment: How much do you earn or save your employer? If you earn or save them more than your annual salaries including your benefit package, then you are earning your keep and then some.

There Is Enough but Only if One Person's Gain Is Another Person's Loss

A common myth for those who hold onto scarcity thinking is that there is only enough for a few and that if you get more, then that means others have to get less. *No!* This way of thinking prevents many from asking for their fair share because it places them in the role of a predator victimizing others by taking away their ability to survive and thrive.

In summary, scarcity thinking results in you making less money than you should. This causes unnecessary financial strain, which can result in negative health consequences, family consequences, and social consequences, not to mention negative financial consequences. Is there another way? Yes, abundant thinking.

Abundant Thinking

Abundant thinking is far less common but far simpler. When you know that there is more than enough, that you deserve more, and that if you get more, then others do not get less, then you are thinking abundantly. Abundant thinking is the enemy of underearning. When you think abundantly, you feel energetic and optimistic. Energy and optimism is the enemy of inertia and procrastination.

Back to the question that opened this chapter: *Have you ever felt stuck like you are in a rut?* For most of us, the answer is yes. After reading this chapter and completing the exercises assuming that you did not procrastinate, you now have some tools and techniques to eliminate or take away the power of procrastination in your financial life, how to overcome inertia and challenge your scarcity thinking, which is often the root of underearning and being stuck in a financial rut. When your financial life is moving, you are deciding and acting with integrity and you are responding to an abundant world filled with opportunities, then you don't have time to be in a rut, and momentum will move you out of most any pothole you may face while you are driving your financial life.

REFERENCES

ACT. (2005). Student Readiness Inventory: Tool Shop. Is College Really Worth It? http://www.act.org/engage/studentguide/pdf/IsCollegeReallyWorthIt.pdf

AHIP Center for Policy and Research. (2009, October). Individual Health Insurance 2009. A Comprehensive Survey of Premiums, Availability and Benefits. http://www.ahipresearch.org/pdfs/2009IndividualMarketSurveyFinalReport.pdf

Baum, S., & Ma, J. (2007). *Education Pays: The Benefits of Higher Education for Individuals and Society.* College Board Advocacy & Policy Center. http://trends.collegeboard.org/downloads/Education_Pays_2010.pdf

Bureau of Labor Statistics. (2008). Current Population Study 2008. www.bls.gov/emp/emptab7.htm

Gal, David. (2006). A psychological law of inertia and the illusion of loss aversion. *Judgment and Decision Making, 1*(1), 23–32.

Judge, T. A., Hurst, C., & Simon, L. S. (2009). Does it pay to be smart, attractive, or confident (or all three)? Relationships among general mental ability, physical attractiveness, core self-evaluations, and income. *Journal of Applied Psychology, 94*(3), 742–755.

Kasper, G. (2004, March 30). Tax Procrastination: Survey Finds 29% have yet to Begin Taxes. http://www.prweb.com/releases/2004/3/prweb114250.htm

Keynes, J.M. (1936). General Theory of Employment, Interest and Money. http://www.marxists.org/reference/subject/economics/keynes/general-theory/

Morrsion, T., Maciejewski, B., Giffi, C., DeRocco, E., McNelly, J., & Carrick, G. (2011). *Boiling Point? The Skills Gap in U.S. Manufacturing*. Deloitte Consulting LLP and the Manufacturing Institute.

Neukam, K.A., & Hershey, D.A. (2003). Financial inhibition, financial activation and saving for retirement. *Financial Services Review, 12,* 19–37.

Newton, I. (1686). *Philosophiae Naturalis Principia Mathematica*. http://www.scribd.com/doc/52635203/Isaac-Newton-Philosophi%C3%A6-naturalis-principia-mathematica-1686

Nyhus, E.K., & Pons, E. (2005). The effects of personality on earnings. *Journal of Economic Psychology, 26,* 363–384.

Stanny, B. (2006). *Overcoming Underearning: Overcome Your Money Fears and Earn What You Deserve*. New York: Collins.

Swann, Jr., W.B. (1983). Self-verification: Bringing social reality into harmony with the self. In J. Suls and A.G. Greenwald (Eds.). *Social Psychological Perspectives on the Self* (vol. 2, pp. 33–66). Hillsdale, NJ: Erlbaum.

Thaler, R.H. & Sunstein, C.R. (2008). *Nudge: Improving Decisions about Health, Wealth and Happiness*. New Haven, CT: Yale University Press.

5

The Deadly Dozen: How to Spot 12 Decision-Making Traps and Avoid Them

Imagine for a moment you're in the woods hunting and your guide tells you to be careful . . . bear traps. You nervously ask, "Where are the bear traps?" Your guide calmly replies, "You can't tell but I can." So, you pause and then wonder whether you should stop hunting or rely upon your guide. After thinking about the possible dangers that may await you as you hunt but also the real possibility of snagging a bear, you nod to your guide that you want to keep hunting.

Financial decision-making is a lot like hunting. There is risk. There is uncertainty. There is danger. And there are rewards. Similar to hunting, you set out to return home safely with the prize. As investors, we set out to "play the markets." The goal is keep our initial investment safe while hoping for reward—returns greater than our initial investment, known as "principal."

Even as "investors" in our careers, we go out to find that job or career that satisfies our soul, rejuvenates our body, and challenges our mind, yet pays enough to free us from the vicissitudes of life and maybe even propels us to the next notch in the economic ladder. Similar to hunting and investing, there is risk and uncertainty. All of three of these—hunting, investing, and "careering"—share not only risk and uncertainty, but also the importance of making smart decisions.

In this chapter, I shall serve as your guide on how to make smarter financial decisions. The reward for learning this information is a greater return on your investments. In the *Journal of Portfolio Management*, a periodical read by professional investment practitioners, Daniel Kahneman and M. W. Pope explain the importance of understanding decision-making traps: "Investors who are prone to these biases will take risks that they do not acknowledge, experience outcomes that they did not anticipate, will be prone to unjustified trading, and may end up blaming themselves or others when outcomes are bad" (page 53).

This chapter outlines 12 decision-making traps that are common to everyday investors and professional investors. These will be referred to here as the "Deadly Dozen." These 12 decision-making traps are also called "biases" or "rules of thumb." In other words, they are shortcuts. When faced with complexity, our brains want to make things simple. Too simple. This process eases our anxiety but interferes with our ability to make smart decisions. This chapter is about teaching you how to spot these 12 biases or rules of thumb before they trip you up when you make important financial decisions that can affect your lifestyle, retirement, and possibly your career.

Understanding these 12 decision-making traps and taking appropriate actions to correct your biases may result in better outcomes, protect you from making poor choices, and give you a sense of control over your financial investments.

After reading this chapter, you'll be able to recognize the Deadly Dozen and avoid them. These 12 decision-making traps are divided into three categories: thinking, feeling, and relating.

THINKING

Eight of the Deadly Dozen involve your thoughts. Alcoholics Anonymous (AA) members remind each other about the dangers of "stinkin' thinkin'." Stinkin' thinkin' is common among individuals who no longer drink alcohol, but who still think like an alcoholic and risk slipping back into drinking. In a way, this chapter is about how to help you recognize when you are engaged in stinkin' thinkin' and then stop thinking that way to protect you from yourself.

This section focuses on how you think when you make a financial decision. As humans, we tend to take shortcuts, which may save time but they can cost you as well. The costs often include money, but also frustration and wasted time. Now, let's begin with the first of the Deadly Dozen.

1. Cognitive Dissonance (Acting one way but believing the opposite)

Cognitive dissonance occurs when your actions differ from your beliefs, and you change your beliefs to match your actions. A psychological study found that people who bet on a horse at the race track increased their estimates of winning *after* placing the bet (Knox & Inkster, 1968). Commitment is not a problem until it borders on irrational. As the saying goes: "The most important thing to do when you find yourself in a hole is to stop digging."

To further drive home the power of cognitive dissonance, let's assume that you believe that eating high-fat foods is not good for you, yet you keep eating high-fat foods even though you know that this is bad for your health. How can you hold an opposing belief and action? We do this routinely as humans. To hold opposing beliefs and actions, we trick ourselves by ignoring or minimizing information that contradicts our beliefs. For example, we may not read an article or watch a news story about the risks of a high-fat food diet or we may say to ourselves, "My great uncle lived to be 89 and he had a terrible diet."

Here's an investment example. In a bear market, investors typically hold two different beliefs:

1. Share prices are low, so stocks are cheap; therefore, I should buy stocks
2. Everybody else is selling stock because the market is dropping.

One way to decrease cognitive dissonance is to ignore the commonly held wisdom to "buy things on sale." A bargain occurs when prices drop, not raise. Why is this different when buying stocks? It's not. Not only are these two beliefs contradictory, but for many investors, they become emotionally attached to their investments. Successful traders on Wall Street, LaSalle Street in Chicago, and Paternoster Square in London will tell you: "Don't fall in love with any stock, bond, or company." The other pull against buying stocks when they are "on sale" is that you are swimming against the tide because the media is reporting how everybody is selling not buying. Do you want to go against the grain? Some investment professionals advocate contrarian investing. Contrarian investors swim against the tide of most investors. For instance, if the masses are buying stocks at the peak of the market (the most expensive price) and selling stocks at the bottom of the market (the cheapest price), then they do the opposite. Why? Contrarian investors buy stocks and other investments like we do for most other purchases. We buy items on sale at their cheapest price for the value, and we sell items at the highest possible price. You have heard the famous saying on Wall Street—"Buy low, sell high."

Cognitive dissonance is a way of avoiding psychological pain. Even if we have to reconstruct our memories to avoid pain, then we do so. We are not intentionally distorting reality and reconstructing the past, but it happens almost automatically. A way of diminishing cognitive dissonance, which may lead to poor decisions, is to pause, reflect, and get some objective information to challenge our internal thoughts and feelings.

How to Avoid the Downside of Cognitive Dissonance?

- ✓ Contemplate how you will explain your decision to others.
- ✓ Grant yourself permission to accept that all decisions are not the best and that it is OK to make mistakes.
- ✓ Choose making a smarter decision over "proving to yourself that you were right."

2. Overconfidence (Acting as if you are smarter than you are)

Overconfidence and optimism are related. Here I will focus on overconfidence and later on optimism under the "Feelings" heading (Deadly Dozen #9). People often refer to overconfidence as a big ego. Overconfidence is caused by two illusions—the illusion of knowledge and the illusion of control. The illusion of knowledge trips up investors because they believe that they have more or better information than others have access to. The illusion of control also trips up investors because of the belief that they can control outcomes, rather than merely influence outcomes.

In studies of confidence, men tend to be more confident than women. Investors are often overconfident too. What's the big deal about investor overconfidence? Overconfidence leads to a number of decision-making traps or biases.

Overconfidence is not simply hutzpah or machismo or cockiness. Overconfidence has four elements.

1. Self-attribution bias
2. Confirmation bias
3. Hindsight bias
4. Over-valuation bias

Self-attribution bias: If you invest in a stock or bond and make a sizable profit, you will assume it happened due to your knowledge and skill as an investor. On the other hand, if you lose a lot of money, then you will assume it occurred because of the market or bad luck. This inclination to view a good outcome as a consequence of knowledge and skill and a bad outcome as a result of fate, luck, or chance is called the "self-attribution bias."

Confirmation bias: Confirmation bias occurs when you choose to interpret a past history of success and failure in a way that protects you psychologically. In other words, you interpret information according to your preconceptions and in a way that aligns with your previously held beliefs. Another way of looking at confirmation bias is that you seek out information that supports your existing point of view and avoid information that is contradictory. We are victims of our own selective perception and filtering. This bias clouds our objectivity.

A popular video used to teach students and managers how to conduct a job interview is titled *Interviewing: More Than a Gut Feeling*. In this training booklet and accompanying video, a simulated interview shows an interviewer asking a job candidate a series of questions, but the interviewer fails to ask questions to get a balanced perspective of the candidate. As a result, the interviewer gains a distorted impression of the candidate. Does this happen with you and your financial decisions? Do you fail to get a balanced perspective?

Hindsight bias: Hindsight bias is the third element of overconfidence. Humans are good at reconstructing the past to fit how we want to view the present situation. This bias is also called the "20:20 bias"—the "I knew it all along" bias. We engage in this bias when explaining our behavior and the behavior of others. If you watch any of the television stock analyst programs or listen to the radio programs, when the stock market makes a major move up or dip down, then commentators report how they had predicted this. Often you cannot find any of these predictions before the event took place. They also fail to comment on their mistaken investment forecasts. This is the hindsight bias in action.

Overvaluation bias: When you make decisions, such as buying and selling stocks or bonds, you may do so because you believe you have access to information or knowledge that is unique and valuable. As such, you may be willing to pay more than the real value of a certain stock. This is why marketers advertise special deals, premium offers, and limited opportunities to a select group of investors, who give access to these "secrets."

All four of the elements of overconfidence encourage you to trade more than you should. The bottom line is that as an investor, you will attribute your success to your stock or bond picking skills, not luck or even a rising overall market. Remember, a rising tide lifts all boats. Furthermore, when suffering from overvaluation bias, you believe your success will continue well into the future.

How to Avoid Overconfidence?

- ✓ Seek feedback from others before acting on the decision.
- ✓ Ask yourself the question, "What if I'm wrong?"
- ✓ Reflect upon times when you thought you were right but you were wrong.
- ✓ Seek out information that contradicts your own point of view.
- ✓ Play the devil's advocate at all times.

The next time you encounter an investment "guru" who appears to be overly confident, stop and identify if they are exhibiting all four of these biases or traps or just a few of them. After you first identify these biases in others, you may be able to check yourself.

3. Representativeness (Seeing patterns and trends where none exist)

Representativeness creates biased expectations. When you imagine the possibility of future events, you will base these probabilities on memories of recent past events. In other words, we construct our realities. You will also make decisions based on stereotypes or preconceived notions. For instance, you may stereotype all Fortune 500 companies as being great investments because they are great companies. Remember, that World Com, Enron, and Global Crossing were all on the Fortune 500 list at some point in time. Also, there are companies whose stock prices have really risen but are not listed on the Fortune 500.

The mutual fund industry plays on this decision-making trap by advertising past returns. As investors, we chase the winners. We consider this past return as advertised to be representative of what we can expect in the future. A famous study dating back to 1985 by Werner DeBondt and Richard Thaler found that it is smarter to invest in the losers than the winners.

Our brains search for and find patterns even when there are no patterns. We are pattern seekers. Reflect back on a vacation that you took to another city, region of the country, or other country. Did you catch yourself thinking—that reminds me of home? If you did, your brain was searching for a pattern and it found a match. A classic example in investing is to confuse a good company with a good investment.

Not only do we search for and create patterns. Once a pattern is identified or constructed, we tend to judge the probability of an event by finding a "comparable known" and assume that the probabilities will be the same. As an illustration, in a survey of high school students, it was found that those who overestimated the percentage of people who smoked cigarettes were also more likely to smoke cigarettes.

A related concept is the gambler's fallacy. This occurs when we believe that a string of good luck or bad luck will continue. The coin toss is a popular illustration of both the gambler's fallacy and the representativeness bias. You are tossing coins with a friend and you have tossed five tails in a row. If you are like most people, you will say, "Heads have a greater chance of coming up now." Statistically, the odds are still 50:50. The odds will always be 50:50. You are at a casino playing a slot machine and you keep losing time and after time, but you think silently to yourself, "It's only a matter of time before I hit it big." Or you are at the casino playing a slot machine and you are winning. You say to yourself, "I'm hot . . . I'm going to keep playing." You play believing that your hot streak will never end. Well, you know the end of that story.

How to Avoid Representativeness Bias?

✓ Treat each event as a separate event.

✓ All "hot hands" and "losing streaks" end at some point in time.

✓ Randomness actually exists in life even if this makes you feel uncomfortable. For instance, flipping a coin always results in a 50:50 chance of heads and tails. *All the time*.

✓ Recognize that patterns exist and randomness exists. Random events and randomness are not bad. Randomness is not to be avoided but managed.

✓ Research your options.

✓ Challenge yourself to question the validity of your stereotypes. In other words, look for exceptions to your stereotype.

4. Familiarity (Believing that what you know is better than what you don't know)

In investing, you are more likely to pick a stock you are familiar with, even if it's not making money. This is called the "home bias" in investing. You know people who root for the local sports team (most people do) and own their own company stock. The sports team and the company are familiar to them. They appear to be less risky because of this familiarity. People prefer things that are familiar to them. Numerous academic studies (French & Poterba, 1991; Huberman, 2001) show that investors over-invest in their own countries, own states, own cities, and own companies. This limits diversification. Diversification protects you against risk.

Familiarity can cause you to make decisions too quickly, often skipping steps that may save you grief down the road. If you think about your favorite food item in your preferred fast food chain, like most people, you probably make your selection fast. If you were to go to an unfamiliar fast food chain, then you would slow down while making your selection. The effect is the same with other decisions, including investing. One of the dangers of familiarity is we tend to view the decision less risky.

If you're heavily invested in the stock of your own company, in your employer's 401(k) or other retirement plan, beware of the home bias decision-making trap. If your company fails, then company stock is likely to drop like a rock, like Enron, AIG, and Lehman Brothers stock did. If the stock in the company plummets, then you are more likely to be a victim of downsizing in this scenario. The home bias decision-making trap can set you up for a double whammy—no job and no more money in your retirement account.

What if your company stock increases in price like WorldCom or Google or Apple? In this case, because you know your company better than other companies, you will invest in your company by buying stock. Why shouldn't you invest in this scenario? Or should you be careful of investing too much in one stock? And as the stock price increases, then you believe that the trend will continue. In this case, you become a victim of two of the Deadly Dozen: home bias or familiarity and representativeness.

Another illustration of the familiarity bias at work when investing is the unfamiliar strategy of selling short. Professional traders will tell novice and uninformed investors that you make money in the stock market if stocks go up, go down, and even side to side. Simply because this investment strategy is not well-known does not mean that is does not work. In fact, some professional traders and investors remind everyday investors that they understand about saving money when bad catastrophic events happen, like house floods, car accidents, and medical emergencies. How so? If you have property and casualty insurance, auto insurance, and health insurance, you are seeking to protect yourself against the risk of potential harm. The same logic applies to your investment and retirement portfolio. To protect yourself against the downside risk, short selling or buying mutual funds that increase when the market decreases is a way to "hedge" your investments against greater losses.

How to Avoid the Familiarity Bias?

- ✓ Recognize there is comfort in the familiar, but that does not necessarily translate into rewards or gains.
- ✓ Venture into the unknown but with a map: Do your homework first.
- ✓ Prepare a contingency or back up plan if something should go wrong. In short, you want to have an exit strategy. Too many investors plan when to buy a stock or bond, but fail to plan when to sell the stock or bond if the market changes. Professional traders always plan an exit strategy, that is, when to reverse the trade.
- ✓ The world has become a global community and your investments should reflect that reality, even if you feel uncomfortable venturing so far from home.
- ✓ It is not unpatriotic to invest overseas.

5. Loss Aversion (it hurts more to lose than to win—twice as much pain)

Loss aversion is also known as "prospect theory" among academics. Two world-renowned psychologists (Tversky & Kahnemann, 1979) were shocked to discover that individuals have a stronger desire to avoid losses than experience comparable gains. Another way of looking at this finding is that losses are emotionally felt twice as strongly as comparable gains.

Losses cause emotional pain. Larger losses cause more emotional pain. When you lose money, you will no doubt react in one of two ways. Your first reaction will be to pull back. Fearing more losses, you may sell your stocks or bonds. Some investors still feel the pain associated with the internet stock bubble burst in 2000, when vastly overpriced stocks went south. Other still feel the sting of the financial crisis of 2008, which melted real estate assets, investment portfolios, and retirement accounts. All of these external events have internal consequences. These internal consequences are loss aversion. The other reaction is to invest with even more vigor to get even. In gambling circles, this is often called "double or nothing."

Central to prospect theory is the anchoring effect. The anchoring effect has been used to explain why people engage in seemingly contradictory behavior. They buy insurance for protection and lottery tickets for financial gain.

One of the most common anchors is a past event or trend. Another major anchor for investors is the current stock price. And for homeowners, the purchase price of the home is an anchor. For instance, a client of mine bought her home in 2002 for $405,000, her home appreciated to $550,000 in 2007, and in 2010 she was struggling to price her house at $480,000, which she later sold for $465,000. In her mind, she lost $85,000 on the deal because she was anchored on the peak price of $550,000. If she were anchored on the initial purchase price in 2002 of $405,000, then she would have realized that she gained $60,000 on the deal.

Another example is an investor who buys a stock that goes up in value by 500 percent in the current year. However, over the past 10 years, the stock has only averaged a 10 percent gain each year for each of the 10 years. Where will the investor anchor—at the most current year with the 500 percent gain or at the 10 year average of 10 percent? Far too many investors will anchor at the peak, and this can result in a poor decision. Statisticians will tell the investor that the current year is an outlier or anomaly. In other words, statisticians will warn the investor in plain English by saying, "Don't expect this to continue." So, remember, where you anchor makes a difference in how you negotiate and how you feel.

How to Avoid Loss Aversion and Anchoring?

✓ Remember that the past is not the present or the future.
✓ Gather information from a variety of sources.
✓ View the decision from another perspective in time.
✓ Acknowledge that you decide where to anchor—at the peak, in the middle, or at the bottom—and this influences how you negotiate and how you feel.

6. Mental Accounting (Don't forget to add up all the money in all the buckets and envelopes)

We like to place people, things, places, and even investments into nice, neat mental compartments. An example of the mental accounting bias is to save money in a low interest vehicle like a bank savings plan, at less than 1 percent, yet use a high interest credit card, at 15 percent interest, for everyday purchases. If you diligently pay off your credit cards each month, then this does not apply to you.

You are probably familiar with people who refer to some of their money as "college money," "play money," "travel money," or "retirement money." This is an example of mental accounting. When people do this, they are not looking at the big picture. Individuals that organize their money into these buckets or discrete categories may know how much money is in each individual bucket or category but not in all the buckets or categories. This type of thinking can lead to an increase in risk taking not to mention not really knowing where you stand financially overall.

I have asked some of my clients to bring all of their investment, banking, and retirement statements and then spread them out on the conference table, take out a calculator, and beginning adding up all of the amounts to a grand total. The typical reaction is usually one of surprise. Good surprise and bad surprise.

Let's take a look at what happened during the financial meltdown of 2008. People had invested in their homes, invested in their company stocks and retirement accounts, invested in stocks of all types from domestic stocks to emerging market stocks, invested in bonds, and invested in commodities such as gold and even cotton. Then, when the stock market crashed, even a diversified portfolio of different types of stocks, bonds, commodities, and real estate dropped in value at the same time. Diversification is supposed to protect people by spreading our risk across different types of investments. Diversification failed in 2008. This does not mean that diversification is an inappropriate strategy, but, like many things in life, it will not work all the time. Remember, randomness happens. Also, you can't predict when randomness will knock on your door or enter your life.

Another common example for middle income households is to sock away thousands, if not tens of thousands, of dollars in retirement plans like 401(k) plans, yet owe credit card companies an equal amount of money. Why do we do this? Mental accounting. We view one bucket of money as savings money and the other bucket of money as spending money. The rational and wise way to use money is to save money at a high interest rate and spend it a lower one. This is how banks get marble floors and how bankers get big bonuses.

Now, let's turn to bonuses. Bonuses are like "birthday money" or a "windfall." Most people, forgetting that bonuses are earned too, spend "windfalls" differently than their hard-earned money. People tend to spend bonuses on what they regard as luxuries and niceties. Even worse, too many individuals who need to use the "bonus" money to pay off their bills, including high interest credit card bills, decide to treat themselves rather than taking care of their debts. Why? Mental accounting. For whatever reason, people often don't view bonus money the same as paycheck money. This also happens with tax refunds.

How to Avoid Mental Accounting?

- ✓ Remember that money is money and the same economic principles apply to all money regardless of its source or how you categorize available funds.
- ✓ Be sure to take out a calculator and tally up all of the money that you have available to spend, save, and invest.
- ✓ Be sure to take out a calculator and tally up all the money that you owe (include the interest).
- ✓ Be sure to subtract the money you owe from the money you have. Then you will know how much you have to spend, save, and invest. This will provide you with the big picture of your financial situation and not just individual, discrete categories of money or mental accounts.
- ✓ Remember that one mental account has an impact (positive or negative) on the other mental accounts. Focus not just on one account but the entire portfolio.

7. Availability Bias (Being lazy in your thinking and paying the price for laziness)

The availability bias results from undisciplined and lazy thinking. It means that you make a decision based on limited information or whatever information is at hand. This is the opposite of "analysis paralysis," in which you over-analyze to the point of inaction.

To make an informed, smart decision, you should consider asking the following questions: What is the quality of the data? How current is the data? How representative is the data? How reliable is the data? How valid or truthful is the data? If you suffer from the availability bias, you may well skip over these questions. You'll get an A for speed, maybe even an A- for efficiency, but you risk getting an F for effectiveness. In short, you are efficiently ineffective.

The internet has made this bias considerably worse because of the volume of information at our fingertips, information that may or may not be reliable, accurate, and so on. With YouTube, we don't even have to read anymore; we can watch a video.

How to Avoid the Availability Bias?

- ✓ Seek information that presents other perspectives.
- ✓ Be sure your information is current and comes from reliable sources.
- ✓ Obtain data from more than one source and see whether the data agrees.
- ✓ Always take time to research your investment and spending decisions. Do not rush.
- ✓ Do not overcompensate and become crippled by "analysis paralysis."
- ✓ Develop and use a decision-making process that gathers data from a number of different sources and formulates more than one course of action.

8. Status Quo Bias (changing is often wiser than staying the course)

If you are someone who dislikes change, then you might suffer from status quo bias. People tend to hold on tightly to investments they own regardless of the returns. You may have heard stories about the dot.com disaster, when people who'd made millions investing in dot.com companies watched their stocks plummet to rock bottom values, even zero. Why did investors keep holding onto these losing stocks? These investors blindly held to the notion that the stocks couldn't possibly continue to fall, and yet they did. So what happened? The endowment effect explains part of the reason. In life, as in investment decisions, we often choose the option that allows us to make the least change.

Studies have found that employees who first joined their company many years ago and decided not to participate in the retirement plan continued not to participate even as they grew older. What happened? Nothing. The status quo bias took effect. The danger of not contributing early in your retirement plan is that you lose the effect of tax-deferred growth and compounding. Also, if your employer matches your contribution, then you are actually leaving money on the table.

You know some of your co-workers who will call payroll if their paycheck is short by a nickel? Yet, these same co-workers will ignore money on the table, free money, by not participating in their retirement plan, because they did not do so at the very beginning. Some change is good.

How to Avoid the Endowment or Status Quo Bias?

- ✓ Recognize that not all change is not bad.
- ✓ Recognize that the decision not to make a decision or to stay the course can have negative consequences, and that such consequences are often preventable had you made a decision or taken appropriate action.
- ✓ Set up automatic accounts like savings accounts and deductions so that you only have to make a decision once and adjustments now and then.

FEELING

The next two of the Deadly Dozen are the result of "feelings," or our emotional state. Investors aim to make rational decisions. Yet, most of us know that before making a decision, while making a decision, and even after making a decision, that we may feel optimistic, pessimistic, guarded, anxious, and lacking in confidence. In brief, the model of the purely rational decision maker is the stuff of academic textbooks, not real life. Below are two powerful emotions that shape our decisions and have an impact on our behaviors: mood/optimism and pride/regret.

9. Mood and Optimism (Because it feels real or right does not mean that it is real or right)

Mood is how you feel right now even as you read this page. You may be sad, angry, happy, bored, frustrated, and so on. Moods are temporary. You wake up sad, but then meet some friends and have a great day at work. Your mood shifted and now you feel happy and satisfied.

As you might imagine, your mood affects your decisions. People who are sad tend to be pessimistic and more critical than usual. On the other hand, people in a good mood tend to be more optimistic and less critical. Let's assume that two individuals, one in a sad mood and the other in a good mood, attend an investment conference. The individual in the good mood is likely to ask fewer questions, read less carefully, and to feel optimistic about the investment presentation. He is ready to make the investment. Grumpy sees the same presentation and finds all sorts of things wrong with it. He does not invest. Which one is right? Which one is better suited to make a decision?

Believe it or not, as an investor, it pays to be in a less than happy state. It is then that your critical faculties are at work. Critical reasoning is the foundation of smart decision-making. I'm not suggesting you walk around in a bad mood, but you should watch out for excessive optimism. The difference between optimism and excessive optimism is a matter of degree. If you find yourself overestimating favorable outcomes in comparison to unfavorable outcomes, then you may be excessively optimistic. Excessive optimism, like overconfidence, often results in impulsive poor decisions.

For example, look at any advertisement of a mutual fund or ETF (exchange-traded fund) and you will find that past performance is highlighted. The ads even go so far as to use colors and stars to distinguish the highest-performing mutual fund or ETF from the others. Investors who respond to these ads reflexively do so out of strong feeling of optimism. These investors are overly optimistic, and would benefit from stopping and thinking before acting.

James K. Glassman, author of *Dow 36,000*, published in 1996, forecasted that the Dow would reach 36,000 from 10,318. In an editorial in the *Wall*

Street Journal, he wrote, "I told readers to tilt their retirement portfolios strongly toward stocks—but with an extra-large dollop of optimism because stocks at the time seemed undervalued" (February 26, 2011, page A15). He further wrote, "I was wrong." This story should remind you that even the experts can be wrong not because of their intellect or education but because of their emotions. In this case, optimism got the best of James K. Glassman. The silver lining in this story is that he recognized it and admitted that he was wrong.

How to Avoid Excessive Optimism?

- ✓ Acknowledge that there is an upside and downside to almost any situation, and then identify what the downsides are.
- ✓ Temper your optimistic feelings by seeking out information or an informed person's perspective that counterbalances your optimistic feelings.
- ✓ Wait for your optimistic feelings to subside before actually making a decision or taking an action.
- ✓ Ask yourself the question, "If I felt differently emotionally, would I make the same decision or take the same action?"

10. Pride and Regret (Being right is not as great as being correct)

If you're like most people, you avoid actions that create regret and seek actions that cause pride. It's natural for people to want to feel good about themselves. Though it sounds counterintuitive, to feel good about ourselves as investors, we sell winners and ride losers. This is called the "disposition effect." How does this work? Imagine that you bought a stock that keeps increasing in price, and then you probably feel good about your decision. When you sell the stock at a higher price than for what you bought it, then you make a profit and you will no doubt feel some pride. The problem is that you may have sold the stock too early because it may have gone up higher in value. But you may also wait too long and then lose money. That's always a problem with stocks. The idea is to set a goal, then sell when you reach that goal without regret.

On the other hand, you buy a stock and the price drops. You do not have to confront your decision until you sell the stock at a loss. If you are like many people, you decide to hold onto the stock to protect yourself from experiencing regret. It makes sense to avoid psychological pain. Will you ride the stock price down to zero?

Remember, investors feel a loss twice as much as they feel a gain of the same amount. The fear is a fear of making an incorrect decision. We all hate to be wrong, don't we? Regret really kicks in for decisions we did not make because we feel we missed out on something good particularly if we find out that others have benefited.

Watch out for a trick that we play on ourselves to minimize feelings of regret. The trick is to have others such as advisors, partners, spouses, or members of an investment club make our financial decisions. After we allow them to make our decisions, then we feel like we do not have to experience regret because we did not make the decision. However, we made a decision to let others make a decision. We can feel regret about that decision.

How to Avoid Pride and Regret?

- ✓ Remember that it is better to be wrong than poor.
- ✓ Acknowledge that all decisions involve risk and that you cannot be right 100 percent of the time.
- ✓ Remember that you need to balance your emotional feelings with your retirement, investment, and saving account balances.
- ✓ Use the time-tested strategy of professional investors and traders, which is, focus as much on the exit (when to get out of the market) as the entry (when to get in the market).

RELATING

The Deadly Dozen are mostly individual decision-making traps, but two involve group decision-making traps: the herd effect and group think. Groups, like individuals, can be irrational, perhaps even more so.

11. Herd Effect (Riding the wave to your own demise)

It is common to hear people make the comment, "Watch out for the blind leading the blind." This happens quite a bit in investing. Not too long ago, there was a rush to buy real estate with little or no money down. People were buying second homes, fixer uppers, and even homes in other countries, largely because people they knew were doing so and because of the barrage of news stories, internet sites, multi-level marketing (MLM) programs, and TV infomercials about the hot real estate market that could only go up—forever. Fast forward to today. The bottom dropped out of much of the real estate market. What explains why rational individuals followed their peers right off the real estate investment cliff? Herd behavior is the answer.

Buffalo are known to blindly follow other buffalo, even if it means jumping off of a cliff. We have to be smarter decision-makers than buffalo. Similar to the buffalo, investors will forget to look where they're headed and just do what others around them are doing, such as buying gold and buying ETFs. Herding takes place when you base your financial decisions on the behavior of others and fail to rely upon your own knowledge.

Since most of us have a strong urge to be part of the crowd, acting independently can be a tough assignment. Furthermore, the crowd is often right but not always. To be a contrarian requires some courage and fortitude.

The herd effect comes in different forms. People may follow the crowd based on what their friends are doing, on internet sites, or as part of investment clubs. The National Association of Investors Corporation is the national organization for members of investment clubs. An investment club is a group of individual investors who pool their money to make investment decisions as a group. The research is pretty substantial that members of an investment club take more risk than individual investors. They invest more in stocks than individual investors, and they invest more in growth stocks than individual investors. The major lesson from this research is that decision-making in groups in not the same as decision-making among individuals.

Perhaps even more so, people follow media reports. Think of all the television shows, from *Mad Money with Jim Cramer* to *The Suze Orman Show*, that focus on investing and personal finance. These investment advisers have a significant influence on thousands of people's investment decisions. Such shows may be as responsible for creating or setting trends as following them. The question is: Should you act on their advice?

In terms of using the internet, if you "Google" finance or personal finance or investing, millions of sites will pop up. Far too many to know whether the information posted is solid, reliable information. It is advisable not to jump into any investment schemes offered on the internet before you've done due diligence.

How to Avoid the Herd Effect?

- ✓ Be aware that collective intelligence is not always superior to individual intelligence and judgment. Trust your own judgment and experience especially if you work on your Deadly Dozen.
- ✓ Group think and/or crowd mentality can be thoughtless and even dangerous. Stay grounded and centered and act as an individual.
- ✓ Swim against the tide if you see a waterfall over the horizon. It is better to stand alone than drown with the crowd.
- ✓ Resist the temptation to get "swept away" by the movement, because movements come and go like stock market bubbles.

12. Group Think/Social Dynamics (Riding the fashion wave and keeping up with the Jones's)

Fashion is the great governor of the world; it presides not only in matters of dress and amusement, but in law, physics, politics, religion, and all other things of the gravest kind; indeed, the wisest of men would be puzzled to give any better reason why particular forms in all these have been at certain times universally received, and at other times universally rejected, than that they were in or out of fashion.

—Henry Fielding

Money is fashion. Fashion is money. Is it vogue to be an investor? Is it fashionable to buy Google stock? Are you considered fashionable if you have read Suze Orman's latest book or watched Cramer's latest television show? We are social beings. As social beings, we care about what others think, about how others view us, and about what others say about us. Past research suggests that individuals make poor investment decisions due to the social situation.

To an extreme, this focus on what others feel or think or say about us drives us to make decisions that are not in our long-term financial interest. We may buy homes, cars, vacations, and electronic toys that we cannot afford not to mention clothes, shoes, and accessories.

We may use our money as a way of not only "keeping up with the Jones's" but "beating the Jones." Our own view of reality changes due to group pressure. Solomon Asch, a famous psychologist, conducted a study in which he showed individuals a long line and a short line and asked these individuals which line was the longest line. This seems like a silly experiment. But some individuals said that the shortest line was the longest line after they heard other individuals in the group says that the shortest line was the longest line. How could a rational individual change what he or she actually sees in the face of group pressure? This not only happens with lines but many financial decisions and behaviors.

How to Avoid Group Think/Social Dynamics?

✓ Stop and pause before making a decision.
✓ Ask the group how they arrived at that decision or action.
✓ Be willing to take the consequences from the group for standing up to be your own person.
✓ Remember that just because more than one person is moving in a direction does not mean that that is the right direction for you.
✓ Use your critical reasoning. Think about the fact that you could also lose money. How much money can you afford to lose? If you want to

keep up with the Jones's, compare your own level of wealth to theirs. Are you equal?

SUMMARY

This chapter walked you through the Deadly Dozen. After learning how to spot these 12 decision-making traps, then you learned how to stop yourself from falling into these traps. Remember, even professional investment professionals can fall into these 12 decision-making traps. We may not always be rational but we are always human. By exposing you to the major pitfalls to avoid, this chapter should help you make smarter financial decisions and even life decisions.

In the end, to make a smart decision you must be sure to make these your new decision-making habits. Why habits? Because habits are nearly impossible to change.

- Habit #1: Develop a process for decision-making.
- Habit #2: Collect as much information as possible from multiple sources.
- Habit #3: Monitor your emotions. If you feel too happy, optimistic, and overconfident or too sad, down, anxious, or mad—do *not* make a decision.
- Habit #4: Categorize your decisions into the following buckets: urgent, routine, and long term.

Beyond these healthy decision-making habits, you must also remember the Deadly Dozen. Before turning to the next chapter, read five ways to overcome the Deadly Dozen:

1. Understand and avoid the Deadly Dozen.
2. Identify your financial goals.
3. Develop criteria for any financial decision.
4. Diversify your investments, remembering what happened in 2008 because it may happen again.
5. Review the results of your decisions. Change course if you are not benefiting from your investment decisions.

REFERENCES

DeBondt, W., & Thaler, R. (1985). Does the stock market overreact? *Journal of Finance, 40*(3), 793–808.

Deems, R. (1994). *Interviewing: More than a Gut Feeling.* Video. American Media International.

French, K. R., & Poterba, J. M. (1991). Investor diversification and international equity markets. *American Economic Review*, Papers and Proceedings, 222–226.

Huberman, G. (2001). Familiarity breeds investment. *Review of Financial Studies, 14*, 659–680.

Kahneman, D., & Piepe, M. W. (1998). Aspects of investor psychology. *Journal of Portfolio Management, 24*(4), 52–65.

Knox, R. E., & Inkster, J. A. (1968). Postdecision dissonance at post time. *Journal of Personality and Social Psychology, 8*(4), 319–323.

Tversky, A., & Kahneman, D. (1979). Prospect theory: An analysis of decision under risk. *Econometrica, 47*, 263–291.

6

Am I an Impulsive-Compulsive Shopper or Spender?

NEIL AND TRAINS

Neil, a metallic train collector, drove from specialty store to specialty store hunting for the latest train to add to his burgeoning metallic train collection. Trains swarmed his basement like a bulging nest of out-of-control yellow jackets. His office was filled with trains, train boxes, and train magazines. Yet all was well from Neil's vantage point. This was not the case for his wife and his boss. Both complained. His wife voiced concerns about "wasting time and money." She also grew increasingly frustrated with Neil's rationalizations and the basement being overwhelmed by metallic trains. For instance, "They're for our two-year old son," or "They'll be worth a mint when we sell them."

Neil's boss at the financial services firm counseled Neil about his "messy office," but he did not focus on just the metallic train collection and magazines. His boss also wondered where Neil went during the day and why he worked such odd hours and always seemed drained and fatigued. Neil sought financial therapy to placate his wife and boss. Neil tried half-heartedly to cut back on his shopping, but he knew deep inside that he couldn't help himself. He couldn't seem to stop. He'd tried but it never worked.

DOES NEIL HAVE A PROBLEM?

It is clear that Neil was struggling with compulsive buying behavior. His relationships were suffering from his buying behavior. Beyond his relationships, Neil's credit card debt was mounting as he racked up late fees and over-the-limit fees. Neil rationalized his debting behavior by promising himself to erase the credit card debt when he received a bonus. Sadly, the bonuses were not predictable or steady.

Does Neil meet the psychiatric definition of compulsive buying disorder (CBD) or impulse control disorder? Let's look at the evidence: Neil thinks excessively about shopping as illustrated by his boss' complaints about him not focusing on his work and his office. Neil engages in excessive buying behavior as evidenced by the large number of trains in his basement, and also the time spent away from home and work shopping for metallic trains. And Neil has impaired marital and occupational relationships. Add it all up and it Neil suffers from CBD. Let's be clear, I am not claiming that Neil is crazy, but he does need help from a mental health practitioner who is both sensitive to and educated about money matters.

NEIL IS NOT ALONE: COMPULSIVE BUYING IS MORE COMMON THAN YOU THINK

Neil is just one example of an increasing number of Americans suffering from compulsive buying. In a study published in the prestigious journal *World Psychiatry*, almost 6 out of 100 individuals will develop CBD at some point in their life. What is CBD? Author Donald W. Black, a noted academic psychiatrist who has dedicated his life to study of CBD, defines it as follows: "Compulsive buying disorder (CBD) is characterized by excessive shopping cognitions and buying behavior that leads to distress or impairment" (2007, 14). Not only does CBD lead to distress and impairment but also serious financial consequences from poor credit scores to bankruptcy.

RECOGNIZING THE SIGNS OF COMPULSIVE BUYING BEHAVIOR

In my work with individuals from varied and socioeconomic backgrounds, I discovered that there are classic signs that strongly suggest an individual has fallen prey to compulsive buying behavior. What are these telltale signs?

1. Falling prey to internal (e.g., feeling anxious, etc.) and external (e.g., fancy stores, etc.) triggers that activate a seemingly reflexive response to buy.
2. Experiencing an urge to buy and not being able to satisfy that urge unless something is purchased no matter how trivial the item.
3. Sensing a feeling of elation almost like a buzz or a high like a "runner's high" when a purchase is made.

4. Feeling guilt or shame after buying.
5. Hiding purchases from others.
6. Rationalizing purchases on issues related to current and past relationships, for instance, blaming others for the behavior.
7. Lying about purchasing behavior.
8. Racking up a large consumer debt and being unable to service that debt.
9. Perceiving one's self as being unable to control buying.
10. Stealing, embezzling, borrowing, cashing in retirement plans, and tapping home equity lines to shop.

This is by no means an exhaustive list of signs. Some of these signs are more serious than others. Obviously impairing one's relationships is detrimental, and so is damaging one's credit score, but when you steal or embezzle you are also exposing yourself to criminal charges. There is a range of compulsive buying behavior, from feeling compelled to buy something daily, even multiple times a day, to wiping out home equity and retirement plans.

In my work with clients, I know that "time does not make it better." To the contrary, the more you engage in compulsive buying behavior, the stronger the urge becomes. You can and should seek help by finishing this chapter and then implementing some of the recommendations I suggest.

This chapter not only focuses upon CBD but also impulsive buying behavior. One of my clients, Maria, exhibits the essence of impulsive buying behavior.

MARIA: WHEN "JUST SAY NO" DOESN'T WORK

Maria views herself as a casual shopper and readily admits that she enjoys the experience of shopping. If you were to observe Maria in a shopping mall or in a downtown shopping district, Maria would blend in with the crowd of shoppers strolling from store to store. Some of these shoppers would have made purchases and others would not.

Maria would not plan to buy anything and has certainly been able to resist buying something on occasion. "I feel caught off guard at times when I shop," says Maria reflecting upon those times when she suddenly buys something for no apparent reason.

Maria is very intelligent and can engage in a dialogue about how shopkeepers "trick us into buying stuff we don't need or want, particularly at the counters while waiting to check out." She also knows that certain stores are riskier for her than others. Maria explains that she has "lots of books that I haven't even read and would love to read." Yet, she goes to bookstores with no intent to buy a book and will browse casually, skimming the titles and even cracking open a book or two and perusing the contents. In an almost blind instant, Maria finds herself having purchased a book and wonders, "How did that happen? Why did I also buy those little chocolates?"

More recently, I remember coaching Maria over the phone. She told me the story of how she came out of her attorney's office feeling depressed and ambivalent about the high fees she was paying him. And yet, she bought something from Neiman Marcus right after her appointment. "I found myself buying make-up I didn't need. I think I bought it to feel better. I didn't need the make-up. I don't even like that make-up."

MARIA IS NOT ALONE: IMPULSIVE BUYING IS MORE COMMON THAN YOU THINK

Maria is another example of an individual suffering from "out-of-control" buying behavior. Like Neil, impulsivity is interfering with Maria's life and well-being. About 62 percent of supermarket sales and 80 percent of luxury-goods sales in the United States are impulsive according to a marketing newsletter and the *Wall Street Journal*. In the *American Journal of Psychiatry*, Eric Hollander and Andrea Allen (2006) estimated that 2–8 percent of the U.S. population are impulsive buyers.

RECOGNIZING THE SIGNS OF IMPULSIVE BUYING BEHAVIOR

In my work with individuals from varied socioeconomic backgrounds, I discovered that there are classic signs that strongly suggest an individual has fallen prey to impulsive buying behavior. What are these telltale signs?

1. Purchasing something spontaneously.
2. Feeling that you lack the willpower to resist buying.
3. Making unplanned purchases.
4. Experiencing pleasure, gratification, or release of tension at the time of the purchase.
5. Buying things you don't need or won't use.
6. Engaging in binge buying.
7. Failing to evaluate the consequences of buying.
8. Calling your credit card company to find out if you are over the limit.
9. Draining your bank account or maximizing the limit on your credit card.
10. Being caught in the buying–returning cycle.

Similar to compulsive buying, impulsive buying exists along a continuum anchored on one end with making unplanned purchases to recognizing after you've bought something that you bought something you didn't need or were not really aware of until after you made the purchase. We all have our fetishes.

ARE COMPULSIVE AND IMPULSIVE BUYING THE SAME OR DIFFERENT?

Compulsive and impulsive buying are different but related. Some individuals have both and others only suffer from one and not the other. Some in the field of psychiatry, like Drs. Eric Hollander and Andrea Allen, argue that the proper term should be impulsive-compulsive disorder. Not only are mental health professionals seeking to better define impulsive and compulsive buying, but so too are marketers. As an example, impulsive buying is defined as the "degree to which an individual is likely to make unintended, immediate, and unreflective purchases" (2006, 306). This definition appeared at an American Marketing Association Conference not at a mental health conference.

Impulsive buyers are attractive to marketers and retailers. Why? When individuals shop without thinking, then they make purchases they don't need. Also, when individuals "can't help themselves," then they will often zero out their bank balances, max their credit cards, and even, tap their home equity lines and withdraw money from their retirement accounts.

Both compulsive and impulsive buyers pay a high price for engaging in such materialistic behaviors or what experts refer to as acquisitive or consumptive behavior. In Tim Kaiser's 2002 book *The High Price of Materialism*, the impact of materialistic behavior is painfully detailed with an emphasis on the negative impact on health and physical, mental, and financial well-being. Kaiser poses the following question in his book, that you should also ask yourself: "What happens to our well-being when our desires and goals to attain wealth and accumulate possessions become prominent" (page 4)?

DO BOTH GENDERS SUFFER FROM IMPULSIVE AND/OR COMPULSIVE BUYING BEHAVIOR?

Absolutely. In this chapter, Neil's story demonstrates compulsive buying behavior that is interfering with his functioning and quality of life. Some may argue that Neil cannot exhibit compulsive buying because he is a male. But, this is untrue. In one study, appearing in the *Journal of Clinical Psychiatry*, the majority of compulsive buyers were women, and yet a more recent study by Lorrin M. Koran and colleagues (2006) found that the frequency of compulsive buyers among men and women is almost equal.

Recognizing Impulsive/Compulsive Buying in Others

As you may well know, most people do not like talking about money. In the financial therapy community, we often say that clients would rather talk about sex than money. Both are taboo topics, for different reasons, but money seems especially difficult to discuss when a person is having financial problems.

I received a call from a married couple who had been married for more than 20 years. The wife, a nurse, was very agitated and felt betrayed because her husband, a sales representative, had failed to pay the mortgage for three months and their son's private school tuition. When she confronted her husband, asking him whether he'd paid the bills, he replied "yes," when in fact he hadn't. The husband regularly spent money in a compulsive manner on tools and equipment for the house and the garage. Also, he could not resist the temptation of ordering books and tapes from online book stores because it was as simple as "clicking one button." The situation grew considerably worse when the sheriff slapped a foreclosure notice on the front door of their home.

What would cause a loving husband of 20 years not to tell his wife that he could not or would not pay the mortgage and private school tuition? The husband felt a sense of tremendous shame about not being a "real man" and not being able to "provide for his family." Instead of telling the truth, he simply withdrew and stopped communicating with his wife.

He had a problem. His problem was not limited to being unable or unwilling to talk to his wife but to face up to his own problematic buying behavior. He was quite similar to both Neil and Maria.

BEYOND LABELS: THE POWER OF PATTERNS

In my work with clients, I have learned that the labels are not the most important thing to focus upon. The key is to describe the compulsive or impulsive behavior, to identify *patterns of behavior*, to discover the *triggers of that behavior* (what we refer to as "antecedents" in the psychological community), and to examine what happens after the behavior, or what we refer to as "consequences."

Not only does compulsive and impulsive buying have an impact on others but others can also subconsciously drive us to engage in such behavior. Neuroscientists have discovered mirror neurons. These neurons enable us to imitate others. The problem is that we imitate both desirable and undesirable behaviors. Imagine that you are out shopping with a friend or relative and you have no intent to buy anything other than a cup of coffee and a pastry. Your friend goes on a buying spree and without thinking, you begin buying too. This is an instance of your motor neurons firing like crazy causing you to imitate your friend's behavior.

Psychologists have a name for everything. I use a model called the A-B-C Model of Impulsive-Compulsive Buying Behavior to really figure out what's going on with clients. I have taught this model to clients and seminar participants, even high school and college students, and I suggest that if you think you might be a compulsive or impulsive spender you learn how to use the following, which includes an A-B-C Impulsive-Compulsive Buying Behavior Chart. First, let's discuss the ABC's and then I will explain how to use it.

A-B-C MODEL OF COMPULSIVE/IMPULSIVE BUYING BEHAVIOR

Let us begin by spelling out the acronym:

A = Antecedents
B = Behavior
C = Consequences

Antecedents Explained

Antecedents are *triggers* of behaviors that prompt action as well as constraints that shape action, indicating what is and what is not acceptable behavior. A trigger could be seeing another shopper with a shopping bag. This may signal to the person to buy something.

Behavior Explained

Behavior is a person's action or reaction to some situation or stimulus. Behavior is measured by its frequency, magnitude, duration, intensity, and appropriateness. Let's dissect each one of these elements of behavior to see how this is related to impulsive-compulsive buying behavior.

Frequency is quite simply how often the behavior occurs. If the impulsive-compulsive behavior occurs more frequently, then that behavior presents more problems. *Magnitude* is the degree of consequences that follow the behavior. If there are greater and more consequences following the impulsive-compulsive buying behavior, the more problematic the behavior. *Duration* describes how long the behavior lasts from start to finish. As it relates to impulsive-compulsive buying behavior, you can observe how long a person engages in the buying behavior in minutes or hours. *Intensity* focuses on the level of energy expended in the behavior. With respect to impulsive-compulsive buying, you can assess the degree of activity and energy expended as well as the amount of money spent. Finally, *appropriateness* assesses how others view the behavior. For instance, if you impulsively-compulsively buy illegal drugs, then this is viewed differently than if you impulsively-compulsively buy dollhouses. *Do you know the antecedents or triggers to your buying behavior?*

Consequences Explained

Impulsive and compulsive behaviors lead to consequences, which may be positive, negative, or sometimes a combination of both. The consequences may be for the person involved or other people. For motivational purposes, the consequences for the person involved are the most important. The positive consequences, like being told by a significant person in your life that the purchase was a good decision, reinforce the impulsive-compulsive behavior.

Other consequences are negative, like feeling guilty, experiencing regret, worrying about being confronted by a loved one, and feeling overwhelmed about where to store the item. Antecedents and consequences together often go a long way toward explaining compulsive buying behaviors. Sometimes the lack of consequences is as important as the actual consequences. Thus, "no consequences" is, in fact, a consequence.

THE THREE PRINCIPLES OF BEHAVIOR CHANGE USING THE A-B-C CHART

Principle 1: Antecedents can be controlled by managing your environment.

Triggers or antecedents to impulsive-compulsive buying behavior are seldom random. There is usually a pattern. I remember one client telling me that the "smell of the store makes me feel so relaxed and calm to the point that I find myself buying something without really thinking about what I just bought." For this client, she has two triggers—olfactory (sense of smell) and an internal state of relaxation (calm and cognitively disengaged). The solution for this client was for her not to frequent this store because of the increased probability that she would buy on impulse. Another client reported that when she felt anxious that buying anything would reduce her anxiety. For this client, anxiety was the trigger.

Principle 2: Negative consequences sometimes change behavior.

In working with clients, I often ask them, "What can you do to negatively consequence your buying behavior?" In response to this question, they will list things like wash the dishes, do not go to the movies, do not go to the Starbucks, or clean the closet. Consequences can be reinforcing or inhibiting. Most of us avoid that which we regard as "painful" or "uncomfortable." This is an inhibiting consequence. As such, if you can identify something that happens immediately after making a purchase that you view as "painful" or "uncomfortable," then it will decrease the probability that you will engage in that same buying behavior. Psychologists call this "aversive conditioning."

Principle 3: Behaviors are often the results of thoughts.

In my work with individuals, I teach them about cognitive cueing strategies as a way of establishing and sustaining self-control over their behavior. A cognitive cueing strategy is quite simply a way of engaging in self-talk and self-questioning that puts time between the thought and the behavior. This technique reduces the reflexive nature of both impulsive and compulsive buying behavior. It is a way to slow down the automatic response to buy. The Seven Questions of Buying, which are listed under the "Seven Questions of Buying" heading in this chapter, is a good example of a cognitive cueing strategy in action.

Now that you know the three principles and how they relate to impulsive-compulsive buying behavior, it is time to work on completing your A-B-C Compulsive Buying Behavior Chart. Follow the example in this chapter and remember to record at least one buying behavior every day for at least two weeks. When I work with my clients, I have them e-mail their A-B-C chart at a minimum of once a week or in many cases every day. The daily recording of buying behavior allows individuals to see patterns that they could not see before and to spot points of vulnerability, which are revealed through identifying triggers.

A-B-C IMPULSIVE-COMPULSIVE BUYING BEHAVIOR CHART

With both my clients and workshop participants, after I explain the A-B-C Model of Impulsive-Compulsive Behavior, I then give them the A-B-C Impulsive-Compulsive Buying Behavior Chart (Table 6.1). This is a tool for their toolbox.

How Is the A-B-C Impulsive-Compulsive Buying Behavior Chart Used?

This direct observation tool has space for the individual to record information on antecedents or triggers, that is, the event that immediately precedes the "problem" behavior, and then record the compulsive buying behavior.

Table 6.1
A-B-C Impulsive-Compulsive Buying Behavior Chart

Antecedents *What triggers your buying?*	Buying behavior *Describe your buying behavior.*	Consequences *What happens after you buy?*
Example: Waiting for a friend in a mall and feeling bored.	Walk into a department store and buy a pair of sunglasses I really don't need.	Feel bad about buying the sunglasses and still feel bored.

Lastly, the individual records the consequences of the "problem behavior." Let's assume that the consequences for this person is a feeling of guilt for spending money, drinking beverages that are not good for your health, and eating candy, which is not good for your dental health not to mention your weight.

For example, a person is feeling down and enters a convenience store and buys a sweet, carbonated beverage and at the check out counter sees some candy and buys that right on the spot. This person would take out their A-B-C Chart and write "feeling down" under "A" for antecedents. Under "B," the person would write down "buying soda and candy." Finally, the person would write, "feeling guilty" in the "C" consequences column. As you complete your A-B-C Impulsive-Compulsive Buying Behavior Chart, respect the power of a fading memory. To be quite direct, do not let too much time pass between when you experience the impulsive-compulsive buying behavior and when you record what happened. The longer you wait, the more likely that what you will record will be not only factually inaccurate but somewhat distorted. Don't procrastinate . . . get r'done.

How Do You Make Sense Out of the A-B-C Impulsive-Compulsive Buying Behavior Chart?

A simple recording of one event is not enough. The pattern is important and interpretable. Let's assume that a person, after using the A-B-C Chart for two weeks consistently, notices that "feeling down" and "working past 6 PM at night" are antecedents or triggers to impulsive-compulsive buying. After observing this pattern, the person can attempt to decrease the frequency and intensity of those triggers. If the person is successful at finding other ways to "pick themselves up" or ways to leave the office before 6 PM. at night, then it is highly likely that the person will not engage in impulsive-compulsive buying as frequently or with the same intensity.

What Do I Do after Completing the A-B-C Compulsive Buying Behavior Chart?

After completing the chart for a minimum of two weeks, preferably each time you shop, look for concrete ways to use cognitive cues to change your compulsive buying behavior. I developed a tool, which I call The Seven Questions of Buying, which is designed to provoke you to confront the reasons you are buying and to think critically about what happens after you make a purchase. Upon careful inspection, you will notice that The Seven Questions of Buying is based on the A-B-C Model of Impulsive-Compulsive Buying Behavior.

I have been a believer in the power and magic of checklists throughout my career even while I was practicing clinical health psychology working with patients to modify their health behaviors, like overeating, not exercising, and in the case of diabetics, failing to check blood sugar levels. Atul Gawande, MD, wrote a book, titled *The Checklist Manifesto,* which focuses on the use of checklists in medical settings to make sure that the right patient gets the right care at the right time for the right reason. Pilots in cockpits use checklists. Special Operations forces use checklists. The Seven Questions of Buying is your checklist.

SEVEN QUESTIONS OF BUYING

No traveler would drive to a place he or she had never been without a road map. Yet only a tiny percentage of all individuals have a written spending plan. By developing a plan, many mistakes, temptations, and urges can be avoided. Therefore, shoppers should not spend any money until they have answered these seven questions:

1. What need or desire is being fulfilled?
2. What is the price and do I have the money to pay for it?
3. If I waited one day, would I still want to buy it?
4. How will I feel when I go home with this item?
5. How will I react, when the credit card bill comes in the mail?

6. Where am I going to store this item?

7. Will I tell anybody that I bought this item or keep it a secret?

Question 1: What Need or Want Is Being Fulfilled?

This first question is a powerful question. If you don't have a need or want for something, then it only makes sense that you should not buy it. This sounds rational. Yet, some people buy things even if they recognize that there is not a need or a want. This is one of the classic signs of impulsive or compulsive buying. Impulsive buyers may make statements like "I can't help myself" or "I was in the store and before I knew it, I had bought it." Compulsive buyers engage in self-talk like "I am going to walk into this store and not buy anything." As they enter the store, they feel a strong urge to buy something . . . anything, and they come out of the store having bought something. Let's focus on the difference between a need and a want.

Needs

Abraham Maslow told us years ago that there is a hierarchy of needs beginning with physiological, safety, social, esteem, and self-actualization. Ask yourself these questions regarding your needs prior to making a purchase:

- *What physiological need will be met today by buying this item?* For instance, an individual may purchase 7–10 Red Bulls within a three-hour period to satisfy the need of sleep deprivation and fatigue. This is obviously not normal behavior because the underlying issue is being masked by high caffeine intake, not to mention an expensive habit on a daily basis.
- *What safety need will be met today by buying this item?* For instance, an individual may buy a variety of safety goggles, steel toe boots, and other safety devices in multiples to feel safe when working outside or inside. The average person, unless he or she is working construction, does not need more than one pair of safety goggles and steel toe shoes.
- *What social need will be met today by buying this item?* An example is a client who goes out to fancy restaurants and cafés and invites friends or another client who shops at specific stores to feel connected with others—the sales representatives. There are less expensive ways to get your social needs met.
- *What esteem need will be met today by buying this item?* An example is an individual who buys expensive, brand name, luxury accessories to let others know that they have arrived and have successfully climbed the social ladder. There should be more to buying that seeking the ap-

proval of strangers. There are less expensive ways to obtain approval of those you care about and those who care about you than buying your approval.

- *What self-actualization need will be met today by buying this item?* Self-actualization is the pursuit of achieving fullness in one's life or optimal well-being. For example, an individual who spends a lot of money and time attending self-improvement workshops and buying hundreds self-improvement books but fails to read or even take the books out of their car. Self-actualization is an internal state. An internal state cannot be bought . . . only experienced.

Another example of how individuals seek to satisfy their needs through consumption is illustrated in this story about one of my clients. I remember working with one client who had her social needs met when she shopped in specific stores. The store clerks greeted her warmly and by name and asked her how she was doing. Additionally, they complimented her on what she was wearing. When she tried on some clothes, she was instantly and routinely complimented. This client felt validated, accepted, and acknowledged when she shopped at this store. This shopping experience was meeting her social needs, but she also felt guilty.

While in Japan, I read an article about the success of knock-offs. Some of the best examples are knock-off watches and handbags. Even while traveling in the Middle East, it is quite easy to see knock-offs being sold to those individuals who want to be associated with a brand despite knowing that it is the faux brand. It is not uncommon for buyers to purchase knock-offs to boost their self-esteem, enhance their social standing, and even feel good about themselves as they look in the mirror. Knock-offs are successful because they meet social, esteem, and self-actualization needs.

If you are about to make a purchase, pause, take a breath and determine what valid need is being met if you buy this object. Also, determine if there is another way to meet this need without having to spend money and buy something. For instance, the client who shopped to meet her social needs, after our working together, began to have these needs met by re-establishing her relationship with her adult children, volunteering in political campaigns, and taking non-credit classes at the local community college.

Wants

When my eight-year-old son was in a store with me, he would often say, "I need that . . ." and I would say, "You don't need that . . . you mean you want it." With a puzzled look on his face, he responded, "No, I need that now." After a pause, I would say, "You need to learn the difference between your needs and your wants." It is true, elementary school-age children have difficulty differentiating between a need and a want. However, they are not alone. Adults also have a hard time differentiating between a need and a want.

A *want* is a feeling of seeking or acquiring something that transcends your needs. For instance, let's imagine that you are actually starving. In this state of hunger, you *need* food of any type and will probably not express a preference for the type of food. However, if you are not actually starving but hungry, then you will probably express a preference for a type of food. The second scenario is a *want*. Living in Chicago, there is a physiological *need* for a coat that keeps you warm when the wind chill is -20 degrees Fahrenheit, but there is not a physiological need to have a blue Armani down coat. This is a *want*.

Question 2: What Is the Price and Do I Have the "Cash" to Pay for It?

I conduct "shopping tours" with some of my clients. I accompany them while they shop. As they are shopping, I am observing what triggers them, what annoys them, and how they interact with the sales staff and other shoppers. I also look for patterns and discrete behaviors, such as whether they even look at the price tag or just pick up the item and buy it only to find out the price at the cash register. For some, money, and hence price, is not an issue. But for most of us it is. And, if you're reading this, you probably are "price sensitive."

In my workshops, I often get the "you gotta be kidding" look when I say pay cash. There are six benefits of paying cash.

1. Saving the change

An immediate benefit of paying cash is that you collect a lot of loose change and even dollar bills. You may have heard the news report of Paul Brant, 70, who used $25,000 in change to buy a new Dodge Ram pickup truck. He had been saving this change for nearly 13 years. When folks say "every penny adds up," that is the truth.

2. Setting limits

Credit cards have limits. Even your bank account has a limit. If you go over your limit, you will pay a hefty fee and penalties. The magic of cash is that you cannot spend more than you actually have in your possession. If you can't set limits on your spending while using credit cards or writing checks, then use cash because the limit will be set automatically. A very popular book called *Nudge* describes the power of choice architecture or the myth of free will. The two authors, Drs. Thaler and Sunstein, advise individuals seeking to change their behavior to rid themselves of decisions, that is, structure the situation so the behavior is automatic. If you stop taking your credit card and checkbook with you, then you are not faced with a decision. So, go with cash.

3. Immediate clearance

You know the drill when you go to a bar or tavern and the bartender asks, "Do you want to put this on your tab?" You stop and think, "How much money do I have with me?" If you have enough for two drinks, you are likely to say, "No, I'll settle up now." But, if you have a credit card or even a debit card, you are likely to say, "Run a tab." If you are not keeping track of what you are drinking and eating, you may be surprised when the bill arrives. On the other hand, if you know how much the food and beverages cost and you pay for them up front or as soon as you finish, then you will not be surprised and you won't have the awful feeling of how much money you just spent.

4. Always accepted

Cash is king. Credit cards are royalty but not kings. You've watched folks go up to the counter in a hotel, store, or restaurant proudly taking out their credit card only to be told, "I'm sorry we don't take that card here. Do you have another card?" If the person has another card, they often say, "Let's try this one." When you pay with cash, you will never be embarrassed, because your money will always be accepted.

5. Less temptation

Using credit cards is somewhat seductive. You pull out your credit card and swipe it and like magic, you have made a purchase with very little effort. It is so easy. Unlike taking out bills and coins, credit cards require no counting, and there are no immediate consequences, as occur when using "real money."

6. Discounts

Many retailers will give you a discount if you pay with cash because they do not have to pay the fee to the credit card company, which can be as high as 1.5 percent on any given sales transaction.

These six benefits of paying with cash should serve as reminders not only for those suffering from compulsive buying disorder, but also for those who may be engaged in impulsive buying. All these benefits are obvious. Yet, as obvious as they are, not enough individuals are switching to cash. The big advantage of using cash is eliminating the risk of debt. It will become a bit more challenging to use cash given the changes in commerce throughout the world.

Futurists predict a cashless world in which cash money will be obsolete. Can you imagine paying for all goods and service by swiping? Now, the cashless world is not quite here. Today, many of us are in the habit of using credit cards and debit cards to pay for everything from gas to a new sofa. The convenience of using credit and debit cards is not offset by the financial trouble that many of us find ourselves in because of being mindless as we shop. For compulsive buyers, the plastic makes it far too easy to keep charging and racking up the debt. The good news for compulsive buyers is that the move toward a "plastic only" world is being challenged as consumers think twice about using credit cards. Because of rising fees associated with using plastic, now more than ever, cash is king.

Question 3: If I Waited One Day, Would I Still Want to Buy It?

Both impulsive and compulsive buyers are subjected to their emotions overpowering their rational selves. The key is to put space and time in between the urge to buy and actually buying. I have found success with two rules that I share with my clients and include in my workshops:

1. **The 30-day rule.** If you want to buy an expensive or luxury item, wait 30 days. For instance, if you are going to buy a Jacuzzi, a diamond bracelet, or a pricey car, then you should wait 30 days before buying. During that time you can examine whether your budget allows for such a purchase, and you might discover that you don't even want (or need) the item.

2. **The 24-hour rule.** For less expensive and/or unnecessary items, I recommend waiting 24 hours. For example, you are shopping for a gift with ample time remaining before it's time to deliver it. Perhaps the gift costs more than you'd planned on spending. Then, instead of buying the gift on the spot, think about it, and buy it later if the need or want persists. Or find another way to satisfy the need or want without reaching into your purse or wallet.

   Another example: You are strolling through a mall or down the street, and in one of the store windows a sign that says "Final Sale" catches your eye. You decide to go into the store to inquire about this great deal. The sales person tells you that the sale will last for two more days. What do you do? If you are like many people, you try to find something to buy because of the great sale and so you buy something. What would have happened if you had waited 24 hours? Based upon my experience, most of you would not have returned to the store and bought something simply because it was on sale.

I made a recent trip to Barnes & Noble to see if there were any new books. While browsing, I spotted several great books I would love to read. I felt that urge creep upon me—the urge to *spend*. Then I thought of the $25 it would cost. I thought about all the books I already own and haven't read. I began to have doubts. "I'll use the 24-hour rule," I told myself. "If I still want this tomorrow, I'll buy it."

Both these rules are simple. They are also surprisingly effective. The rules work especially well because you aren't actually denying yourself, you're simply delaying gratification. The 30-day rule has another advantage: It gives you a chance to research the item you want to purchase. This can save you from overspending and aggravation.

Question 4: How Will I Feel When I Get This Home?

For most of us shoppers, we buy something, bring it home, and do not experience any negative emotions or seek to hide the purchases. This is not the experience of compulsive buyers who feel guilty, shamed, embarrassed, defensive, or even depressed when they bring the package into their home. One of my clients used his trunk as a storage closet and waited until his wife went to bed to bring purchases into the home. When confronted, he would react defensively and occasionally with some degree of hostility. What his wife did not know was the anguish, guilt, and shame that he experienced. He never expressed his vulnerability to his wife. He only expressed his defensiveness and hostility. In our work together, we focused on expressing the whole picture and not just part of the picture. After some time, this client was able to express his discomfort about these compulsive behaviors to his wife and asked her to support him in changing by encouraging him to stay out of certain stores, stay away from specific internet sites, and reward him when he shopped less and in a more controlled, deliberate manner.

Question 5: If I Decide to Charge an Item, How Will I React When the Credit Card Bill Comes in the Mail?

The immediate consequences of buying are typically a positive feeling at the moment of purchase. For those who use credit cards, there is little thought given to whether they can actually afford the item. This is not the case with cash. With cash, either you have enough money or not. With credit, your credit could be maxed out but many individuals have more than one card. Also with credit, you might spend on superfluous items and then not have cash necessary for the basics like food and utilities.

Because there is a time lapse between purchase and payment for an item when using a credit card, it makes it far easier to be less mindful of cost, and of the purchases themselves. With cash, you have to be mindful. For example, if you are going clothes and grocery shopping in the same day, and you carry $100 cash, then you know that if you spend the entire amount at Macy's, you won't have money for food. Not so with a credit card. You could purchase $300 worth of clothing and $100 of groceries without even thinking about the "day of reckoning." I'm sure most of you have experienced this more than once. In my practice, I have had clients who either "lose" their credit card statements or knowingly do not open them out of fear that they cannot pay the bill. And sadly, often enough they can't.

Question 6: Where Am I Going to Store This Item?

Households are getting smaller in the United States yet houses are getting larger and an increasing number of individuals are putting things in storage facilities. There is a cliché—stuff expands to fill the space available. Whatever the size of the home, you manage to fill it up with stuff.

In rare cases, impulsive-compulsive buyers buy so much stuff that people label them a "pack rat." How do you know if you suffer from clinical compulsive hoarding? If you agree with all three of the following statements, then you may suffer from clinical compulsive hoarding behavior.

- I acquire and fail to discard a large number of possessions that appear to be useless or of limited value.
- My living space is sufficiently cluttered as not be able to use those spaces for which they were designed.
- I experience significant distress or impairment in functioning caused by hoarding.

These three statements come from a landmark article appearing in *Behavior Research and Therapy* (1998) about clinical compulsive hoarding behavior. One of my clients bought items, like shoes, in multiples. For instance, she wouldn't just buy one pair of shoes that she liked, but she would buy as many shoes as the store carried in her size and in as many colors as available. This buying behavior was clearly compulsive. Her behavior led to piling up these purchases all over the house much to the angst of her husband. Instead of confronting the compulsive buying behavior and clinical compulsive hoarding, this couple decided to add a room to their house by tapping into their home equity line. When the real estate market tumbled, they found themselves "underwater," that is, paying more on their monthly mortgage than the house was actually worth.

My recommendation to both clients and workshop participants is to think through and plan where you will physically put an item once you purchase it. This sounds easier than it actually is for individuals suffering from compulsive hoarding behavior, which often results from impulsive-compulsive buying. In my work with clients, I go to their homes to understand how they have organized their belongings and what the items they purchase symbolize.

I remember one of my clients who was quite sad because her grown daughter refused to visit her because, as she said, "I can't even get into my old room with all of my mom's stuff and junk. Why come home?" This tore the mother apart but she was at a loss of how to de-clutter her house not to mention her daughter's bedroom, which you literally could not enter. I asked the mom if she knew what was in the closet in her daughter's bedroom and she did not know. I then asked her if she knew what was in all the garbage bags, shopping bags, and boxes piled up in her daughter's bedroom and she did not know. After a series of these questions, my client became noticeably upset and began tearing up. I asked her permission to toss out things like old newspapers, magazines, spoiled food, or other dated items. After physically assisting her with this task, I remember saying, "Let's take this and dump it in the trash." Compulsive hoarding often results from compulsive and impulsive buying. It also tears apart relationships.

As we move to a digital age with music and books, one of the emerging dangers is that compulsive buyers will not have to contend with physical storage but with electronic storage, where there is no physical limit. In my college classes, some students brag to other students about the thousands of songs that they have on their MP3s. It's not just college kids. Among some of my professional colleagues, they too brag about the thousands of books, videos, and songs loaded onto their iPads and other electronic devices. This clutter cannot be seen, but this clutter can be felt as time and energy is wasted sorting through reams of data and organizing data even with all of the fancy organizing applications. This clutter is also costly in terms of money even if it is digital money. Digital money is not play money.

It's not just about deciding where you are going to put that recent purchase, but also making room for that purchase if your residence is overwhelmed with "treasures" and junk. I know that "one man's treasure is another person's junk," but if we are honest with ourselves, most residences in the United States have more junk than treasure. When my clients and workshop participants ask me, "Marty, how to do I get rid of all this stuff?" I offer them three simple rules to make the decision whether to keep, toss, or give something away:

1. **Rule Number One:** Didn't Know I Had It Rule

If you go on an expedition in your closet, your attic, your basement, your garage, and maybe even your car, you will be amazed at what you will discover. You may even say to yourself, "When did I get that?" Statements like this are often the fruit of impulsive shopping. If you stumble upon this "surprise find," then most likely it needs to be given away or tossed out.

2. **Rule Number Two:** Haven't Used It/Worn It Rule

My wife and I kid each other about clothes in our closet, primarily her closet, that she used to wear not years ago but decades ago. The fantasy is that "one day I will be able to get back in that dress." The reality is that it won't happen and that the outfit is out of style. To be fair, I have some biofeedback equipment that I used when I was practicing clinical health psychology years ago that I have not used in years. Why am I keeping it? No rational reason. So, what did I do? I gave it away to a training program. I had to let go of the fantasy that I would practice clinical health psychology again and use the biofeedback equipment.

3. **Rule Number Three**: Hate It Rule

Shopping in stores can be deceiving and tastes change over time. When you're shopping in a store, the lights are set in a specific way, the ambiance is designed in a particular way, and everything looks "just right." What happens when you get home? Suddenly, the article of clothing does not look the same and you think to yourself, "What in the world was I thinking?. . . . This is ugly." Yet, it looked good in the store and you looked good too. The other aspect of the Hate It Rule is that your tastes change and what you may have really liked five years ago, you can't stand today. How many of you would go out and buy platform shoes and bell-bottoms today adorned with a tie die shirt? If you hate it, toss it or give it away.

Question 7: Will I Tell Anybody that I Bought This Item or Keep It a Secret?

Most people do not hide purchases or keep purchases a secret unless there is some reason to do otherwise. It is quite common for compulsive buyers to report feeling guilty and experiencing regret and even shame after making a purchase. The experience keeps many individuals from seeking help because they feel the urge to "sink into the floor" or simply "hide." For some individuals, this emotion of shame carries with it a moral aspect. Prudence and financial stewardship are two of the qualities of many religious teachings, including the Judeo-Christian ethic and the Buddhist tradition.

One of my clients, a woman in her fifties, sought my help because she had embezzled some money from her employer to pay off credit cards that she had abused. This particular client had gone to a number of mental health professionals but she stated, "I felt judged." It was hard to know if she was actually judged or her sense of shame was so great that she believed she ought to be judged.

During my training as a psychologist, it was drilled into us that we should demonstrate "unconditional positive regard" for the client and their presenting problem. In this case, with this client, it was not my place to judge her as a person but to evaluate her behavior and to get her to become more mindful and in control of her feelings, thoughts, and actions. This is an extreme example but it shows how shame can interfere with individuals getting help from others, including professionals. How do you know if you are experiencing shame about your buying behavior? There are several indicators that I use with my clients:

1. Do you hide purchases from those you care about?
2. Do you hide or destroy receipts?
3. Do you have credit card statements sent to an address other than your home address?
4. Do you have a storage facility or secret storage place that only you know about?
5. Do you sneak purchased items into your residence while others are not home or not paying attention?
6. When you've been shopping, do you become defensive or even hostile when asked where you've been and what you've been doing?
7. Do you promise yourself that you will stop, but find that you cannot?

Affirmative answers to these questions indicate that you are experiencing shame about your buying behavior. This is not unusual. However, shame can stop people from seeking help. If you have answered yes to these questions, I encourage you to seek help.

SUMMARY AND KEY POINTS

This chapter includes tools like the A-B-C Chart and the Seven Questions of Buying that anybody can use even if you are not a compulsive or impulsive buyer. If you feel that you do suffer from compulsive or impulsive buying disorder or both, then be gentle with yourself and seek professional guidance. Below are the key points from this chapter, followed by action steps, and a daily reminder.

Key Points

✓ We all have a 6 out of 100 chance (6%) of developing compulsive or impulsive buying disorder in our lifetime.

✓ We all engage in compulsive buying behavior and impulsive buying behavior from time to time but not to the point that we have a clinical diagnosis.

✓ We all can change our compulsive and impulsive buying tendencies and support those we care about to modify their tendencies.

Action Steps

✓ Ask yourself The Seven Questions of Buying when you make purchases that are sizeable from a financial point of view or if you find yourself buying things you do not need or want.

Daily Reminder

✓ Complete the A-B-C Chart on a daily basis for at least two weeks to identify your buying triggers, buying behaviors, and the consequences of buying both positive and negative.

REFERENCES

Abrahams, Ben. (1997, March 27). It's all in the mind. *Marketing*, 31–33.

Agins, Teri. (2004, September 3,). For men, fancier pants—and pricier boxers. *Wall Street Journal*, W. 12.

Black, D. W. (2001). Compulsive buying disorder: Definition, assessment, epidemiology and clinical management. *CNS Drugs*, 15(1), 17–27.

Black, D. W. (2007). A review of compulsive buying disorder. *World Psychiatry*, 6(1), 14–18.

Christenson, G. A., Faber, R. J., de Zwaan, M., Raymond, N. C., Specker, S. M., Ekern, M. D., Mackenzie, T. B., Crosby, R. D., Crow, S. J., & Eckert, E. D. (1994). Compulsive buying: Descriptive characteristics and psychiatric comorbidity. *Journal of Clinical Psychiatry*, 55(1), 5–11.

Frost, R., Kim, H-J., Morris, C., Boss, C., Marta-Murray-Close, & Steketee, G. (1998). Hoarding, compulsive buying and reasons for saving. *Behavior Research and Therapy*, 36(7–8), 657–664.

Frost, R. O., & Hartl, T. L. (1996). A cognitive-behavioral model of compulsive hoarding. *Behavior Research and Therapy*, 34, 341–350.

Hollander, E., & Allen, A. (2006). Is compulsive buying a real disorder, and is it really compulsive? *American Journal of Psychiatry*, 163(10), 1670–1672.

Kaiser, T. (2002). *The High Price of Materialism*. Cambridge, MA: MIT Press.

Koran, L.M., Faber R.J., Aboujaoude, E., Large, M.D., & Serpe, R. T. (2006). Estimated prevalence of compulsive buying in the United States. *American Journal of Psychiatry, 163*(10), 1806–1812.

Mowen, J. (2000). *The 3M Model of Motivation and Personality: Theory and Empirical Applications to Consumer Behavior*. Boston: Kluwer Academic Press.

Thaler, R.H., & Sunstein, C.R. (2009). *Nudge: Improving Decisions about Health, Wealth, and Happiness*. New York: Penguin.

Weun, S., Jones, M.A., & Beatty, S.E. (1997). A parsimonious scale to measure impulse buying tendency. In W.M. Pride & G. T. Hult (Eds.), *AMA Educators' Proceedings: Enhancing Knowledge Development in Marketing* (pp. 306–307). Chicago: American Marketing Association.

7

Why Can't We Talk about Money?: Equipping Yourself with Skills to Talk about Money like Adults

As usual, Roberta showed up on time for her appointment. Waiting for her husband, she was slightly annoyed, but not surprised. About 5 to 10 minutes later, Hector rushed into the meeting, gasping for breath. "I'm sorry I'm late," he said, tightly gripping his blinking BlackBerry. Roberta looked at me with faintly sad eyes, "Let's get started now that Hector is here."

I scanned the room, making intentional eye contact with both Roberta and Hector, and noting that Roberta responded, but Hector was trapped in the sliding quicksand of the seducing BlackBerry. "Hector," Roberta whispered. Startled by his wife's soft voice, Hector glanced at Roberta, then me, then his BlackBerry, then back at his wife of 15 years, and finally responded, "What?"

Realizing that this communication roadblock needed to be broken, I intervened with the following comment, "What would you like to accomplish today?" Roberta jumped in confidently, declaring, "Hector and I need to find a way to agree on what we spend and what we should save for retirement." Waiting for Hector to respond, and then waiting a bit longer, I turned gently toward Hector. "Hector, what are your thoughts about what Roberta wants to focus on today."

Hector, lifting his eyes from his BlackBerry, responded, "That's fine, but there is no urgency about retiring now or even saving a lot now."

A deep sigh echoed throughout the room. Roberta said, "You are just like my father and that really disturbs me because I had hoped that our marriage would be different, that we could talk about money, but it looks like we can't, just like my parents . . . we can't talk about money and I hate that." Roberta nervously folded and unfolded a piece of paper, to the point of practically shredding it.

BASIC COMMUNICATION: MORE THAN
WORDS AND BEYOND INSTINCT

Effective communication is not instinctual. Communicating is something that we typically do without really thinking about it. But how much do we really know about communication? Here are some interesting communication statistics to keep in mind:

- Eighty-five percent of what we know we learned through listening.
- Confident people tend to listen to content better than insecure people.
- Spoken words only account for 30–35 percent of the meaning of any interpersonal communication. The rest is transmitted through nonverbal cues.
- The average person speaks at a rate of about 125–175 words per minute, while we can perceive at a rate of up to 450 words per minute.

If Roberta and Hector knew these communication facts, they may have approached the topic differently and talked to one another differently. For Roberta and Hector, attention to body language may have changed the way they respond to each other. Would paying attention to body language change the quality of your communications overall? Communication is challenging enough, but when you talk about money, it becomes even more difficult. To ease the burden of talking about money and make it easier to talk about one of the more challenging yet vital topics in your life, the Financial Communication Model walks you through seven important steps to communicate better about money.

FINANCIAL COMMUNICATION MODEL

This give-and-take between Roberta and Hector is unfortunately quite common. All too common. Spouses argue more often about money than sex and chores, according to a 2008 PayPal Valentine's Day survey. Researchers like Ragnaar Storaasli and Howard Markman (1990) now know that money and good communication are two key ingredients to a satisfying marriage. Paul R. Amato and Stacy J. Rogers (1997) found in a scientific study that problems in communication predicted divorce.

Talking about money becomes especially challenging if you don't understand the basics of interpersonal communication. The Financial Communication Model begins with these basics. In my work with couples, this model emerged after I gave couples numerous handouts and drawing diagrams on yellow pads as ways to help them make tough financial decisions about retirement, estate planning, and career choices without arguing, digging up the past, or trying to outscore one another.

The Financial Communication Model walks you through the seven steps of communication when talking with family and other significant people in your life about money or money-related matters. In this model, there are two individuals—you and one other person. The goal is to connect meaningfully. The first three steps (1–3) begin with you, followed by the next three steps (4–6) based upon the other person, and finally, the last step (7) ends with you.

You (Steps 1–3)

1. The financial communication process begins with a thought that you want to convey to the other person. For example, you wish to talk about saving money for retirement.

2. After being clear on the thought to be conveyed, then you run the thought through your talking filter. This filter takes out messages that may be confusing, inappropriate to the situation, and even hurtful. For instance, you are upset that your spouse/partner does not currently save for retirement and you know that they should, but you also know that anger will not motivate them to save. So, you filter out the judgment and resentment that you feel and stick to the wish—"Let's begin saving for retirement."

3. The filtered thought is then sent across the communication bridge to the other person. The communication bridge is constructed out of three communication building blocks: (a) verbal communication; (b) non-verbal communication; and (c) paralinguistics, or vocal elements. Psychologist Albert Mehrabian published a famous study reporting that words contribute to 7 percent of communication, nonverbal communication accounts for 55 percent, and vocal elements account for 38 percent. The exact percentages have been debated among scientists. The key takeaway is to remember that quality communication consists of three building blocks: words; vocal elements; and facial expressions as well as gestures. Going back to our example of saving for retirement, the challenge is how to remain composed given the emotions associated with sending the message ("let's begin saving for retirement"). Do you monitor your volume, your tone, and the rapidity of your speech? Do you watch out for facial expressions of anger and judgment and other physical gestures? If you want the other person to focus on the message, then you must be sure that the message, the nonverbal cues, and vocal elements are all aligned.

Other Person (Steps 4–6)

4. Let's start with this truism: People hear what they want to hear. In other words, after hearing the message sent by you—with a focus on

your words, vocal elements, and nonverbal cues—the other person filters out any messages, feelings, or vibes that are perceived as unsettling or that do not fit their own beliefs and values.

So, there is a gap between step 3, which you control, and step 4, which is controlled by the other person. In step 3, you intend to communicate a particular message, and in step 4, the other person experiences the impact of your message, which may or may not fit with your intention. For instance, though you verbalized, "Let's begin saving for retirement," what the other person heard was: "Why aren't you saving for retirement? Don't you care about your future—our future?"

5. Once your message has traveled across the communication bridge and been filtered by the other person, then the other person considers how to respond. This response may be directly related to your message or seem to have little or nothing to do with what you intended to communicate. The message received may vary tremendously; a person may have heard everything from:

- "Why aren't you saving for retirement?" to
- "Don't you care about your future-our future?" to
- "Who do you think you are telling me what I should and should not save?" to
- "How do you know I'm not saving? How dare you? You're not saving your damn self."

In those situations in which person #2 responds irrationally to person #1, then person #1 ought to say something like the following to make sure that their intent is matched with the impact that person #2 experienced.

- "Allow me to be clearer. I meant to let you know that I am concerned about us not reaching our saving goals. I did not mean to purposefully upset you but to let you know that I feel upset when we are not able to save. Does that make sense or shall I say it in a different way?"

6. Ideally, after person #2 has formulated his or her thought, he or she runs it through their filter, which serves the same purpose as your filter. Person #2, not wanting to pick a fight, cleans up the thought a bit and says, "Look . . . I know that we need to begin saving for retirement, but you actually do not know whether I've begun saving for retirement or not. How about you? Have you begun?"

You (Step 7)

7. You mechanically hear the message from the other person and now filter the message to derive meaning.

The lesson here is that communicating about anything is complicated, but communicating about money is a bit more puzzling because it is often associated with emotions—typically negative emotions. Money can stir up feelings of survival, insecurity, vulnerability, and control. All of these emotions energize our interactions with others. Unfortunately, the energy is often negative rather than positive.

This Financial Communication Model begins with the seven steps of basic interpersonal communication. Over the years, in my work with couples, I have emphasized the following key points about communication of any kind, but especially communication about money.

- Communication is complex, not simple.
- Communication is more than speaking and listening.
- Communication is connecting with meaning.
- Communication is the foundation of problem-solving and decision-making.
- Communication is a learned skill that can be improved with feedback and practice.

Each of these key points will be briefly explored, and done in the same way that I discuss them with both individuals and couples who work with me in person.

1. Communication Is Complex, Not Simple

Thousands of books have been written about communication. Consultants in nearly every industry recommend communicating more and often to address almost any problem facing an individual, couple, group, team, or organization. If only it were that simple, but it ain't. Communication is complex. The Financial Communication Model identifies seven steps to communicating with another person. Think about the fact that most babies walk before they talk. Developmentally, communicating is a highly developed skill.

2. Communication Is More than Speaking and Listening

It is widely assumed that communication is simple; that is, if you speak clearly and really listen, then high-quality communication happens. Does it really boil down to speaking clearly and really listening? No, it involves a bit more. Here is what you need to know, practice, and do. When speaking, you must attend to the words (content); the volume, pitch, and tone (paralinguistics); and body language (nonverbals). The three of these together send the signal to the other person. The goal is to align all three aspects of speaking.

When receiving the signal (listening), you have to attend to at least three levels: content (words), feelings (nonverbal + paralinguistics), and values (words + nonverbal + paralinguistics). You do not need a PhD in linguistics to speak and listen effectively, but you do need to remember that it is a skill, a skill that requires practice to perfect or improve.

3. Communication Is Connecting with Meaning

Poor communication results in gaps between intent and impact. One person intends to send the signal that they are worried about paying the mortgage, and the other person hears that they are a reckless spender. The impact of the message sent is not aligned with the intent of the messenger. This is very common. To remedy this common occurrence, the messenger should state their intent clearly, focusing upon the words, feelings, and values, and then be sure that the receiver understands, but not necessarily agrees, with the full intent of the message at all three levels. This communication would sound like this, "I meant to let you know that I worry when we're behind on our mortgage. And I value our credit score and peace in our relationship."

4. Communication Is the Foundation of Problem-Solving and Decision-Making

Effective problem-solving and decision-making with others about money and all other matters related to money like moving, changing careers, and retiring must rest on a solid foundation of good communication skills. Beyond the seven-step Financial Communication Model, what else is there to linking good communication skills to effective financial problem-solving and decision-making? First, it is essential that the problem be accurately portrayed, second that the options are vividly described, third that the process used to select the most viable option be clearly articulated, and fourth that the criteria to evaluate the selected option be painstakingly described, pointing to measures, and time frames.

5. Communication Is a Learned Skill that Can Be Improved with Feedback and Practice

Similar to other highly developed skills, you communicate better and better as you practice more and more. Practicing is learning. Learning can be frustrating. Learning something new and becoming more skilled at what you think you already know can feel clumsy and awkward. This is expected. This is normal.

My clients have taught me that it is worth doing that which feels uncomfortable, clumsy, and awkward if it means that your skill improves. Is your relationship worth more than the discomfort of feeling clumsy and awkward? Will your communication skills about anything, but particularly money, improve without your involvement? No. Deal with the discomfort, and begin improving your communication skills today. To prove to yourself that it was worth the effort, reflect back on any skill that you feel you are very good at and ask yourself this question: Did I become really good at this without a lot of feedback and practice? If the answer is no, then I would predict that the same process works with communication skills.

BEYOND CRUCIAL CONVERSATIONS . . . BEFORE CRUCIAL CONVERSATIONS

The *New York Times* bestseller *Crucial Conversations: Tools for Talking When Stakes Are High* teaches readers how to better communicate in situations characterized by the following:

- The stakes are high.
- Opinions vary.
- Emotions run strong.

Returning to our couple seeking to begin saving for retirement: *Are the stakes high?* Yes, because the safety net for average retirees, woven together by the government, unions, and large corporations, is disappearing. *Do opinions vary on whether the stakes are high?* Yes, Roberta appears to view the stakes as higher now than Hector. *Are emotions strong?* Yes, because statements were made that were perceived as allegations. Roberta seems to be experiencing heightened emotions not only about her husband, Hector, but also how she felt about her parents' ability to talk about money and their relationship. Psychoanalysts tell us that if we wish to "unpack" emotional baggage from the past that we must focus on the here and now by first recognizing when the past is facing us versus the present, or, in this case, Roberta needs to focus on Hector and their relationship, not what happened in her parents' relationship. And Hector needs to demonstrate good attending behaviors by tossing his Black-Berry aside, maintaining eye contact, and letting Roberta know that he is following along in the dialogue even if he does not agree. You can listen and understand without agreeing.

Communicating about money can be a crucial conversation, but it does not have to be all the time. Here are some concrete ways to prevent a crucial conversation.

1. Talk before the Fuse Is Lit

The key is to talk before the fuse is lit. One of the key elements of a crucial conversation is that emotions run high. When talking about money, opinions may still vary and the stakes may indeed be high, but emotions do not have to become overheated. This is one of the three elements of a crucial conversation that you can control. Later in this chapter, you will learn how to talk before the fuse is lit.

2. Put the Topic of Conversation into Perspective

To go one step further, another way to prevent a crucial conversation is to place the discussion about money into perspective. For example, the couple who is talking about beginning to save for retirement will approach the topic differently depending upon factors like current savings, anticipated retirement income and inheritance, life expectancy, and current age. If the two people are in their mid-thirties, then the stakes are actually not so high. But, if they are in their early fifties and have not set aside any or little money for retirement, then the stakes are higher. The older the couple, or the closer to retirement age they are, the stakes keep rising.

3. Differences Are Not Deficits

What about varying opinions? One person wants to save for retirement by putting money into safe investments like certificates of deposit (CDs) because they are insured by the FDIC (Federal Deposit Insurance Company). This meets that person's need for predictability and security. The other person wants to take on more risk for a greater return. This person suggests saving for retirement by putting some money in CDs, some money in bonds, and some money in mutual funds and ETFs (exchange-traded funds), including emerging markets like Brazil, Russia, India, and China (BRIC).

So how will these two come to agreement about how to save for their retirement? Successful couples frame the decision as a grey decision versus a black-or-white decision. A grey decision is a compromise that represents give and take. A black-or-white decision is an absolute decision in which there is no compromise only winning and losing. In the case of this couple, they could select a portfolio that includes the investment vehicles of their choosing and then the discussion moves to the proportion and weighting of selected investment vehicles in the portfolio.

Over the years, I've done a lot of work with couples who had differing views on money. In fact, the research across numerous disciplines is clear that a diversity of views leads to better decisions and greater options. This assumes that conflict can be managed with these different views. I ask couples with differing views on money to do a number of things, such as complete a money autobiography (discussed in an earlier chapter), but I also have them identify the strengths of the other person's view on money and their opinion about the particular issue being discussed. Each party writes down the other's strengths on a sheet of paper and reads it silently before reading it out loud to each other. I then ask them to write down their collective strengths based upon what they have written individually. In most cases, what happens is that a shift takes place. Instead of judging one another and feeling negatively about the difference of opinions, the couple usually comes to recognize and appreciate the different views. Ultimately, opinions may still vary, but they are framed in an appreciative manner rather than being viewed as deficient.

F. Scott Fitzgerald (1936) once said, "The test of a first-rate intelligence is the ability to hold two opposed ideas in the mind at the same time, and still retain the ability to function." From my standpoint, this quote would suggest that couples must learn to understand each other better and recognize and accept each other's point of view. When you love but don't fully appreciate each other, you'll be destined to have a rocky journey ahead. When couples are willing to talk about everything and step into each other's shoes to look at problems, then that will be the starting point of an ideal committed relationship.

COMMUNICATION UNDER STRESS

Not all crucial conversation can be prevented. There are times when the stakes are high, emotions are flaring, and opinions widely vary. How do you communicate under these circumstances? Imagine talking about an impending bankruptcy, notification of a big bill from the IRS, an announcement that your company will lay off 1,400 workers and you are one of those to be laid off, the decision to leave money to your children in your will, or a diagnosis from your physician that you will need an expensive surgery that is only partially covered by your health insurance, leaving you and your loved one to cover thousands of dollars on your own. Communicating under stress is different for most people, and you must learn how to communicate in the best of times and the worst of times.

Do you communicate the same way under stress as in normal circumstances? Are you as clear? Do you listen as attentively? Do you raise your voice? Roll your eyes? Rush to judgment? If you're like most of us, we communicate differently under stress.

When under stress, the "fight or flight" response kicks in. You are now ready to run like crazy or fight like a prize fighter to get rid of the threat . . . to protect yourself. Roberta shouts at Hector, "Did you really need to buy another fishing rod?" Feeling attacked by his wife, Hector turns red with clenched fists, and looking at his wife with piercing eyes he screams back, "I'll buy whatever I damn well please . . . who are you to tell me what to buy and what not to buy . . . it's my money!"

Hector just became emotionally hijacked. His ability to problem solve, make decisions, and communicate were sideswiped by his emotions and his biological need to protect himself from a perceived threat. The threat in Hector's mind was Roberta's comments about him buying the fishing rod. Hector is not crazy. Nor is he "out of control." He is simply under stress and this impacts his ability to communicate clearly and caringly.

If we were to give Hector another shot at responding to his wife's comment, "Did you really need to buy another fishing rod?" then Hector would have responded in the following ways, assuming that he did not allow himself to become "emotionally hijacked" by Roberta's question:

- "Roberta, you're right . . . I didn't need another fishing rod, but I really wanted this rod."
- "I can understand your point of view and why you're upset."
- "Roberta, I was thinking the same thing before I bought the rod."
- "Tell me what really upsets you about me getting another fishing rod."
- "I should have let you know before I bought the rod."

These responses would have led to different results for sure. If you are a skeptical reader, you may be thinking that Roberta started this mess, not Hector. Well, to be fair, what could Roberta have done differently? She could have said:

- "Hector, I noticed that you bought a fishing rod."
- "Do you have a minute; I thought we agreed to talk to each other before we bought things."
- "Hector, I was surprised when I saw the fishing rod . . . it looks new?"
- "I was disappointed when I found out that you bought the fishing rod."

It is true that Hector could still have become "emotionally hijacked" by any of these comments, but it is less likely. The key is to be careful with your words, tone, facial expressions, and body language. The other key is to really work on becoming less reactive when thinking and talking about money. This is easier said than done, but what follows are five steps to becoming less reactive when thinking and talking about money.

FIVE STEPS TO BECOMING LESS REACTIVE WHEN THINKING AND TALKING ABOUT MONEY

There is a science to communicating effectively. In fact, linguists earn PhDs in communication, and universities have colleges and schools of communication. You do not need a graduate degree in communication to communicate effectively, but you can benefit from the key lessons arising from the research in effective communication. Below are the key lessons for you to use in your communication with important people in your life about everything, including money.

These five steps will help you become less reactive if you commit to practicing each one of these steps. As you practice these five steps, you will find that over time your communication skills will get better.

1. Breath In, Vent Out

Have you ever noticed that you nearly stop breathing when you talk while stressed? Or you're talking so fast that you can barely catch up with yourself. To slow down, take a deep breath . . . several deep breaths. As you breathe deeply and more rhythmically, allow the stress, strain, and hurt to leave your being. Breathe in . . . stress out. Breathe in . . . strain out. Breathe in . . . hurt out.

2. Take a Time Trip

Trips and vacations change us. After a trip, we feel rejuvenated. We experience the world from a different point of view. For many of us, trips make us look at our current reality differently, even at times with a greater sense of appreciation and gratitude for what we have rather than what we don't have. So, take a trip into the future when feeling stressed while communicating and ask yourself this question, "If I look back on this situation as if it were 10 years from now, would I be as upset or would I even remember it?" For most of you, the answer will be "no." If the answer is "no," then why are you sweating this so much now, when in the long run it does not carry much significance.

3. Prepare to Listen and Connect

Listening involves more than simply hearing. Hearing is mechanical. Listening is heartfelt. Our ears and brains equip us to hear. You can hear but not understand. You can understand but not appreciate. You can appreciate but not connect. The goal is to listen, understand, appreciate, and connect. Listening is a critical tool to make it easier to discuss money, so critical, in fact, that a section is devoted to this skill later in the chapter. The magic of listening when talking under stress is that you "get out of yourself" and focus on the other person, rather than staying stuck in your internal dialogue and stuff. Challenge yourself to identify one or two statements that you appreciate. Appreciative listening is akin to "First Seek to Understand, then Be Understood," the title of a chapter in Stephen Covey's 2004 highly acclaimed book, *Seven Habits of Highly Effective People*.

4. Focus on the Issue/Decision

During my career as a financial psychologist, and earlier as a clinical psychologist, I observed couples in my office start off talking about their budget, and in about 10–15 minutes, they were arguing about something that happened years ago, or they found themselves discussing global politics and economics. In short, they got off the track. They lost focus. They got distracted. They got hooked by a behavioral pattern of migrating away from the topic and talking about something completely unrelated to the intended conversation. My advice to these couples, although many at first frown at this suggestion, is to use a written agenda. For many, this does not sound romantic or spontaneous. I agree, but the purpose of these dialogues is to be financially intimate not romantically intimate. There is a time and place for everything, and written agendas work, especially if you stick to them.

5. Discuss with Curiosity

How often do you listen with your ears perked up trying to catch the other person in an inaccuracy or lie, or trying to find fault with what they say? If you cannot listen with curiosity, then you cannot discuss with curiosity. If you listen and discuss with curiosity and not judgment, then you will find that you will better understand that person's point of view (even if you do not agree). You may also find that by being curious and open to viewing the problem from another perspective that a creative solution is more likely to occur.

Mindfulness is the glue that holds all five of these recommendations together. Mindfulness is being aware of the present moment. It begins with a single breath. And it ends with a single breath.

TWO SIDES TO COMMUNICATION . . . AND A GAP . . . AND THE KEYS

Kim Allen, PhD, MFT, and Christina Crawford, MA, (2009) of the University of Missouri Extension, came up with a very useful acronym for effective communication: SPEAK/HEAR. This acronym really drives home the point that there are two sides to communication and, if we are not careful, a gap between the two sides. I have found this acronym to be very helpful with couples who struggle to communicate effectively. In fact, I give them this acronym as a handout and encourage my clients to pull it out when talking about money and finances.

Start with a positive. Start by saying something positive about your concern, such as "I know that it is important for us to be financially safe" or "I'm glad that we agree that the bills must be paid first." We are all more eager to listen when the tone of the conversation starts with a positive.

Pay attention to what you say and how you say it. Be careful about the words you use, your tone of voice, and your body language. You are more likely to be listened to if you speak in a gentle, nonthreatening way.

Explain how you feel, using details. Share how something makes you feel and what specific situations have upset you. Use an "I" statement to take charge of your own feelings. Name the specific behavior that concerns you and how that behavior makes you feel. For example, "I feel frustrated when you say you will save money and instead you spend money on expensive coffeehouse drinks."

Avoid trigger words, like always and never. Trigger words are words that can quickly turn a conversation into a fight. These include words like *always* and *never*. Everyone has their own set of trigger words as well. Recognize these words and avoid using them.

Keep it brief, and then give your partner a chance to talk. Briefly share your concerns with your partner, and then allow your partner a chance to paraphrase what you said and share his or her thoughts.

Once you have had a chance to share your side of the story, give your partner a turn to use the SPEAK skills while you listen using the HEAR skills. Use HEAR skills when you are listening to your partner share thoughts, feelings, or concerns. When using the HEAR skills, you are only listening to your partner's viewpoint, not sharing your own.

Honor your partner's thoughts and feelings. Honoring your partner is about making your partner feel valued and showing respect for his or her thoughts and feelings. Show your partner that you value him or her by listening and focusing on what your partner is saying, not what you want to say next.

Empathize: Put yourself in your partner's shoes. Empathizing with your partner means that you understand and can imagine how your partner might be feeling. Show your partner that you respect his or her feelings as being real and valid.

Allow a difference of opinion. Even if you disagree with your partner, your job as the listener is only to listen to what your partner is saying and to repeat back what you hear. Don't judge your partner or share how you feel.

Repeat respectfully. After your partner is done sharing his or her feelings, repeat what your partner said as closely to his or her words as you can. Repeating your partner's words helps you to really focus on what your partner is saying.

Couples who use these skills when talking about tough issues are often able to do so with less conflict. If you think you are going to have a discussion about a difficult topic, plan a time and a place where you can talk and use these skills to help you have a positive conversation with your partner.

APPRECIATIVE COMMUNICATION

Think about how different life looks when seen through the eyes of appreciation. When you are with friends and loved ones you really appreciate, life's inconveniences just don't seem as significant.

In the HeartMath System, appreciation is one of the most effective sentiments for giving you an energy boost and changing your perspective. HeartMath is an organization dedicated to incorporating the concept of appreciation into assisting individuals to better manage their stress and improve their relationships with others. According to Rollin McCraty and Doc Childre (2002), the word "appreciation" means to be thankful and express admiration, approval, or gratitude. Appreciation also means that something has increased in value. Material things, such as art, collectibles, and property, are said to "appreciate" when their market value rises. Appreciation here is more than an increase in material value. It is an increase in the quality of relationships and quality of life-yours and others.

COMMUNICATING IS MORE THAN TALKING: GREAT LISTENING

Some couples shut down when talking about money. They shut down not because they have nothing to say but because they feel that nobody is really listening. Communication seminar and workshop leaders teach participants how to paraphrase. Paraphrasing is a key communication tool, but showing others that you really listen is more than paraphrasing. To improve your listening skills, add the following listening tools to your listening toolkit.

- Appreciative listening.
- Empathic listening.

Appreciative Listening

In appreciative listening, the goal is not only to listen with curiosity, but also to listen and identify what part of the communication resonated for you or you connected with. Or perhaps you feel in sync with the way the other person crafted the message. You must be fully present to listen with appreciation. Turn off your internal and external distractions. Toss out your tape recorder with outdated communication scripts and stereotypes. Know that you can listen with appreciation and still not agree.

Roberta, despite feeling upset about Hector's multitasking, could have worked on this internal distraction and sought to be curious about whether he could attend to both, and after he started speaking, she might have shifted into listening mode, rather than staying stuck in her own annoyance. Hector, on the other hand, could have set the smart phone aside and demonstrated nonverbally that he was present, alert, awake, and interested. He would also have had to turn off his internal smart phone to get into a listening state of appreciation.

Empathetic Listening

When you listen empathetically, you go beyond sympathy to seek a truer understanding of how others are feeling. Unlike sympathy, you do not actually feel what others are feeling. You can relate to how they feel without experiencing their feelings. Empathy ain't about you. It's about the other person. When you listen empathetically, people talk more. People talk less about superficial stuff. People get real and talk real.

Both Roberta and Hector have conditioned themselves to listen with judgment and self-protection. Their pattern is such that one talks while judging the other and the other avoids or attacks to protect from being judged. What would happen to their ability to listen to each other with empathy if judgmental verbal attacks ceased? Would they stop piercing each other's heart? You would find that they connect at a deeper level beyond the surface of understanding words and concepts and into the feelings and motives underlying the words and concepts.

You know that people are listening with appreciation and empathy when they talk more, share more, move away from facts and figures, get physically closer to you, and when you both feel as if time has passed and the dialogue is effortless, when it flows like a gentle spring winding down a mountain.

TRAPS TRAP MORE THAN BEARS . . . THEY TRAP US TOO

The other part of your listening toolkit is to know the traps that impede effective communications. Knowing these three listening traps will prevent you from stepping on communication mines that may blow up your ability to talk about money and may even ruin your relationship with others.

- Critical listening
- False listening
- Initial listening

Critical Listening

Critical listening is listening to judge and form an opinion about what is being said. When you listen critically, you are not really listening carefully but listening to agree, disagree, approve, or disapprove. *Am I trying to prove the other person wrong so I can be right?* This is a popular question among critical listeners.

False Listening

False listening is an art for some individuals. These individuals maintain meaningful eye contact, nod while you talk, and encourage you to talk more by saying "uh-huh." Is the person really listening? Or are they pretending to listen? If you suspect that they are faking, then you may challenge them, "What did I just say?" And to your surprise, they tell you word for word, but something is missing. The spirit of your message is missing, and you know it and now they know that you have discovered they've been faking you out. If you are not ready to listen, then let the other person know by saying, "Now is not a good time for me to really listen and understand. I want to fully listen, so let's pick a time when I can devote my full attention to what you have to say."

Initial Listening

Like a flick of a switch, you are listening and BANG!—the listening stops. What are the triggers for shutting down listening? Boredom, repetition, attacks, hostility, strong feelings, overpowering memories, specific topics, time of day, place, or some other factors. One of the more common triggers is preparing your response to what the other person just said. This can be awkward because the other person may respond, "If you were listening, you would have heard me just say that, but you were too busy thinking about what you wanted to say." Hold the thought, but jot it down on a piece of paper or electronic device by saying, "That's really important. I'm writing it down to capture it." Only do this if you feel like you will forget the point.

Now that you are equipped to handle the basics of talking about money, let's move to some of the most difficult money topics that you will have to talk about with important folks in your life.

HANDLING TOUGH MONEY TOPICS

You have all the skills available to humankind and still find yourself getting very upset. You know that there are certain topics that set you and the other person off. In most cases, you cannot simply refuse to talk about those topics because of the consequences. But you can learn how to talk about those topics without gravitating toward a fight.

Reframing is a skill practiced by therapists and savvy negotiators. Skeptics may refer to it as "spin." It is more than spin. Reframing is expressing a thought in such a way that it is more likely the other person not only hears the message but will also resonate with the message and is primed to further think about the topic or act on the topic. For instance, you say, "Why can't you make more money?" This statement is likely to produce a feeling of being attacked in the other person. To reframe the statement, but stay true to the intent of the message, you might say, "I'm wondering if there are ways for us to make additional money as we try to catch up with our bills." The reframed statement does not begin with an accusation, it does not begin with a demand that the other person explain their story, and it uses the words "I" and "we," which convey that the emotion is with you as the sender, but that both of you are in this together. This reframed statement does not trigger defensiveness, but might trigger curiosity about making more money and how you will support one another to get through this together.

MORE ON HANDLING TOUGH TOPICS

There are some fairly common topics that are tough to handle when talking about money with loved ones. All of the "tough topics" cannot be addressed here, but we shall begin with these:

- Saving more and spending less
- Setting aside an emergency day fund in the midst of struggling to pay bills
- Deciding to invest in investments with varying risks and returns
- Letting adult children know that they have to be financially independent
- Deciding on how to take care of an aging relative

Saving More and Spending Less

Couples often disagree about how much to save and spend. Research demonstrates that opposites do attract and establish committed relationships. Savers are drawn to spendthrifts and vice versa. The key is to move the discussion away from saving and spending and focus on life goals. A focus on life goals requires that you ask and respond to these questions:

- What type of life do you want to live in the next 25 years, 15 years, 10 years, 5 years, 3 years, and year?
- What do you have to do today to achieve these long-term life goals?
- How do your spending and saving habits have to change to match your life goals?

Setting Aside an Emergency Day Fund in the
Midst of Struggling to Pay Bills

Financial advisors are quick to recommend that individuals set aside at least six months of living expenses as an emergency fund. This is sound advice but can create tension among couples. The tension results from disbelief and fear. The disbelief is related to the notion that it is not possible to save that much money if you are living paycheck to paycheck. The barrier to establishing an emergency fund is fear. To begin, pay yourself first. If it's $25 a week, begin with $25. The key is to develop a new habit. Habits take at least six to nine months to develop. Set up an account that makes it difficult to take out money and transfer money. This is your emergency fund. This is your insurance plan. How would you feel if your auto insurance company ran out of money and could not pay your claim after an accident? If you run out of money, then you are just like your auto insurance company.

Deciding to Invest in Investments
with Varying Risks and Returns

Risk tolerance is different for different individuals. Some will see the glass as half full and others as half empty. Some will be able to sleep well at night knowing that they could lose 20 percent, or 1 out of every 5 dollars, of their investment portfolio. Others would feel so worried and stressed that they could not sleep knowing that much is at risk. They could sleep better, with 5 percent at risk, or 1 out of 20 dollars. A few could sleep even better at bank rates of 1 percent, or 1 out of 100 dollars. These individuals would probably be less likely to sleep well if they knew that there money is safe at 1 percent, but if inflation is at 3 percent, then they are actually decreasing their spending power by 2 percent every year. This is akin to taking a pay cut of 2 percent. If you were to make $100,000, then you would be making $98,000—a 2 percent pay cut. Couples would be well served to ask a financial advisor to give them a risk tolerance survey and then talk about how they will feel if their retirement and investment portfolio is up, down, or just treading water.

Letting Adult Children Know that They
Have to Be Financially Independent

Adulthood is not defined by turning 18 or 21. Sociologists argue that adolescence is becoming more and more delayed in the United States. This delay to fully taking on the role and responsibilities of adulthood occurs due to rising unemployment, increasing educational requirements for jobs, and heightened income needs to actually live independently. Parents need to view financial independence like other developmental tasks, such as cognitive learning in school or the development of motor skills associated with driving. Chapter 8 goes into greater detail about what is appropriate developmentally for children from toddlers to adult children regarding handling money responsibly—from spending to saving and investing money. For adult children beyond their mid-twenties, you ought to discuss money from the point of view of guiding them to take on responsibility, not bailing them out, financing them, or protecting them from experiencing the natural consequences of mishandling money, such as missing a mortgage payment or even worse racking up thousands of dollars in frivolous credit card expenditures and the resultant debt. To enter into this conversation, you have to step out of parenting your little baby or young child and step into parenting your now adult son or daughter.

Deciding on How to Take Care of an Aging Relative

The good news about living longer is that we get to spend more time with our mothers and fathers. The bad news is that many of us are raising children (remember delayed adolescence) and taking care of our aging parents. It used to be that taking care of our aging parents was much easier because we lived nearby, our siblings lived close by, and there were other social support systems, such as religious communities. With the mobility of our society, the erosion of support structures, and the backing out of social obligations on the part of governments, it appears that you will have to take on this responsibility to a much greater degree than in the past.

My initial advice is to reach agreement with your parents, your siblings, and even your aunts and uncles as soon as possible. The best time to reach agreement is when everybody is mentally, emotionally, and physically healthy. It has been my observation, over the years, that this conversation is best had in a neutral setting, not in your or your parents' home. Do not forget to talk about money when having this discussion, and find out how much money your parents have set aside to care for themselves and also let your parents know what you think you can afford and what you are willing to set aside. Honesty is very important in these conversations. Recognize that these conversations may not be comfortable, so focus on their purpose and the importance. You do not want to have this conversation in the ICU or at the admission desk of a skilled nursing facility when all hell has broken loose.

QUICK TOOLS TO ENHANCE TALKING ABOUT MONEY

1. Use an agenda.
2. Select the optimal time and environment.

3. State the purpose of the conversation and intended outcomes both in content and feeling.
4. Evaluate the conversation.
5. Take and share minutes and agreements.

REFERENCES

Allen, K. & Crawford, C. (2009). Money Talks: Using Communication Skills to Discuss Finances. http://missourifamilies.org/features/divorcearticles/relations 70.htm

Amato, P.R., & Rogers, S.J. (1997). A longitudinal study of marital problems and subsequent divorce. *Journal of Marriage and the Family, 59*, 612–624.

Covey, S. (2004). *The Seven Habits of Highly Effective People*. New York: Free Press.

Fitzgerald, S. (March, 1936). The crack up. *Esquire, 2*.

Mehrabian, A., & Ferris, S. (1967). Inference of attitudes from nonverbal communication in two channels. *Journal of Consulting Psychology, 31*, 248–252.

McCraty, R. & Childre, D. (2002). *The Appreciative Heart: The Psychophysiology of Positive Emotions and Optimal Functioning*. Boulder Creek, CA: Institute of Heart Math.

Pay Pal (2008). Pay Pal's Valentine's Day Survey Proves Money Still Can't Buy Love. Available at: https://www.paypal-media.com/press-releases/20080122005212

Storaasli, R.D., & Markman, H.J. (1990). Relationship problems in the early stages of marriage: A longitudinal investigation. *Journal of Family Psychology, 4*, 80–98.

8

Talking with Your Kids about Money and Preparing Them for Financial Independence

Even before money existed as we know it today, parents have taught children how to survive in their environment. Children learned how to grow crops, hunt, prepare food, save for hard times, and demonstrate their relative worth/ value and power based upon the objects they owned. Before money, we exchanged actual objects, such as crops for lumber. Now we exchange an object with perceived value, such as currency, stocks, and futures. Should children know the difference between the real value and utility of a $50 pair of tennis shoes and a $150 pair of tennis shoes with a designer label, sneakers that happen to be popular among the cool kids?

In this chapter, the focus is on doing what parents have done for centuries, but with a modern-day and future focus. The lessons to be learned and mastered by children include the following:

- Knowing the value of money—real and symbolic.
- Recognizing the difference between needs and wants.
- Acknowledging that saving is difficult in a media-saturated, consumer world.
- Identifying the difference between consuming, producing, and creating as well as "having," "being," and "doing."
- Realizing that in a capitalist society, financial literacy, competence, responsibility, and prudence are as important as the three R's (reading, writing, and arithmetic).

Learning the best time to share money lessons with your children will be shared with you in this chapter. Given significant changes in the economic landscape in the United States and abroad as, well as in the labor market, it is now even more important that children and teens are equipped with the necessary skills to navigate the turbulent waters of making a living as an adult, and how to prepare themselves for what some economists are calling the "New Normal."

NEW NORMAL

The New Normal is an era marked by structural unemployment, low inflation (including wage inflation), declining home prices, and anemic economic growth as measured by GDP (gross domestic product). For parents, the New Normal is the chalkboard-scratching anxiety of knowing that your children will not be better off economically than you. This is the first generation in America to face this new reality. The New Normal is new but not pleasant.

The Economic Psychology of Everyday Life, written by a team of researchers (Webley et al., 2001), states that the dangers of economic life are no longer shielded from children today. First came the dot.com bust of the early 21st century; this was followed by the collapse of the housing market in 2008, which engendered the Great Recession and lingering unemployment; and in the summer of 2011, another stock market decline triggered the S&P downgrade. This has brought tighter budgets to the dinner tables across America. (In fact, it is estimated by some experts that one out of five families in America goes to bed hungry each and every night.) According to a 2010 American Express survey of parents with children between the ages of 6 and 16, nearly three-fourths (71%) of the parents say that children understand the country is in a recession. Moreover, almost all (91%) of parents say they are committed to teaching their children how to be financially responsible. This chapter is for parents and others who bear responsibility for the children in your life.

Given the increasing importance of financial competence and prudence in the lives of children and teens today, you would predict that financial literacy would be relatively high. Wrong. Lewis Mandell, the author of a widely acclaimed 1990 report titled "Our Vulnerable Youth: The Financial Literacy of American 12th Graders," exposed the dismally high rates of financial illiteracy among high school seniors in our nation. I have provided three sample questions from the report. Each of the three questions has an asterisk. The asterisk is the correct answer. The percentages are the percentage of children who chose which answer. For example, the first question indicates that nearly two out of three (61.3%) answered this question correctly.

- If each of the following persons had the same amount of take home pay, who would need the greatest amount of life insurance?
  - *61.3% (a) A young single woman with two young children.
  - 4.4% (b) A young single woman without children.

- 30.0% (c) An elderly retired man with a wife who is also retired.
- 4.2% (d) A young married man without children.
- Which of the following statements is true?
  - 10.0% (a) Your bad loan payment record with one bank will not be considered if you apply to another bank for a loan.
  - 11.6% (b) If you missed a payment more than two years ago, it cannot be considered in a loan decision.
  - *70.9% (c) Banks and other lenders share the credit history of their borrowers with each other and are likely to know of any loan payments that you have missed.
  - 7.5% (d) People have so many loans it is very unlikely that one bank will know your history with another bank.
- Inflation can cause difficulty in many ways. Which group would have the greatest problem during periods of high inflation that last several years?
  - 8.7% (a) Young couples with no children who both work.
  - 33.9% (b) Young working couples with children.
  - 13.3% (c) Older, working couples saving for retirement.
  - *44.1% (d) Older people living on fixed retirement income.

The gap between what children and teens ought to know financially and what they actually know is sizable. The growing gap has five specific dangers that loom over the next generation:

1. Their lack of financial knowledge challenges their ability to make wise financial decisions.
2. Their lack of financial knowledge hinders their chances to make the most out of limited financial resources marked by a current and possible future job market looking more like a desert than a rich, lush rainforest with abundant jobs.
3. Their lack of financial knowledge may result in wasted time, energy, and effort at work; as well as arguments with loves ones.
4. Their lack of financial knowledge may not protect them from the perplexing and often predatory media messages and merchandise messages slickly produced by retailers, credit card sellers, and advertisers.
5. Their lack of financial knowledge will handicap them from determining the price, both paid today and in interest tomorrow, for spending on their needs and wants.

Not only do children and teens have to be financially competent and prudent to make smart money decisions and engage in financially constructive behaviors, but they must also resist the seduction of marketers, advertisers, and sales professionals urging them to, "Spend your money . . . buy this . . . you need this . . . you deserve this . . . treat yourself . . . you can't take it with you . . ." Consumerism is the new capitalism. The dangers of consumerism were discussed in chapter 6. Consumerism is swallowing up children, teens, and their parents into suffocating sinkholes of consumer debt and financial stress.

Economists define consumerism as valuing and using money for non-utilitarian reasons, such as escape from boredom, social prestige, and entertainment. Teach children about the three rudders of financial orientation as presented in chapter 2: "having," "being," and "doing." Consumerism is all about "having" not "being' and not "doing." After your children have been introduced to three rudders of financial orientation, then it is time for them to learn about the differences between consuming, producing, and creating. In fact, now is the time. Right now.

CONSUMING

As animals, we must consumer food and drink to survive physically. Is there a level of consumption that extends beyond meeting physical needs? Yes. In his classic book—written over a century ago in 1899—*The Theory of the Leisure Class*, Thorstein Veblen lays out the concept of "conspicuous consumption," or how consumption beyond meeting your physical needs symbolizes being a lady, a gentleman, or a master not a commoner. In his own words painting a picture of conspicuous consumption, he writes: "He consumes freely and of the best, in food, drink, narcotics, shelter, services, ornaments, amulets, and idols or divinities" (page 47).

According to Motoko Rich and Stephanie Clifford (2012), consumer spending accounts for 70 percent of all spending. What's alarming about this? What happens when consumers stop spending like they did after the financial crisis of 2008 and once again in the summer of 2011 is that the engine of the economy sputters along or even stops completely. As Margaret Magnarelli (2011) notes on the website www.parents.com, "Marketers invest more than $14 billion a year to turn out little children into huge consumers."

As a parent, you have to proactively fight against the markets armed with $14 billion to immunize your children. You may not be able to win the fight with dollars but you can win the fight with providing love, nurturance, financial parenting; and being a great financial role model. Consuming is all about "having." There is nothing inherently wrong about "having" and consuming but somebody somewhere somehow at some time has to produce, or else there is nothing to consume.

PRODUCING

Production is making a good or service that has economic value to be sold in the marketplace. But not everything that is produced is sold or even produced for economic gain. Art and music is made and sometimes without any interest in being sold but appreciated. The nursery rhyme "Simple Simon Met a Pieman" teaches children the differences between consumers and producers.

> Simple Simon met a pieman going to the fair;
> Said Simple Simon to the pieman "Let me taste your ware"
> Said the pieman to Simple Simon "Show me first your penny"
> Said Simple Simon to the pieman "Sir, I have not any!"
>
> Simple Simon went a-fishing for to catch a whale;
> All the water he had got was in his mother's pail.
> Simple Simon went to look if plums grew on a thistle;
> He pricked his fingers very much which made poor Simon whistle.
> He went for water in a sieve but soon it all fell through;
> And now poor Simple Simon bids you all "Adieu."

The lessons to be learned in this nursery rhyme are that to buy something, somebody must have made something.

In our current society, you cannot make a living by consuming alone. You earn a living in our society by producing. Producing is associated with the financial rudder of "doing."

CREATING

Lastly, to consume, something must be produced, and to produce, something must be created. Apple's iPad is a good example of the economic ecology of creating, producing, and consuming. First, Steve Jobs created the iPad. Second, the iPad was produced or manufactured. Third, the iPad was sold. Fourth, the iPad was consumed by those who bought the iPad.

Where was money exchanged and between whom? Creators typically get paid by a company to create or they create for no money in their garages. In fact, Apple began in a garage in California, and the founders did not get paid for their first technological creations. Steve Jobs and his co-founder created for free—at least monetarily. After the creators create, then they manufacture or produce what they have created. The creators often have to pay the producers to manufacture. The manufacturers have to pay the producers of resources and materials to build the product. For instance, an iPad is made of plastic, wires, and chips. The iPad manufacturer, Apple, has to pay producers of plastic, wires, and chips to make the iPad. Finally, after the iPad is made and is sitting on a shelf to be sold, then consumers must give retailers money to take home the iPad. The money that is given to the retailer is distributed along to the producer and the creator. Creating is often associated with "being" and "doing." You cannot force creativity.

Now that you know the differences among consuming, producing, and creating, and "having," "doing," and "being," what lessons are you teaching your children; and if your children were to follow you for a full week (168 hours), what would they observe?

- Observe you consuming more than producing and creating?
- Observe you "having" more than "doing" and "being"?
- Hear you talking more about consuming than producing and creating.
- Hear you talking more about "having" more than "doing" and "being"?
- Notice you watching television programs or listening to radio programs focusing on consuming more than producing and creating?
- Notice you watching television programs or listening to radio programs focusing more on "having" than "being" and "doing"?
- Praying or hoping for the ability to consume more rather than produce more or create more?
- Praying or hoping for the ability to "have more" rather than "do more" or "be more"?

After really thinking about these eight self-observations, then make a decision, today, to change what you say, what you do, what you watch, and what you pray and hope for to send your children a message that prepares them to not only consume but to produce and create. How often do you hear parents saying, "I just want my kids to be productive members of society and love what they do?" It is also true that you overhear parents remark, "I want them to have all the things I did not have." But how often do you hear, "I want my kids to consume, to buy more, and keep getting more and more." You will have to tailor your money message to meet the specific needs of your child or children taking into consideration what is developmentally appropriate based upon their age and maturity, which may not be reflected by their actual age.

Children are unique as individuals. Also, children do not develop randomly. There are patterns to how children and teens develop. Knowing these developmental patterns will guide you as a parent to teach and support your children and teens by exposing them to concepts about money at the right time developmentally. It would be foolish to try to teach an infant to ride a bike but it would be developmentally appropriate to teach a six year old to ride a bike. The same holds true for teaching lessons about money and finances.

DEVELOPMENTAL STAGES

Leading child development authorities have documented that as children progress through developmental stages, their ability to understand economic and financial concepts change. A key question is: What is developmentally appropriate for children to understand about money? A famous developmental psychologist by the name of Jean Piaget introduced a model of children's cognitive development that has been used worldwide by educators, including parent educators (1952). This model will be used to hear to answer this question: What is developmentally appropriate for children to learn about money?

1. Sensorimotor (0–2 years)
2. Preoperational (2–6 years)
3. Concrete operational (7–12 years)
4. Formal operational (12 years–adult)

These ages are general benchmarks, not absolute rules. So, perhaps you know a 5 year old who is functioning at the concrete operational stage? Likewise, you may know a 14 year old, or even an adult, who is functioning at the concrete operational stage. Before applying these four stages of cognitive development to money, a brief description of each stage will be presented. The question of whether to provide a child an allowance of any type will also be answered with a fuller explanation of the three types of allowances later in this chapter.

Sensorimotor (0–2 years)

The infant and toddler explore the world with their five senses (sight, sound, touch, taste, smell). Touch is one of the more notable senses that children at this age use to explore the world. Parents often say, "Do not touch that . . . do not put that in your mouth." At this stage, children are developing object permanence. This means that if an object, such as a bright yellow duck, is out of their sight, that object still exists even if they cannot see it. They are also developing the ability to separate from their parents without triggering an intense, distressing feeling known as "separation anxiety."

At this stage, money represents only another physical object to be explored with their five senses. An allowance is not necessary. To be frank, it is does not make much sense developmentally. This does not mean that you should not tuck away money in a savings account or designated investment account for college.

Preoperational (2–6 years)

The young child now progresses to the preoperational stage. Some regard this as the pre-school stage. At this stage, the child begins to develop a vocabulary for describing objects as well as ideas, a vocabulary that accelerates and builds with each year. The other major aspect of this age is that children begin to imagine and pretend. Finally, at this stage, children are focused on meeting their own needs and expressing their feelings with little or no regard for others. Developmental psychologists call this stage "egocentric." Others refer to this as, the "it's all about me" phase.

At this stage, money is still recognized primarily as an object, though now children have a vocabulary to describe money. They can draw and recognize money. They may even "have" money, but at this point money is similar to any other object that the child does or does not value. The value, at this stage, is not linked to the "actual" value of money, but to some other physical and/or sentimental characteristic, such as being a shiny silver coin given to them by their grandmother who they miss and love.

As early as three to four and a half years old, children can identify money from other objects. Yet, at this age, they cannot discriminate between different coins, and they have no understanding about the source of money. Children around the ages of four to five associate size with cost. For instance, if asked which costs more, a chocolate bar or a loaf of bread, children will say a loaf of bread because it is larger.

At this stage, an allowance is considered developmentally appropriate. If you decide to give a young child an allowance, it is better to show, not explain, the value of money and that it be done in the simplest of terms. For instance, buy a clear piggy bank so your child can see how money accumulates when saved and how money diminishes when spent. If you are worried that your young child is a spendthrift, then pretend to place the object that they want to buy, such as a candy bar or toy, next to the clear piggy bank and remove the amount of money required to make that purchase and ask, "Does your piggy bank have more money in now or before your bought [name the object]?" If they say, yes. Then say, "What happened?" Remember, you have placed the object that they bought right next to the clear piggy bank. If they bought a candy bar, the young child may not notice the difference. If they bought a big object, then the young child will probably notice the difference with your prompting.

Concrete Operational (7–12 Years)

The school-age child is beginning to use reason and logic to understand the world around them. Their vocabulary continues to increase, grammar begins to function, and conversations can be started and held with others. Basic math concepts are introduced at home and at school. Children at this age can add, subtract, multiply, and divide. These newly found skills in the four basic math functions enable children to count money, distribute money, and talk about money with others.

Unlike children at the age of 4 to 5, beginning at about 7 or 8 years of age, children associate the cost of an object not with its size but with its function or usefulness. For example, if asked which costs more, a loaf of bread or a watch, children of this age usually choose a watch because you can tell time with a watch, but only eat a loaf of bread. Closer to 10 years of age, children begin to associate cost with the degree of work and materials put into an object. For instance, if you were to ask a 10 year old which costs more, a watch or a gourmet cupcake, they would most likely pick the watch because of the degree of work and materials used to make the watch.

At this stage, school-age children should have an allowance. In addition to the piggy bank, open a savings account in your child's name and let them know you will deposit gifts and their allowance in this account. These deposits have three purposes: saving, spending, and giving. At this stage, do not use electronic banking, although it is convenient, but instead take your child to the bank and physically go through depositing and withdrawing. Remember, school-age children love to do and get involved. Get your school-age children actively involved in saving.

Formal Operational (12 Years–Adult)

Middle school marks the transition between concrete operational and formal operational. This time also signals adolescence. At this stage, teens and adults can reason abstractly and think in hypothetical terms. They can ask and answer "What if . . . ?" questions such as "What if I save my allowance for a year, will I have enough to buy a new iPad?" Not only can teens and adults perform the four basic math functions, but they can also perform higher level math depending upon their progress and success in middle school, high school, and, for some, higher education. You do not need to be a college graduate to be financially competent and prudent. In fact, most of the underlying math skills required to be financially competent and prudent are acquired during the concrete operational stage. Likewise, the reasoning skills to make decisions about money are also developed at this stage.

Children at this age and stage of development should be receiving an allowance. At this point developmentally, your emerging adult is ready to demonstrate financial literacy, competence, and prudence at a very basic level. As such, you should encourage them to earn their own allowance and get off

Table 8.1
Money and Development Stages: Timing is Everything!

Developmental stage	Age	Developmentally appropriate money skill
Sensorimotor	0–2	• None.
Preoperational	2–6	• None.
Concrete operational	7–12	• Can add, subtract, multiply, and divide money. • Knows that money is different from other physical objects. • Recognizes that money has value. • Realizes that money can be earned, saved, lost, destroyed, and wasted. • Senses that loved ones can argue about money. • Learns that people sometimes steal, hurt, and kill others for money.
Formal operational	12 +	• Makes decisions about earning, saving, spending, and investing money. • Makes plans about earning, saving, spending, and investing money. • Develops behavioral patterns or habits about earning, saving, spending, and investing money. • Performs what-if scenarios to reduce uncertainty and anxiety about money. • Understands the difference between owning something of value and borrowing something of value. • Talks about money with others. • Acknowledges that money symbolizes more than an economic exchange.

the parental "payroll," even during tough times. And times are tough. Not only should your emerging adult open a savings account, but also a checking account with a debit card. Credit cards will be discussed later in the chapter.

Table 8.1 shows each of the four developmental stages and developmentally appropriate money skills. In this table, each stage is the foundation for the next stage.

FINANCIAL PARENTING

The family is the primary provider of financial lessons for their children. The lessons children learn depend not only on the information provided, the way in which the information is delivered, the example that the parents model, but also the amount and source of income that children actually control. Academics specializing in child development, parenting education, and family consumer sciences write that the goal of financial parenting is to financially socialize your children and teens. What is "financial socialization"? In the journal *Financial Counseling and Planning*, a researcher named Dr. Danes offered this definition: "the process of acquiring and developing values, attitudes, standards, norms, knowledge, and behaviors that contribute to the financial viability and well-being of the individual" (1994, page 128).

Five Targets of Financial Parenting

To break down this definition into its simplest parts, Dr. Danes suggests that the targets of financial parenting ought to focus on the following:

- To teach your children and teens appropriate *attitudes* regarding money. An attitude is a preference. Simply put, an attitude is felt as a like or dislike. Some children have a favorable attitude toward putting their allowance in the bank and some do not.
- To teach your children and teens facts and concepts or *knowledge* involving money. For instance, explaining what interest and interest rates are and how this works.
- To teach your children and teens about *standards* related to money is all about setting expectations. For instance, setting an expectation that half of his/her allowance must go into the savings account creates a standard related to how much of the allowance can be spent and how much must be saved.
- To teach your children and teens about *norms* surrounding money boils down to viewing what is "right" and what is "wrong" from an ethical or moral point of view. For instance, is it ethically or morally acceptable to cheat on your school examinations? Of course not. Is it ethically or morally acceptable to give your child money if they receive an A in class? Yes, perhaps. If your child is reinforced by getting paid for higher grades by all means necessary including cheating or lying to you about their grade, then they have learned that money overshadows truth telling and their relationship with their parents.
- To teach directly or indirectly through modeling *behaviors* concerning money, such as making deposits into the saving account after each birthday or major holiday, when the child or teen receives a monetary gift.

These five lessons together will help your child move closer to knowing the difference between a want and a need. Looking back on my own parenting, I often would say to my elementary school child, "Do you mean you want to have [name object]?" Automatically, the almost defiant response was, "No, I need . . . I really need [name of object]." Sometimes, depending upon my parenting energy and assessing the openness and receptivity of my elementary school child, I would remark, "There is a difference. A need is for survival such as food, clothing, and shelter. A want is just because I want it." Each one of these factors of financial socialization will be reviewed below to guide families in better preparing their children to lead financially competent and prudent lives. These five lessons will also give you more confidence as a parent that most of the bases are covered with regard to developing a child that will be more likely to be financially wise, financially prudent, and financially savvy. You may be asking, "Marty, how can you be so sure?" Psychologists will tell you that real change, lasting change is based upon addressing attitudes (how we like and dislike), knowledge (what we know), behavior (what we do), standards (expectations by self and others), and norms (rewards and consequences for not meeting standards). Look back on these five lessons and you will notice that all five bases are covered. This is how I can be so sure. But there are no guarantees.

Financial Information Provided

Knowing what is and is not developmentally appropriate is the first step in financial parenting and then knowing the target that you aim to seek as a financial parent is the second step. The third step is to deliver the information that demands the attention of your child in a way that appeals and excites their senses.

Kids hate dry boring lectures as much as we all do. Communicating with your child about finance and saving is made more difficult because you must compete with the exciting graphics and interactivity of gaming technology. Instead of complaining about the alluring almost hypnotic control that gaming companies have on our children, learn from them. If a gaming company were to put out a financial education game, it would definitely have these attributes:

- Children and teens would experience the concepts, not just be taught the concepts.
- Children and teens would be hurled into a simulated environment that required them to apply newly taught concepts.
- Children and teens would be bombarded by content tapping as many senses as possible and using diverse learning styles.
- For males in particular, the element of competition would be a key focus of the lesson, and unfortunately a dire consequence if the money is not managed well.

These four tips to talk about money to prevent your child from whining out, "I'm bored" or "Are you finished yet?", are helpful tools in your financial parenting toolbox. Combining the five targets of financial parenting and these four tips on how to deliver financial information all result in the development of financial schemas or scripts.

Financial Scripts Being Developed

Underlying our decisions and behaviors, even among children, are our beliefs. These beliefs are called "schemas" by psychologists. Schemas guide our choices, actions, and interactions. Suzan Cross and Hazel Markus (1994) suggest that we even have self-schemas. A self-schema is a belief about the self. For children, do they believe that they can wait and eat only one marshmallow to get three more in five minutes? Or do they believe that they can't wait for five minutes to get three more?

Because of the purposeful or accidental modeling related to finances and economics by parents and caretakers, children develop financial scripts or schemas often referred to as "money scripts." Hibbert, Beutler, and Martin (2004) published an article in *Financial Counseling and Planning,* the official journal of the Association of Financial Counseling and Planning, describing how financial scripts or schemas come to be: "Children are likely to observe and absorb attitudes and behaviors from the prosaic or commonplace financial processes embedded in home and family life such as: spending or saving, making payments late or timely, and wise use or misuse of credit" (page 51).

The concept of financial scripts or schemas were introduced in chapter 3. Just like an actor or actress, you do not have to follow the financial scripts or schemas that were modeled to you growing up as a child and teen. The key lesson for those influencing children is that your purposeful money lessons and your own actions, words, and expressed emotions determine the financial scripts and schemas of the children in your life. Be purposeful and mindful because you are being watched and imitated.

Children and teens can also develop healthy financial scripts. These scripts or schemas are associated with smart financial decisions and behaviors. Two purposeful and healthy financial scripts to be developed are financial prudence and debt avoidance.

1. Financial Prudence Scripts or Schemas

- I save money.
- I live within my income.
- I pay my bills on time.
- I recognize that some of my debts are the result of unwise decisions and behaviors.

2. Debt Avoidance Scripts or Schemas

- I buy what I need or want within the limits of my budget.
- If I borrow money, I take my time to calculate how I will pay the money back.
- I try to minimize my living expenses.
- I use cash for daily purchases even if a debit or credit card is more convenient.
- I know that using a credit card is like taking out a loan from a bank. It is borrowed money.
- I recognize that all borrowed money must be paid back with money I have to earn.

It is critical for parents to realize that while they are developing financially healthy schemas and scripts, marketers are also seeking to program your children with consumption schemas and scripts. Noted researcher Karen E. Wohlwend in an article titled "Damsels in Discourse: Girls Consuming and Producing Identity Texts through Disney Princess Play," writes: "Toys that are associated with children's popular animated films or television programs encourage children to play and replay familiar scripts and character roles" (page 59).

The good news is that early in children's development, parents are by far the dominant influencer and shaper of children's schemas and scripts. Many of the schemas and scripts that children learn are taught through modeling.

THE ROLE OF PARENTS

It is never too early to introduce investing to your children. As a parent, if you don't know much about investing yourself, educate yourself first. This is akin to flying in an airplane when you hear the pre-flight safety announcement say, "In case of a change in cabin pressure, the oxygen masks will drop from overhead; if you are traveling with small children, put on your mask first, and then your child's." So, increase your own financial literacy, and then begin to educate your children. If you don't feel comfortable teaching them, you might find a place that teaches financial literacy to children. It is increasingly being taught even to pre-schoolers. In an iVillage and American Express online survey of U.S. moms, nearly half (41%) of moms reported wanting to know more about financial matters themselves so they could pass that knowledge on to their children.

Models of Financial Well-Being

A study by Jeffrey R. Hibbert, Ivan F. Beutler, and Todd M. Martin (2004) found that financial stress and strain can be reduced among children and teens if financial prudence was demonstrated by their parents. What were the behaviors associated with financial prudence in this study?

- Living within their income.
- Paying their bills on time.
- Avoiding unnecessary debt.
- Consistently saving.

The good news from this same research study was that parents should not pressure themselves to become financial experts and gurus to teach their children and teens about money in general and financial prudence in particular. Knowledge about finances and economics is important, but even more so are the four behaviors associated with financial prudence.

Amount and Source of Income under the Control of Children

Teaching children and teens about money is important, but unless these lessons are grounded in their daily reality, the impact will not be as strong. Can you imagine trying to learn how to play a musical instrument without ever being allowed to touch the instrument? You would no doubt learn something, but you would learn a lot more if you could actually practice the instrument. The same case is made here.

Teens have three major sources of income: (1) allowance; (2) earnings from part-time jobs; and (3) gifts and other money received from parents and family members. Children under the age of 10 generally only have two sources of income: (1) allowance and (2) gifts and other money from family. Each one of these will be discussed in greater detail because there are lessons to be learned.

Allowance

Two researchers in a paper titled "The Role of Allowances in Adolescent Socialization," published in the prestigious journal *Youth and Society,* argued that there are three types of allowances for teens (Miller & Yung, 1990). This also holds true for some children depending upon the family.

- *Earned allowance.* This is income earned by performing chores or other assigned tasks. It also includes monetary rewards for achieving specific goals such as good behavior or grades. The lesson to be learned here is that money is based upon performance and that more money can be earned when you achieve or engage in socially appropriate conduct. Obviously, this type of allowance prepares children and teens for the world of work, including the concept of incentive compensation or bonuses.

- *Educational allowance.* This is income exclusively for the purpose of educating your child or teen about making better financial decisions and engaging in financially prudent behavior. This includes giving them savings bonds or money to invest in a "child friendly" mutual fund. The lesson is that learning about money is as important as learning about subjects taught in school. This sends the signal to your child or teen that money is important and that there are parental expectations about mastering money and becoming financially literate and prudent.

- *Entitled allowance.* This income should be used to pay for the basics, such as clothing and school supplies as well as the extras like dolls or video games. This is money given "just because you are our child" and has no strings attached. There is a danger lurking with the "entitled allowance." Beware of associating how much you love your child with how much money you give, and inadvertently delivering the message that money can buy love. After all, money can't buy love.

Earnings from Part-Time Employment

Earnings from work both inside and outside the home are a source of income worthy of debate and discussion. Some of the sources of debate arise from the following questions about work and children:

- Should children and teens be more focused on school or on combining work with school?
- Is it ethical for children and teens to work?
- Are there any life lessons to be taught from working that cannot be learned at school?
- Are there any money lessons to be taught from working that cannot be learned at school?

Each of these four questions will be answered here.

Should children and teens be more focused on school or on combining work with school? Kids ought to have the experience of learning how to work and benefiting from working. In our work-driven, capitalistic society, teaching children about work and how to work are essential survival skills. If children and teens fail to develop what human resource professionals call "work readiness" skills, then parents have failed the next generation. Imagine a mother bird failing to teach her baby bird how to eat and survive. What will happen to the baby bird? It will die. The same is true with us as humans. Our children as they grow up may not be able to survive without us teaching them the valuable lessons about to the importance of work, how to find work, and how to wisely save and spend the money they receive from legitimate work.

Is it ethical for children to work? The ethics of children working or not is a subject of debate and is beyond the scope of this chapter from a public policy point of view. As parents and guardians of children and teens, the question may be framed around what benefits arise for children and teens from working and likewise what harm may occur. If the benefits outweigh the harms, then perhaps it can be reasoned that working is ethical.

Are there any life lessons to be taught from working that cannot be learned at school? Work offers many life lessons for children and teenagers, ranging from demonstrating dependability to accepting authority and responsibility, and being accountable. Another lesson is that work is not simply about performing a task well; it's also about relating well to others, resolving conflict, and learning to navigate office politics. Life lessons can be learned when teens are exposed to disruptive bosses, rude customers, and less than friendly or cooperative co-workers. Through such experiences, they'll learn to develop coping skills.

Are there any money lessons to be taught from working that cannot be learned at school? There are numerous money lessons to be gained from work. For instance, budgeting is an important lesson. Learning how to make your money last until the next paycheck is critical. For many teens, work provides the lesson that "money does not grow on trees," and if all goes well, that hard work results in increased wages. Other lessons learned from working is what economic value is placed on the type of work you do and how this is related to labor market supply and demand. One learns the value of getting educated and skilled in various professions, and learning where current and future shortages lie. Depending on the work/career path, some children and teens may learn the lesson that the more they invest in their knowledge, skills, and experience, the greater financial return they will receive.

Gifts and Other Income

Birthdays and special holidays are times when children and teens receive money. Parents may give restricted, unrestricted, or decision-making gifts for special times during the year.

A restricted gift coming from the parent might sound like this, "In celebrating your birthday, we have decided to give you not only a card, but also $50.

You can spend $25 as you like, but the other $25 has to go into your savings account." This is restricted because the child does not have complete control over how to use the gift.

An unrestricted gift sounds like this, "In celebrating your birthday, we have decided to give you not only a card but also $50. You can spend it all as you like." This is unrestricted because the child has complete control.

A decision-making gift sounds like this, "In celebrating your birthday, we have decided to give you not only a card, but also $50. You can spend it or you can save it or spend a little and save a little. It is your decision." This is a decision-making gift because it requires that your child or teen choose among three options: (1) spend all of the $50; (2) save all of the $50; or (3) spend some and save some.

DOES IT TAKE A WHOLE VILLAGE TO RAISE FINANCIALLY PRUDENT CHILDREN AND TEENS?

The popular slogan and philosophy—"It takes a whole village to raise a child"—can and should be applied to ensuring that children and teens grow up to be financially competent and even prudent. This philosophy will quickly surface tensions and finger-pointing among the relevant stakeholders. These stakeholders include the family, the school, and even financial institutions, like banks and credit card companies. The role and responsibility of the family has already been discussed. The role and responsibility of the school and financial institutions follows.

The Role of the School

The role of the school will be briefly explored here because the real focus of this chapter is on the role of parents. According to the National Council on Economic Education in a 2007 survey of personal finance in schools, just over half (28) of the states mandate personal financial education as part of the curriculum in their schools. Programs like "I Can Save" begin as early as elementary school. Another program used in elementary school is Money Savvy Kids which uses a piggybank as an educational tool along with eight classroom lessons. The Money Savvy Kids piggybank has four slots, not just a single one for money. The four slots are for the basic four functions of money:

- Saving
- Spending
- Borrowing
- Investing

Beyond these four basic functions of managing money, I would also add:

- Sharing
- Donating

If only adults could remember these six basic functions of money. The key is that balance is terribly important.

Among middle school students, Junior Achievement rolled out a program many years ago called Economics for Success. This program focuses on personal finance, careers, and the benefits of staying in school. There are also programs in high school and college. This is not the only program but an example of one of the more well known and long lasting. There are also programs for high school students and college students. For instance, De Paul University in Chicago has a Financial Fitness Program for students that covers many aspects of financial planning including budgeting.

The Role of Financial Institution: Banks and Mutual Funds

Similar to the role of schools, financial institutions have a role to play in developing the financial knowledge, behavior, and attitudes of children. It must be emphasized that banks and other financial institutions may have ulterior motives, like selling financial services and gathering deposits to loan out at a higher interest rate, but there still remains a role for financial institutions.

Imagine that your child is graduating high school. As you proudly watch your child receive her diploma, you feel proud as you should. You are confident that your child has earned an education that will prepare her for the next challenge in life, whether it is going to college, serving in the military, or working at a job. How confident are you that your high school graduate is financially literate? How confident are you that your high school grad will know how to responsibly handle money, ranging from college financial aid to earnings from the military or to money from their paycheck? Almost one in two parents (45%) of high school seniors is unsure about whether their high school senior can manage their own banking and personal finances, according to a 2010 Capital One survey. As parents, you have a role to play, as do the schools and even financial institutions.

Banks and other financial institutions have a role to play in making the bank more "child friendly and teenage friendly." The Federal Reserve Bank of San Francisco even recognized the role of financial institutions when it wrote, "Financial institutions have a vested interest in supporting or providing financial literacy programs. Relative to cost, financial literacy provides both immediate and long-term returns. The most obvious is brand recognition and market share" (2002, page 1).

Beyond saving, investing is also a major financial lesson to be taught to your children and modeled by you. One of the simplest ways to teach your children about investing is to introduce them to mutual funds.

Mutual Funds

Kids learn best by doing. To really make it interesting, have your children actually invest in a mutual fund. There are a few mutual funds that are exclusively focused on children and several more that are "child-friendly." At the end of this chapter, a list of "child-friendly" mutual funds is presented. Consider following these simple rules before investing in a mutual fund. Before making any decisions, consult a financial advisor, particularly one that has earned his or her Certified Financial Planner designation and is fee-only. Fee-only planners do not earn a commission for selling specific mutual funds, ETFs, or stocks.

- Select a stock fund not a bond fund. Keep it simple. The goal is to educate children about how investments work in general, using a mutual fund as a relatively simple way to invest.
- Select a large-cap stock fund, which is viewed as a "buy-and-hold" fund. Such funds will allow your child to track how the fund moves up and down with changes. Remember, you are not teaching your children about trading but investing. There is a difference.

A real concern among parents is whether you can afford to open a mutual fund in your child's name. The answer is yes. There are mutual funds that require $5,000 or even $10,000 to get started, but there are also mutual funds that cost $100 or less. Do your homework and select a fund that fits within your budget. For children with a steady income from a job or allowance, set aside a portion of their total monthly income for a mutual fund.

Perhaps you are wondering if a child can legally invest in a mutual fund. If the child is under 18, you, as a parent, simply set up a custodial account with an adult as a custodian. After this is set up with the mutual fund company, then your children can begin contributing their own money from allowances, gifts, or earnings, and you can even kick in some dollars as you see fit.

Credit Card Companies

There is a purpose for credit cards and credit card companies. For example, in situations when you need access to more money than what you have in your wallet (e.g., when buying a flat screen TV), a credit card is quite handy.

But what about using a credit card for everyday items like candy or magazines? You can carry around that amount of cash so you don't really need to
use a credit card or debit card. Paying with cash keeps you in touch with how
much you spend because of the sensory experience of handling money and
even smelling money.

Without credit and credit card companies, you would have to use cash
for all purchases small and large, which is not always convenient. Another
good use of credit cards are when you do not actually know how much a bill
will be for services such as dental office visits, plumbing, or rental cars. Or
an emergency arises unexpectedly and you don't have sufficient cash. In such
instances, you can rest easy knowing you can use your credit card.

It makes no sense to invest when you are paying off unnecessary credit card
debt at 18–25 percent interest or more. It is very, very important to teach
your children about how to use credit cards prudently and responsibly. The
first lesson is to remind them that they are taking out a loan each and every
time they use a credit card. The second lesson is to teach them how to deci-
pher the "secret code" when reading a credit card billing statement. Credit
cards, if used imprudently, can be dangerous.

In an online article on MSN's Money Central, M. P. Dunleavy (2006) told
the following story about the dangerous mix of teens and credit cards.

> Like a lot of hard-working women, Andrea Alba has moments of finan-
> cial despair. Between juggling three jobs, paying her bills and trying to
> get out of debt, she feels overwhelmed. "I just want to pay everything
> off," she says, "I wish I didn't have to struggle so much." But Alba is no
> debt-weary baby boomer. She's only 19 and a couple of years out of high
> school.

Given these dangers and the move toward a cashless society as predicted
by some futurists, teaching your children about how to use credit cards becomes more important. In this cashless society, individuals are paying not
just for daily basic items like gas and food, but for all purchases and services
with debit and credit cards. However, there is one thing to beware of: The
misuse of credit. How does a child or teen know the appropriate use of credit
versus the misuse of credit? With the high interest rates credit card companies
charge, it's best not to leave it up to the credit card companies to teach these
lessons. I don't recommend even leaving it up to the schools. It is up to you as
a parent. What happens when your children graduate from high school and
to a community college or college?

Credit card companies and banks promoting credit cards are part and parcel of freshman orientation on college and university campuses from coast to
coast. Even as college students are checking into dorms, registering for classes,

and meeting new friends, banks are offering to help students set up checking accounts and sign them up to receive their own credit cards. Just like personal checking and saving accounts, credit cards have become a rite of passage marking entry into adulthood. Though many students will use their credit card responsibly, it is important to educate your sons and daughters about the pitfalls of credit card usage. For example, research has shown that the use of credit cards makes compulsive buying worse. As a parent, you want to treat your college age student like an adult, but you also know from your own life experience that the misuse of credit cards can have disastrous consequences.

Most often parents are still paying the bills while children are in college, which means you can have control over how and when the card will be used. Perhaps the single best way to avoid misuse is to be a co-signer on the card and set a credit limit of perhaps $500 to $1,000. Along with giving your child a credit card, you earn the right to give them one of your rare lectures. What are five lessons to teach your college student as part of your family orientation to college?

1. Discuss the importance of a good credit history—how to build and protect your credit history.
2. Shop for credit with your college student, showing them how to interpret a credit card marketing flyer and how to manage their own credit by understanding the terms, conditions, and rates.
3. Explain why you are restricting the credit card limits, which includes letting them know that as they show good judgment and use the card responsibly, you will allow them to increase the credit card limit.
4. Describe the financially smart way to use credit. My suggestion is to pay for items with cash, except when it is more convenient or necessary to use a credit card.
5. Allow your college student to experience the consequences of misusing credit cards by reducing their credit limits, taking away their credit cards, refusing to pay their unpaid credit card bills, and refusing to co-sign. The real test is what happens after they have access to credit.

FINANCIAL PARENTING NEVER ENDS

You will no doubt continue to model healthy financial behaviors as a parent as you pass through developmental milestones, such as preparing for retirement, being retired, and preparing for your legacy. Be intentional and purposeful about your financial decisions and behaviors knowing that you are a role model. As your children have their children, guide and coach your children to make sure that they fully accept and take on the role of being a financially healthy parent.

RESOURCES

The following is a list of some mutual fund companies that have specific funds for children. This is neither an exhaustive list nor am I making a recommendation to purchase a particular mutual fund.

- USAA First Start Growth (UFSGX)
- Monetta Young Investor Fund (MYIFX)
- Stein Roe Young Investors Fund (SRYIX)

The following is a list of recommended books:

- Donati, E. (2008). *The Ultimate Allowance: How to Teach Your Children the "Wealth Rules" They Need to Grow Up Happy, Wealthy, and Wise.* Santa Barbara, CA: Inner Wealth Publishing Company.
- Foster, C. (2005). *Financial Literacy for Teens: The Teen's Guide to the Real World of Money.* Conyers, GA: Rising Books.
- Lea, T., & Lora, T. (2004). *When I Grow Up I'm Going to Be a Millionaire (A Children's Guide to Mutual Funds).* Victoria, B.C., Canada: Trafford Publishing.
- Olsen, T. (2003). *The Teenage Investor: How to Start Early, Invest Often, and Build Wealth.* New York: McGraw Hill.

Another resources is a website that allows you to purchase one share of a stock so you can frame it and give it your child, grandchild, or any other youth as a gift. Visit www.oneshare.com.

Visit www.drmartymartin.com, the companion website and social networking site for this book, and go to "Children and Money" and download the Budget for Kids/Teens.

REFERENCES

American Express. (2010, February 16). Children Clued in to Recession and Family Finances. http://home3.americanexpress.com/corp/pc/2010/cci.asp

Capital One. (2010, June 17). Capital One Survey Finds nearly Half of Graduating High School Seniors Lack Confidence in Ability to Manage Personal Finances. http://phx-ir.net/phoenix.zhtml?c=70667&p=irol-newsArticle&ID=1439250&highlight

Cross, S. & Markus, H.R. (1994). Self-schemas, possible selves, and competent performance. *Journal of Educational Psychology, 86*(3), 423–438.

Danes, S.M. (1994). Parental perceptions of children's financial socialization. *Financial Counseling and Practice, 5*, 127–146.

Dunleavy, M. P. (2006, November 21). How teens get sucked into credit card debt. http://www.casb.uscourts.gov/html/care/Articles/how_teens_get_debt.pdf

Federal Reserve Bank of San Francisco. (2002). *Guide to Financial Literacy Resources*. http://www.frbsf.org/community/webresources/bankersguide.pdf

Hibbert, J.R., Beutler, I.F., & Martin, T.M. (2004). Financial prudence and next generation financial strain. *Financial Counseling and Planning, 15*(2), 51–59.

iVillage. (2010, September 15). iVillage and PASS from American Express (SM) Partner to Launch the Talk to Mobilize Moms to Talk to Teens about Money. http://americanexpress.com/news/pr/2010/thetalk.aspx

Magnarelli, M. (2011, August 29). Teaching Kids about Money: How Corporations Turn our Kids into Consumers. http://www.parents.com/parenting/money/family-finances/how-corporations-turn-kids-into-consumers/

Mandell, L. (1998). Our vulnerable youth: The financial literacy of American 12th graders. Jump $tart Coalition for Personal Financial Literacy.

Markus, H. (1977). Self-schemata and processing information about the self. *Journal of Personality and Social Psychology, 35*, 63–78.

Miller, J., & Yung, S. (1990). The role of allowances in adolescent socialization. *Youth and Society, 22*(2), 137–159.

Piaget, J. (1952). *The Origins of Intelligence in Children*. New York: International Universities press.

Rich, M. & Clifford, S. (2012, January 3). Signs point to tepid consumer spending for 2012: High levels of debt make rapid growth unlikely. *New York Times*. http://www.msnbc.msn.com/id/45852507/ns/business-us_business/t/signs-point-tepid-consumer-spending/

Roberts, J. A., & Jones, E. (2001). Money attitudes, credit card use, and compulsive buying among American college students. *Journal of Consumer Affairs, 35*(21), 213–240.

Sherraden, M. S., Johnson, L., Guo, B., & Elliott, W. (2009). Financial capability in children: Effects of participating in a school-based financial education and savings program. CSD Working Papers No. 0–16. Center for Social Development-Washington University in St. Louis.

Veblen, T. (1994). *The Theory of the Leisure Class* (originally published in 1899). New York: Penguin Classics.

Webley, P., Burgoyne, C. V., Lea, S.E.G., & Young, B.M. (2001). *The Economic Psychology of Everyday Life*. Philadelphia, PA: Taylor & Francis.

Wohlwend, K. E. (2009). Damsels in discourse: Girls consuming and producing identity texts through Disney princess play. *Reading Research Quarterly, 44*(1), 57–83.

9

Am I Searching for More Money or More Happiness?: Insights and Evidence from the Emerging Science of Positive Psychology and Happiness Studies

Happiness has been on the human agenda probably since humans were able to think about aspects of living beyond survival. It is probably fair to assume that happiness has been on your mind too? If you haven't thought about it for yourself, then perhaps for your loved ones? Or even society at large?

In recent years, psychologists and philosophers as well as mainstream media reporters have written about happiness. In fact, an academic discipline in happiness studies is emerging, with courses on happiness being taught at such world-renowned universities as Harvard and with peer-reviewed research being published in the *Journal of Happiness Studies*.

MONEY AND HAPPINESS: FACTS AND FICTION

Numerous studies in economics and psychology have investigated the link between money and happiness, wealth and happiness, and income and happiness at the individual level. This research reveals six notable facts to be reviewed later. The landmark study exploring the effects of money on happiness was conducted by Richard Easterlin. As reported in his 1973 essay titled "Does Money Buy Happiness?" Easterlin's first answer to that question was "no" in absolute terms that we shall discuss later in this chapter. This chapter cannot cover all of the research that has been done in this blossoming area but can offer you a limited tour presented in a concise, easy-to-understand way of asking the question: What is the link between happiness and money, wealth, as well as income?

Facts

Fact 1: High Income Increases Life Satisfaction Not Happiness

Daniel Kahneman, the first psychologist to be awarded the Nobel Prize in Economics, and Angus Deaton (2010) concluded in their article titled "High Income Improves Evaluation of Life but not Emotional Well-Being" appearing in *PNAS Journal* that high income results in more life satisfaction but not happiness. Life satisfaction is a more enduring characteristic in contrast to happiness, which is fleeting. Both are meaningful but differ in their degree of permanence.

Fact 2: Happiness Follows Investments in Time More than Investments in Work

It was discovered in rigorous scientific study that happiness results from spending more time with others not working to generate more money. Cassie Mogilner, the author of the study titled "The Pursuit of Happiness: Time, Money, and Social Connection" in *Psychological Science* (2010), describes the focus on time by harkening back to a classic written by Charles Dickens: "Still, the message is clear: Despite the belief that money is the resource most central to Americans' pursuit of happiness, increased happiness requires a shift in attention toward time" (page 1353).

Count your social connections not your pennies. Focus on relationships not your bank or investment account. How long does happiness last when you see a gain in your retirement account in comparison to enjoying a great time with friends and family?

Fact 3: Individual Happiness Is about Others Not Just You

Individual happiness is not only about you and your income, money, and wealth but also the income, money, and wealth of others in two ways. First, feeling "rich" is relative based upon social comparison theory. Second, as Americans we are not as happy if we know that there is greater income equality or more simply a larger gap between the haves and have-nots. Three researchers named Shigehiro Oishi, Selin Kesebir, and Ed Diener (2011) wrote a paper in *Psychological Science* titled "Income Inequality and Happiness" and found that this decline in individual happiness with an increase in income equality violates our sense of trust and fairness.

Fact 4: You Don't Need to Win the Lottery to Be Happy or Rich Either

In the study titled "High Income Improves Evaluation of Life but not Emotional Well-Being" (Kahneman & Deaton, 2010), it was found that $75,000 is the magic annual income number beyond which happiness (emotional well-being) hits the ceiling or the limit. In other words, if you are looking for more happiness by generating more annual income, then you are looking in the wrong place.

Fact 5: A High Standard of Living Does Not Equal Happiness

Higher income equals a higher standard of living. This is what many folks pursue. But does this necessarily translate into greater happiness? In a recent review of the research literature by researcher Dr. Biswas-Diener (2008), it was found that happiness takes place among those with low and high individual incomes. There is more to happiness than a high standard of living as demonstrated by studies showing that as economic growth increases in countries that happiness does not follow this economic growth step by step.

Fact 6: Happiness Is Temporary but Life Satisfaction Is Stable

Life satisfaction is not happiness. Federal Reserve Chairman Ben Bernanke gave the commencement address at the University of South Carolina in 2010 and talked about the difference between life satisfaction and happiness: "The story points out that, sometimes, happiness is nature's way of telling us we are doing the right thing. True. But, by the same token, ephemeral feelings of happiness are not always reliable indicators we are on the right path. Ultimately, life satisfaction requires more than just happiness."

Knowing these six notable facts about the relationship between money and happiness should stop you from focusing too much on the wrong things in your life if your goal is to experience more happiness and greater life satisfaction. This is the goal for most of us. Before concentrating on the nature of happiness, a quick review of these six notable facts is shown in Table 9.1 with a recommendation to achieve more happiness for each of the six notable facts.

THE NATURE OF HAPPINESS: BE CLEAR ABOUT WHAT YOU WANT OR DESERVE

Focusing on happiness can be tricky. Happiness has to be gingerly unpacked, much like defusing a bomb. Some of you may say, "How can you write on happiness with so much misery in the world?" You have a valid point. It

Table 9.1

Tips to Increase Happiness in Your Life Today

Money and happiness fact	Recommendation for experiencing greater happiness
High income increases life satisfaction not happiness.	To experience greater happiness, concentrate on daily activities and experiences not generating more income.
Happiness follows investments in time more than investments in work.	To experience greater happiness, invest more in relationships and experiences not working more to make more money.
Individual happiness is about others not just you.	To experience greater happiness, broaden your focus beyond you and your needs and connect with others who you care about and who care about you regardless of your net worth or income.
You don't need to win the lottery to be happy or rich either.	To experience greater happiness, stop wasting your money on the lottery hoping that the winning ticket will bring you lasting happiness and realize that happiness is available for you every day.
A high standard of living does not equal happiness.	To experience greater happiness, continue to earn a higher standard of living but don't assume that this will provide more happiness in your life.
Happiness is temporary but life satisfaction is stable.	To experience greater happiness, know the difference between happiness and life satisfaction and be willing to embrace happiness in your life.

is true; the world is a place of too much misery. For example, over a billion people live without adequate toilets, and hundreds of millions are on the brink of starvation from famine. While ideally we would like every individual on the planet to experience happiness, in this chapter, it is assumed that you can experience happiness and at the same time be generous, caring, compassionate, and committed to increasing the happiness of others. The two are not mutually exclusive. In fact, researchers have demonstrated that spending money on others promotes our own happiness.

Curiously, happiness is viewed by some as pathological or abnormal. Richard P. Bentall (1992), in his article "A Proposal to Classify Happiness as a Psychiatric Disorder," argues that happiness should be included in the American Psychiatric Association's *Diagnostic and Statistical Manual*. Bentall makes the argument that because happiness is statistically abnormal, then happiness is abnormal. This argument is a bit silly. Why? There are many sought-after things in life such as a great job or the right home or a specific feeling that are not experienced by the general population but are also not regarded as abnormal even if abnormal statistically. People generally do not live their lives based upon statistical definitions of normal and abnormal but in terms of an internal compass or shared values with like-minded, like-hearted, and like-spirited people in their community.

In his article on happiness as a psychiatric disorder, Bentall (1992) brings up an interesting concept about whether happiness is reactive or endogenous, that is, existing within regardless of external circumstances. This is a question that you should pause to ask yourself now and perhaps even write down the answer.

- Is my happiness reactive, that is, does it depend upon external circumstances such as a good income, happy loved ones, or freedom from pain or suffering? Or does my happiness come from within regardless of what is happening around me or even in the face of pain and suffering?

Write answer here:

DO HUMANS HAVE A HAPPINESS GENE?

Science is a long way from definitively answering this question. Researchers estimate that our genes account for about one-third of our happiness. Scientists measure happiness by using questionnaires that ask about our satisfaction with life and our subjective well-being.

What else accounts for our experience of happiness beyond our genes? Our environment . . . both external and internal. Our external environments involve situations and circumstances beyond our control and influence. Our internal environments are comprised of our thoughts, values, beliefs, habits, and long-standing feelings about our external environment. The genetics of happiness is like any other "nature versus nurture" debate, such as the question of how much of our intelligence and aggression is the result of inherited genes or external factors. The take-home message is that you may be genetically predisposed to exhibit happiness or not, but this does not mean that your genes spell out your entire destiny.

There is a poem that I often use in closing presentations that drives home the point that your genes are not your destiny, but rather your thoughts, words, actions, habits, and character *are* your destiny:

Watch your thoughts: They become your words.
Watch your words: They become your actions.
Watch your actions: They become your habits.
Watch your habits: They become your character.
Watch your character: It becomes your destiny.

After reading this poem, I receive enthusiastic responses from the audience. I am commonly asked, "Where did you get that poem?" or "Can I use it because I know somebody who can benefit from it?" or "Who wrote it?" I encourage my audience to not only share it with others but also to live it . . . live the message. So, I am telling you to live the message before sharing it with others.

Matthieu Ricard, a Buddhist monk and formerly a cellular geneticist, tells his readers that happiness is a habit and a skill in his book *Happiness: A Guide to Developing Life's Most Important Skill*. If happiness is a habit and acquired through practice, then happiness can be taught. If happiness can be taught, then it is influenced by our environment and can be nurtured. Who nurtures happiness in our lives? For many of us, our parents, teachers, mentors, and occasionally kind strangers nurture us. Nature versus nurture is the wrong way of asking where happiness arises. It comes from both nature and nurture. Even our sociopolitical values nurture happiness for Americans.

HAPPINESS IS A HABIT AND SKILL:
THE ROLE OF NURTURANCE

One thing is clear in the United States of America, and that is the American psyche has happiness encoded in its cultural DNA. "The pursuit of happiness" can be traced back to the Declaration of Independence: "We hold these truths to be self-evident, that all men are created equal, that they are endowed by their Creator with certain unalienable Rights, that among these are Life, Liberty and the pursuit of Happiness."

What did the writers of the Declaration of Independence intend when they wrote these words? Was it the pursuit of happiness in and of itself? Was it the pursuit of things that we believe will make us happy? The key lesson is that there is an expectation in the United States that the pursuit of happiness is a worthwhile endeavor regardless of how you define happiness. Barbara Ehrenreich, the controversial author of *Bright-Sided: How Positive Thinking Is Undermining America*, criticizes this pursuit of happiness for profit. Not only does Ehrenreich point to the focus of individuals and corporations on happiness but also organized religion (see Ehrenreich's chapter 5, "God Wants You to Be Rich").

Other than the tiny nation of Bhutan, nestled in the Himalayas, we are the only country to place the happiness agenda as a cornerstone of our political structure. Bhutan emphasizes the "delivery" rather than the "pursuit" of happiness. As recently as August 2011, the General Assembly of the United Nations accepted a non-binding resolution to make happiness an indicator of development along with other measures such as gross domestic product (GDP). Bhutan has had a gross national happiness (GNH) indicator for some time and advanced the process to get the United Nations to accept this resolution.

Beyond the politics and economics of happiness, there are others, including ourselves, who nurture happiness. You may hear a conversation between a father and a daughter reflecting this nurturing.

Daughter:	Why don't you accept the fact that I want to be a singer?
Dad:	Baby, you sing beautifully but I'm worried that you won't be able to make a living.
Daughter:	It's what I love and what I'm really, really good at . . . how come you can't see that?
Dad:	I can see that. I'm just concerned and don't want to see you working as a struggling artist. I just want you to be happy.

Or you may overhear a dialogue between a husband and a wife illustrating how couples strive to nurture happiness as individuals and as a couple.

Husband:	We've worked hard and built a wonderful life for ourselves.
Wife:	Yes, I never thought we could be this happy.
Husband:	What do you mean by happy?
Wife:	Content. Looking back over our lives and knowing that with the ups and downs . . . it was always, well, you know, happy.

My college philosophy professor who taught logic would say, "This conversation is not rational. This is an example of circular logic." It may be true that this conversation is not rational or even logical. Happiness is an internal experience that cannot and should not be judged based on logic or according to other people's standards. Argyle (1987) argues that people have a right to view themselves as being happy without being challenged by others. In short, it is acceptable to claim that you are happy. You probably know better than anybody else about your own happiness and even your own suffering.

Happiness is not solely determined by your genes, and you play a major role in creating your happiness and deciding when you are happy.

YOUR JOURNEY BEGINS: THE GREAT THINKERS ON HAPPINESS

Aristotle, the famous philosopher who today may be regarded as a life coach, believed that happiness is voluntary. In essence, nobody can make you happy. You have to commit to happiness. Aristotle went further, describing happiness as an end and as a general condition, not a fleeting moment of euphoria. For Aristotle, pleasure is an element of happiness. Yet, happiness and pleasure are not the same. Aristotle wrote about happiness in his book *Nichomachean Ethics*.

Aristotle's writing on happiness has lasted for centuries. Psychologists in the 20th century differentiated between hedonic and eudemonic happiness. Eudemonia is based on Aristotle's notion of happiness, or the "good life." In contrast, hedonia is temporary and fleeting. Life is a long series of moments.

YOUR JOURNEY CONTINUES: GETTING OFF THE HEDONIC TREADMILL

Researchers Brickman and Campbell (1971) studied a process called "adaptation." They found that when we want something and then attain it, we don't seem to be any happier in the long run. They called this the "hedonic treadmill." It's like walking on a treadmill, but not really getting anywhere or any happier because we are adapting to things. They studied lottery winners and found that a couple of years after they won, life satisfaction was not significantly greater for the winners. This process of adaptation explains why we are not significantly happier despite significant increases in the standard of living over the last 50 years.

At this point in this chapter, important questions shall be explored and a framework offered to begin increasing your own happiness in your life regardless of your net worth or annual income. However, there are two key assumptions: (1) you are not struggling to live from paycheck to paycheck, and (2) you are not wealthy either. Why are these two assumptions critical? Happiness is both created and experienced by many individuals along the income and wealth continuum as long as you are not dealing with survival and even if you are listed on Forbes's Richest Americans list. It is not a stretch to see how poverty is a barrier to happiness, but it is a stretch to see how being rich is a barrier to happiness. In the prestigious *Journal of Consumer Psychology*, one of the journals widely read and respected by marketing dynamos, the authors Elizabeth W. Dunn, Daniel T. Gilbert, and Timothy D. Wilson offer you a glimpse into why happiness is a barrier for the wealthy: "It is not surprising that when wealthy people who know nothing about wine end up with cellars that aren't much better stocked than their neighbors', and it should not be surprising when wealthy people who nothing about happiness end up with lives that aren't that much happier than anyone else's" (page 115). The key lesson from this quote is that knowing how to get wealthy and knowing how to get happy are not the same. The basic reason is that happiness and wealth are not the same. If you are working tirelessly, depriving yourself of sleep, exercise, and nutrition, and eroding the quality of your relationships to be wealthy, then you are bound to make yourself depleted, not happy. This is especially true if you hate or dislike what you do for a living. One of the major keys to happiness is knowing the difference between relative and survival materialism.

WHAT IS THE DIFFERENCE BETWEEN RELATIVE AND SURVIVAL MATERIALISM?

Oliver James, the author of *The Selfish Capitalist: The Origins of Affluenza*, distinguishes between relative materialism and survival materialism. Relative materialism is captured by the cliché, "Keeping up with the Joneses." Survival materialism, in contrast, is captured by the saying, "I'm hanging on" or "I'm just surviving."

Relative materialism can put you on the hedonic treadmill. It becomes like a nuclear arms race with a "stuff" buildup instead of a weapons buildup. Perhaps you feel tempted to buy an item because a new version has been released, or an innovative product just hit the market and buyers are lining up, and you don't want to miss out. Or perhaps you're visiting a family member or friend and think, "If they can have a 52-inch, high resolution, 3D TV, then so can I," even though you already have a 42-inch TV and can't really afford a new one. Relative materialism has no end. You will always be behind if relative materialism is the driving force behind your purchases. Setting aside the factor of money, the other danger of living your life based upon relative materialism is that you "live to have" rather than "live to be."

This question has real world impact. Living on and off in New Orleans for nearly 20 years, I have had to make fast decisions about what to pack in a car, realizing that after the wrath of a Gulf hurricane I may return to an apartment or house that is no longer there or one that has been damaged by wind, water, fire, and vandalism.

What would you pack if you had less than 12 hours to prepare your home for rain and 100 mph winds? Instead of just casually contemplating this question, use the space provided here to write down your answer. It's too late to buy a U-Haul, you cannot ship goods, you have to take what you can with you and put it in your car along with however many family members you have. And don't forget your pets. So, for most of you, people and pets go first, and then possessions. What possessions would you pack?

Write Your Answer Here:

Most people pack essential documents, including identification (birth certificates, passports, social security cards, etc.), and insurance and other critical papers needed to keep your life on track. After that, most folks pack some photos and items associated with their deepest values, ranging from family to spiritual. Many leave room for jewelry and art objects. Not surprisingly, people leave behind TVs, but take a picture made by their child; leave behind clothing, but take a treasured heirloom. Why? The former objects are replaceable and not highly valuable as compared to those possessions connected to the core of who we are. TVs and clothes are simply material objects that fulfill a transitory need at some point in time.

Once you get off the Hedonic Treadmill, catch your breath and turn within and check your internal compass or your own personal global positioning system (GPS). Richard Carlson, PhD, the author of two best sellers, *Don't Sweat the Small Stuff* and *You Can Be Happy No Matter What*, writes about our internal guidance system:

> You have at your disposal a foolproof guidance system to navigate you through your life. This system, which consists solely of feelings, lets you know when you are off track and headed toward unhappiness and conflict, away from healthy psychological functioning. Your feelings act as a barometer, letting you know what your internal weather is like . . . We recognize the powerful connection between our thinking and our experience of life. When we think, we immediately feel the effects of our thoughts. (2006, page 57)

To promote thinking and to develop your internal compass, Richard Carlson suggests you ask questions. Questions have great power. A single question asked at the right time can change your perspective—it can even change your life. Rather than telling you what you need to do to be happy in your life, our journey along the path to happiness will continue by asking you these eight questions.

- Is happiness possible if I am struggling to survive?
- Is happiness possible if I am responding to media messages?
- Is happiness lasting if I am wealthy?
- Am I sure money can't buy happiness?
- Is happiness all about me or my loved ones?
- Does the small stuff really matter when it comes to positive moods?
- What is my *real* reason for giving to others?
- Do you mean that if I like nice things I won't be happy?

Answering these questions with courage and brutal frankness will move you along your path or help you to create your path toward happiness. It is your path. It is your happiness. It is your journey. To begin, I would suggest that you set aside a week. On each day of the dedicated week, ask yourself one question and write down the answer in a journal or a notebook. It is through writing that you can create greater meaning for yourself. Writing also functions as a visualization practice, because what you are thinking and feeling is projected onto a page through linguistic symbols and images.

I would even suggest that you physically write it down in your own handwriting not type it into a computer. The benefits of writing longhand are prominent, as indicated in the article by Gwendolyn Bounds titled "How Handwriting Trains the Brain," which appeared in the *Wall Street Journal* on October 5, 2010. Writing by hand reinforces what you are thinking and even allows you to better express what you are feeling. Some even suggest that it may help sharpen the brain for aging baby boomers.

Most of us would agree that writing is intimate. Imagine it is your birthday and you get three cards in the mail:

1. An electronic birthday card sent via your e-mail with an electronic signature.
2. An actual birthday card sent via the U.S. Postal Service but signed with a digital signature.
3. An actual birthday card sent via the U.S. Postal Service but with a handwritten address, a handwritten message, and a handwritten signature.

If you are like most people, you would admit that a card written in longhand is a bit more special. Why? You may identify several reasons, but one reason was probably that a person who sent such a card really seemed to care because he or she took the time to actually write a message inside.

As you answer the following questions, it is important that you be honest with yourself. This is not the time to be efficient or even effective, but present. Now, it is time for the first of the eight questions.

Is Happiness Possible if I Am Struggling to Survive?

Probably not. If you are spending every waking hour figuring out how to survive, then it is likely that you will not be focusing on happiness. Survival is a lower-order need that takes a priority over higher-order needs such as self-esteem, belongingness, and happiness.

If material survival is the aim of the day, the struggle of the hour, the pursuit of the minute, and the anxiety of the long, seemingly eternal second, then happiness is far over the horizon. When are you struggling to survive, you are obsessed with satiating your visceral needs, such as food, clothing, shelter, and safety. The good news is that your physiological needs unlike your material needs are limited. You can feel full. You thirst can be quenched. There is an actual physical limit to how much you can eat even if you try to force down more food. Your body will send a signal to your stomach and you will feel increasing discomfort until you stop stuffing yourself. Is there a physical limit for satisfying your need to survival in a relative way, that is, keeping up with the Joneses?

Do you have a physiological signal shouting, "Stop buying more electronic devices or shoes because it hurts"? Will your body send a signal to your nervous or musculoskeletal system and cause you to become numb so that you drop your credit card and money or throw your muscles into paralysis so that you cannot physically reach for your money or credit card? No. What your body cannot control, you must control. Or you are out of control. If you are out of control, then some force outside yourself is in control. Part of happiness is about getting in control. Getting in control is about resisting the temptations of being bombarded with slick ads designed by consumer psychologists and marketing professionals armed with MBAs and PhDs.

Is Happiness Possible if I Am Responding to Media Messages?

Media Matters reports that the average person is exposed to 600–625 ads each day in a variety of formats (Our rising ad dosage, 2007). How much is 600–625 ads per day? A stack of paper for a printer or copier holds 500 pages. That's a lot of exposures. How can you not respond to so many exposures? Many of these ad messages are about buying something for some reason. Or buying for no conscious reason. Or buying for no good, rational reason. These ads are designed to stimulate your material urges.

Beside becoming a hermit or buying TIVO, how can we resist the pull of these advertising messages? Conduct a self-assessment to see how vulnerable you are to buying goods and services based upon media messages by responding to these three questions:

1. *Do I watch media while I am sleepy, hungry, irritable, or under the influence?* If not, fine. If yes, then make sure that you are fully present and mentally in control to decrease your vulnerability to succumbing to these media messages. Why do you think the gaming/casino industry serves alcohol for free?
2. *Do I watch media with family and friends, and do we influence one another to respond to the messages and then buy what we've experienced?* If no, great. If yes, then minimize how much you watch media messages with these folks and engage in a compact for both of you not to talk about the media messages.
3. *Do I have a pattern of buying what I experience in a media message?* If no, fine. If yes, then break the connection by not buying the item or experience at all, waiting for a longer period of time to buy the item or experience, or contracting with a strong family member or friend to confront you when you do buy in this way and reward you when you do not.

Is Happiness Lasting if I Am Wealthy?

The most interesting answer to this question is to determine what happens to lottery winners. Many of us fantasize about winning the lottery and then being able to be happy forever or at least free from the worry about money. Research from numerous studies has found that lottery winners do experience happiness. But their happiness is not sustainable. They experience short-term happiness. The reason why happiness is not sustainable among lottery winners has to do with the adaptability of humans.

As humans, we are very adaptable to changing circumstances both desired and not desired. Imagine that you are earning $50,000 per year, your IRA has a balance of $140,000, and you have $7,000 in savings and a $13,000 credit card balance. Life is not great but you are also not struggling with survival. You often play the lottery. On a cold, winter day, you hit. You hit big. You have to decide whether to receive $10,000,000 after taxes in one lump sum or $1,000,000 after taxes for the next 10 years. You decide to take it all—$10,000,000 at once.

Are you happier once you know that you have won the lottery? Yes. Are you happier when you deposit $10,000,000 into several accounts? Yes. Are you happier knowing that you can pay your bills and be completely out of debt? Yes. Are you happier realizing that you can quit your dull, boring job? Yes. Are you happier recognizing that you have enough money to do what you really love even if that means doing nothing? Yes.

As a big lottery winner, you do what most lottery winners do initially— you shop, you spend, and you do so without too many cares or concerns. You probably buy a new home, a new car, new clothes, and take several really, really nice vacations. You no longer ask about the price tag on anything. If you desire it, you buy it. If you want it, you get it. Over time, you discover that your desire and want of things are beginning to disappear because you can meet all of your needs, desires, and wants. Your fantasies are now your reality.

Yet, in spite of being able to buy anything you desire, you still experience sadness, nervousness, loneliness, and anger. How could you still experience these unpleasant emotions when you have won $10,000,000? Furthermore, you feel good about what you now own and what you have experienced in your travels, yet there is still a lack of fulfillment and contentment. How could you not be feeling content and fulfilled with so much money available to you? Could it be that happiness cannot be purchased once you pass the survival threshold? Most of the research to date suggests that happiness can't be bought. Money helps, but only to a point.

Am I Sure Money Can't Buy Happiness?

On a recent trip to Wellington, New Zealand, on a Lord of the Rings tour, the 40-something tour guide shared his story of how he left the turbulent, high-paying corporate world as an IT manager to work in the relatively low-paying, unpredictable tourism industry. Why would this bright individual say no to money and yes to a relatively risky, low-paying, and low prestige occupation as a tour guide driving a bus full of tourists? He loved it. He really loved it.

In his own words, he described how he found his passion. He also relayed how he found this path to happiness in his life. In his late thirties with a wife and children, he committed to internally discovering those attributes that he needed in his life to feel happiness and to feel true to "his spirit." He described how he dedicated a long weekend beginning on Friday night and ending on Sunday evening with himself locked away in a corner of his home, with all electronics turned off, and all means of communication disabled. He embarrassedly admitted that he drank quite a bit on Friday to decrease his inhibitions and to allow his "inner voice" to surface. He recalled, "This is similar to what the Aztecs and Incas did with peyote. To access the soul and the spirit. They used substances."

On Sunday evening, he emerged from his retreat having discovered a job that met 80 percent of his list of requirements. He knew that he could not achieve 100 percent. He was quite satisfied with an 80 percent fit. The lesson for me, as he told this part of the story, is that happiness is not about perfection. "Good enough" can get you to happiness. His list included the following requirements:

- Travel
- Talking to people
- Movies
- Driving
- Outdoors
- Photography
- Pizza

His challenge was to discover a job that could weave together 80 percent of these attributes. He discovered that a tour guide fit this portfolio of criteria. At the time, he was living in the Netherlands and made contact with several tour operators. In the back of his mind, he was struggling with how this might disrupt his family but yet he also knew that there was a lesson here for his children.

One tour operator offered this gentleman the chance to travel as a tour guide with one family for 28 days to Egypt. The dilemma was that he was scheduled to return to New Zealand so he told the tour operator about his travel plans. The tour operator responded, "I have a job in New Zealand, in Wellington in fact, are you interested?" The answer was "yes." Happiness was not only the job, but living a high-quality life.

For the skeptical reader who does not believe in stories and anecdotes, there are numerous scientific studies that conclude that money brings happiness up to the point of providing necessities (survival materialism), but affluence (relative materialism) has little effect on happiness as measured by subjective well-being.

Is Happiness All about Me or My Loved Ones?

Growing up in America, we are socialized to view happiness as an individual aspiration, pursuit, or right. I agree that individuals deserve happiness. What about families, communities, and nations? Families strive for and attain happiness as do communities and even nations, such as tiny Bhutan, which measures not just the gross domestic product (GDP) but gross national happiness (GNH).

To promote happiness beyond yourself while at the same time benefiting yourself, here are five tips:

1. Demonstrate kindness toward others without expecting anything in return.
2. Donate you time, talent, and treasure to others.
3. Help others in need.
4. Count your blessings and include others in your blessings.
5. Be present with others.

Is it fair to claim that giving to others causes happiness? This cannot be answered in a scientific way because most of the research is correlational. This means that the science is not to the point of declaring that if you give to others that your happiness is guaranteed. But the scientists will tell you that the more you give to others, the more likely you are to be happy. This is similar to what your physician may say about eating five fruits a day. Eating five fruits a day is statistically associated or correlated with better heart health but your physician will not say, "Eat five fruits a day and you will be heart healthy."

Putting aside science for a moment, if you feel or believe that giving to others increases your happiness, then the answer to the question "Is it fair to claim that giving to others causes happiness?" is *yes*. Furthermore, two prominent researchers by the name of Isen and Levin back in 1972 found that if you are in a positive mood, then you are more charitable.

What does it take to get in a positive mood? Not much. These two researchers, Isen and Levin, conducted an experiment in which people were given a cookie or found a dime in a phone booth. Guess what happened? A cookie and a dime boosted their positive mood. It does not take much to increase our positive moods.

What Is Your Real Reason for Giving to Others?

After reading about the benefits of giving to others, you may switch from retail therapy to boost your happiness to giving to boost your happiness. *Stop.* If you do, you are likely to find that this will boost your happiness for a short while. It will not result in any dramatic changes in the quality of your life. This is just like retail therapy. You get an adrenaline rush shopping, charging, getting a deal, and socializing with friends. You are all jazzed up. How long does it last? Three hours after you get home, a day after you get home, a week or longer after you get home. Not long. The same is true for giving to others.

Check yourself. Are you giving for selfish reasons, that is, to feel good about you or for others to view you favorably, or are you giving to really help the other person? You cannot do both. The longer term benefits of happiness accrue to those who are altruistically motivated expecting nothing in return.

Does This Mean that if I Like Nice Things I Won't Be Happy?

Absolutely not. Two researchers, Charles Carver and Eryn Baird, wrote an article for *Psychological Science* titled "The American Dream Revisited: Is It What You Want or Why You Want It That Matters?" (1998). They discovered that buying things is not harmful to your happiness but what is important is your motivation for buying things. If you really enjoy and derive pleasure by having beautiful objects around you, and others who you care about also find pleasure in these objects, and as a result you relate to each other in a more meaningful, connected, and deeper way, then you can argue that these objects are contributing factors to your happiness, but not controlling factors.

Reflect for a moment about a major purchase that you made recently—a new wide-screen TV or a vacation that was beyond your budget or a really, really nice dinner in a lovely restaurant that was too pricey. What motivated you to make these purchases? Were you driven internally to make these purchases, or was there some environmental trigger or external reward that motivated you to make these purchases? If you responded: I did these things because I wanted to impress others, I wanted to uplift my spirits, or I wanted to be happy, then you probably only achieved these three states for a temporary period of time, which is fine, but you should recognize it for what it is . . . short lived.

Yet, if you responded I bought the TV because I really love watching television on a screen that is wider and the pictures are more detailed and clear, which allows me to be fully present and engaged, and then this is an internal motivation. Or if you thought to yourself before enjoying that pricey dinner, "I love the tastes, the smells, and the atmosphere of this restaurant. It allows me to really savor the food and the experience while taking in every delightful moment." Then, this is also an internal motivation. Even if internally motivated, will this result in happiness or guarantee happiness? No. But they are one of the paths to happiness, even if only temporary.

YOUR JOURNEY ENDS FOR NOW: PULLING IT ALL TOGETHER

Now that you have answered and written down all of your answers to each of the eight questions in long-hand, it is time to pull it all together. Like the end of many journeys, you began your journey by packing your bags, doing safety checks, then you took the journey with starts and stops and some near misses along the way, as well as some good laughs and breathtaking views or memorable conversations, and as you prepare to leave your destination, you begin to pack up knowing that you are a bit different after taking this journey and that is OK because that was one of your motivating reasons for taking this journey along your path.

You began this journey along the path to happiness with these eight questions. Sit back and take a look at your written answers for all of these eight questions.

- Is happiness possible if I am struggling to survive?
- Is happiness possible if I am responding to media messages?
- Is happiness lasting if I am wealthy?
- Am I sure money can't buy happiness?
- Is happiness all about me or my loved ones?
- Does small stuff really matter when it comes to positive moods?
- What is your *real* reason for giving to others?
- Does this mean that if I like nice things that I won't be happy?

After reviewing what you have written for each of question, do you notice any common themes, patterns, or trends? Are your surprised? Are you delighted? Are you saddened? Are you elated? Pulling together these answers is both a cognitive and emotional exercise.

COUNT YOUR BLESSINGS NOT YOUR BURDENS: A GREAT WAY TO BEGIN AND END EACH DAY

Before closing this chapter, take an inventory . . . a gratitude inventory. Over the years, I have found working with my clients that acknowledging thanks and capturing what you are grateful for in your mind or on paper or on your tablet is a great way to remind you of the particular pearls of experiences, moments, and memories that make up the string we call happiness. Remember, happiness consists of not just a single pearl, but a multitude of pearls in a string of pearls. As you know, real pearls, which are far more valuable than fake pearls, are imperfect unlike synthetic pearls, which are perfect but fake.

Stop counting your burdens and start counting your blessings. Gratitude acknowledges the good in your life or the life of loved ones. And gratitude recognizes that this gift that results in a positive emotion or more long-lasting view on life is generated by more than you and you alone. Expressing gratitude or blessings connects you with others in the world including higher powers if you have a more spiritual or religious philosophy of living.

Shake out the kinks in your tired muscles, clean out the cobwebs in your old ways of viewing the world, soothe the roar of your running mind with flying thoughts, and take out something to write with you, preferably by hand. In the space below, write down what you are grateful for in your life overall and then write down what you are grateful for today even if it is the beginning of the day. Gratitude is both a view of life and a momentary state.

Overall, in my life, I am grateful for . . .

Today, I am grateful for . . .

What did you notice? Any patterns or themes? The beauty of capturing what you are grateful for on a daily basis is that it proves to you that happiness is within reach because of all the daily gifts we receive in our life. As the saying goes, "It's the small things that count." To be honest, you have far more control over the small things in your life than the big things in your life.

In closing, happiness cannot be guaranteed no matter how many books you read, seminars you attend, DVDs your watch, or coaches you work with throughout your life. Happiness is your responsibility. Happiness is your pursuit. Be honest with yourself and pursue happiness in your own unique way because happiness does not "rolls off the assembly line" like a mass-manufactured product. Happiness is customized. It is customized to fit you.

Be truly thankful for all of the blessings and gifts that are available to you and your loved ones. Accept the power of money in your life. Respect the power of your financial decisions and behaviors. In the end, it is not what you make but what decisions you make and what behaviors you decide to engage in along your path in your life. My hope is that after reading this book you can now make better financial decisions and engage in healthier financial behaviors for you and your loved ones. Now it is time to turn to the final chapter in this book but hopefully a new chapter in your financial life.

Be Well, Marty Martin

REFERENCES

Argyle, M. (1987). *The Psychology of Happiness.* London: Methuen.

Bentall, R. P. (1992). A proposal to classify happiness as a psychiatric disorder. *Journal of Medical Ethics, 18,* 94–98.

Bernanke, B. (2010, May 8). University of South Carolina Commencement Ceremony. Columbia, South Carolina.

Biswas-Diener, R. (2008). Material wealth and subjective well-being. In M. Eid & R. Larsen (Eds.), *The Science of Subjective Well-being* (pp. 307–322). New York: Guilford Press.

Bounds, G. (2010, October 5). How handwriting trains the brain: Forming letters is key to learning, memory, ideas. *Wall Street Journal*. http://online.wsj.com/article/SB10001424052748704631504575531932754922518.html

Brickman, P. & Campbell, D.T. (1971). Hedonic relativism and planning the good society. In M.H. Appley (Ed.), *Adaptation Level Theory: A Symposium* (pp. 287–302). New York: Academic Press.

Carlson, R. (1996). *Don't Sweat the Small Stuff, It's all Small Stuff.* New York: Hyperion.

Carlson, R. (2006). *You can Be Happy no Matter What: Five Principles of Keeping Life in Perspective.* Novato, CA: New World Library.

Carver, C.S., & Baird, E. (1998). The American Dream revisited: Is it what you want or why you want it that matters? *Psychological Science, 9*(4), 289–292.

Dickens, C. (1988). *A Christmas Carol.* (originally published in 1848). New York: Bantam Books.

Dunn, E.W., Gilbert, D.T., & Wilson, T.D. (2011). If money doesn't make you happy, then you probably aren't spending it right. *Journal of Consumer Psychology, 21*(2), 115–125.

Easterlin, R. (1973). Does money buy happiness? *Public Interest,* Winter, 30, 3–10.

Ehrenreich, B. (2009). *Bright-Sided: How the Relentless Promotion of Positive Thinking has Undermined America.* New York: Metropolitan Books.

Isen, A.M., & Levin, P.F. (1972). The effect of feeling good on helping: Cookies and kindness. *Journal of Personality and Social Psychology, 21,* 384–388.

James, O. (2008). *The Selfish Capitalist: The Origins of Affluenza.* London: Vermilion.

Kahneman, D., & Deaton, A. (2010). High income improves evaluation of life but not emotional well-being. *Proceedings of the National Academy of Sciences Journal, 107*(38), 1649–1693.

Mogilner, C. (2010). The pursuit of happiness: Time, money, and social connection. *Psychological Science, 21*(9), 1348–1354.

Nes, R.B., Czajkowski, N., Røysamb, E., Reichborn-Kjennerud, & Tambs, K. (2008). Well-being and ill-being: Shared environments, shared genes. *Journal of Positive Psychology, 3*(4), 1–13.

Oishi, S., Kesebir, S., & Diener, E. (2011). Income inequality and happiness. *Psychological Science, 22*(9), 1095–1100.

Our rising ad dosage: It's not as oppressive as some think. (2007, February 15). *Media Matters, 21*(3), https://www.mediadynamicsinc.com/UserFiles/File/MM_Archives/Media%20Matters%2021507.pdf

Ricard, M. (2006). *Happiness: A Guide to Developing Life's Most Important Skill.* New York: Little Brown & Company.

10

Are You Ready to Change Your Money Habits?: A Five-Step Approach to Making and Sustaining Healthy Money Behaviors

After reading the first nine chapters of *The Inner World of Money: Taking Control of Your Financial Decisions and Behaviors*, you have no doubt identified some financial decisions that need improvement as well as discovered some financial behaviors that need to be modified—for example, splurging on expensive dinners too often or not putting money into your 401(k) retirement plan. Knowing that you need to make these changes is not enough. What you need before you implement this five-step approach to financial behavior change is a "tipping point" and a way to assess your readiness for change.

YOUR TIPPING POINT: THE POINT OF NO RETURN IN YOUR FINANCIAL LIFE

Malcolm Gladwell is the author of the bestselling book *The Tipping Point: How Little Things Make a Big Difference*. This book presents three potent forces in creating change: the law of the few, the stickiness factor, and the power of context. Gladwell defines the "tipping point" as the point of no return regarding a change. Although this book describes social change such as the decline of smoking in the United States and more recently the increase in savings after the financial crisis of 2008/2009, the three core principles apply to individuals too.

1. The law of the few.
2. The stickiness factor.
3. The power of context.

The Law of the Few

The first principle, the law of the few, illustrates specific types of people who help tip the scales: connectors, mavens, and salespeople. The connectors are individuals in your life who put you in touch with resources of all types to help you. For instance, a connector would let you know about a financial planning professional or a group dedicated to helping people learn more about money or retirement. The information mavens connect you with the latest information, tools, and products, such as an app to manage your budget that you can load onto your smartphone or tablet. The salespeople in your life influence you to change. This is the person that convinces you to do that which you want to do and even do not want to do but should do. *Do you have a connector, maven, and salesperson in your life helping you to achieve your financial goals and change your financial behaviors for the better?*

The Stickiness Factor

To illustrate the second principle, the stickiness factor, Gladwell uses *Sesame Street* and *Blues Clues* to exhibit repetition as a learning tool. Not only is repetition key to any behavior change (including a financial behavior change) but so too is memorability or salience. *How can use memorability and repetition to help you make permanent changes in your financial behavior?*

The Power of Context

In discussing the third principle, the power of context, Gladwell uses the example of how cleaning up graffiti shows others that the larger environment is changing. Also, he points out in this chapter about the magic number of 150. He argues that groups under 150 are best for helping individuals change while groups larger than 150 can take on some toxic qualities. *Does your daily environment at home, work, and in other settings trigger you to make changes in your financial behavior even while you interact with others personally or online?*

If you apply these three principles in your financial life, then not only will you be making a financial behavior change but you will not be bumping up against strong headwinds. In fact, you will move even faster because the supportive winds of change will be moving in the same direction that you are headed based upon your specific financial behavior change goals.

The power of individual behavior change is great for those who are do-it-yourselfers; however, many of us are not do-it-yourselfers and really need to rely upon others or prefer to have others in our corner. Finding the tipping points as you make your financial behavior change will accelerate and solidify your financial behavior change. Why make it hard on yourself when you can make the change in a way that is less stressful and a bit easier although it will still be challenging?

The following pages will walk you through the five-step process of making a financial behavior change based upon a widely accepted and effective model of change—the Transtheoretical Model of Change (TTM). Before we proceed to describe the TTM and teach you how to use it, you ought to answer the following question: Are you ready for financial behavior change? Yes? Then, read on.

ARE YOU READY TO CHANGE YOUR FINANCIAL BEHAVIOR OR MONEY HABITS?

After identifying your tipping point, it's time to assess your readiness for financial behavior change. To answer the question "Am I ready to change my financial behavior?" it is essential to focus on a specific financial behavior using a SMART goal framework and then filling out the Declaration of Financial Behavior Change Goals worksheet (following the SMART goal framework).

When writing your financial behavior change goal, you want to make sure that you use the SMART goal framework to increase the chances of achieving your goal. Goal setting is a powerful way to clarify and plan your journey to change specific financial behaviors. In a nutshell, SMART is a handy acronym:

Specific
Measurable
Achievable
Relevant
Time driven

- A *specific goal* is simple and easy to describe. Set goals such as: "I plan to put away $100 per paycheck towards my 401(k)," not: "I plan to put away money for retirement."
- A *measurable goal* is one that has an exact result. Which one of these two goals is measurable? "I'm going to save more for retirement" or "I'm going to contribute $2,400 per year to my retirement plan." Obviously, the latter is more measurable because you have indicated a precise dollar amount.
- An *achievable goal* can be accomplished, but it might involve a "stretch." The research that difficult goals are more readily achieved than easy goals is crystal clear. However, if the goals are too difficult, then frustration will surface. For example, if you earn $50,000 per year and you

decide to save $20,000 per year for retirement, then this goal is very likely unachievable because dedicating almost half of your total income to retirement would put a too heavy a financial burden on your day-to-day expenses. On the other hand, if you commit to saving $5,000 toward your retirement contribution, this is a more achievable and realistic goal as it represents only 10 percent of your total income.

- A *relevant goal* is one that is important to you. There is some real meaning for you in achieving that goal. It answers the question: *So what?* If saving for retirement is not something that reflects your values or expresses your larger financial life, then this goal is irrelevant for you. A useful tip for you may be to remember the previous exercise on identifying your tipping point and assessing your readiness for financial behavior change. After going through these exercises, if the goal still has value for you, then you know that it is relevant.
- A *time-driven goal* is one that has a deadline. You well know that many things do not get done unless there is a deadline staring you in the face. Deadlines can be energizing and assist with accountability. So set a deadline, for instance, "By December 31 of this year, I will have contributed $5,000 in my retirement account for the year."

What does a SMART financial behavior change goal look like in real life? Take a look at the example below:

"By December 31 of this year, I will contribute 10 percent of my gross income every pay period to my 401(k) retirement plan with the goal of saving $5,000 by the end of the year."

Does this goal meet the requirements of setting SMART goals? Let's walk through this now to see.

- Is this goal *specific*? Yes, note the date and the two metrics (10% and $5,000).
- Is this goal *measurable*? Yes, refer to the date and the two metrics (10% and $5,000).
- Is this goal *achievable*? Yes, more than likely 10 percent of your gross income is a realistic number and one that may also represent a stretch.
- Is this goal *relevant*? This depends upon the person that set the goal and whether this goal has some personal meaning.
- Is this goal *time driven*? Yes, note three dates (December 31, every pay period, end of the year).

In summary, it seems that this goal meets the SMART goal requirements. Jim Rohn (n.d.), a well-known business philosopher, remarked, "We want to set the goals that our heart conceives, that our mind believes and that our bodies will carry out." Remember, goals are part of the process that moves you closer toward your desired and deserved financial life.

Below is the Declaration of Financial Behavior Change Goals worksheet, one of the more important rules in goal setting is to write out your goals. By writing out your goals, you begin creating momentum for taking positive action toward achieving your goals. Not only must you simply write out your goals, but you must also ask yourself this question: *Do I believe what I am writing or am I just going through the motions?* If you are simply going through the motions, then stop. You cannot fool yourself with regard to achieving your goals. Achieving goals takes work, inner certainty, and tenacity. Now is the time for you to write your SMART financial behavior change goal in the space provided here:

Declaration of Financial Behavior Change Goal:

I intend to:

Before reading any further, test your goal to see if it meets the SMART goal requirements by answering each the of the following questions. You might even ask a friend or relative whether they believe your goal meets the SMART goal requirements:

- Is this goal *specific?*
- Is this goal *measurable?*
- Is this goal *achievable?*
- Is this goal *relevant?*
- Is this goal *time driven?*

If you answered yes to all five questions, then you know that your financial behavior change goal is a SMART goal. Knowing this should give you the confidence and certainty to move forward, because SMART goals have a greater likelihood of being achieved than vaguely worded goals. If, on the other hand, you did not respond yes to all five questions, rewrite the goal until it meets all five requirements.

The next step, after writing your financial behavior change goal, is to move toward achieving your financial life goals by asking yourself this question: *How do I achieve my goals?* This five-step model is your recipe to bringing your goals into action and feeling pride upon accomplishing your goals. This simple model has worked for many. And it can work for you, but only if you are ready for change. *Are you ready . . . really ready . . . truly ready for change?*

AM I READY . . . REALLY READY . . . TRULY READY FOR CHANGE?

To make sure that you are ready to change your financial behavior, framed as a SMART goal, take the time to use a powerful technique which can assess your readiness to change. This tool is called the Readiness for Change Ruler (Table 10.1). Psychologists, coaches, and behavior change professionals use this tool with their clients.

The Readiness for Change Ruler is a 10-point scale beginning with Not Ready and ending with Ready. Plot where you think you are in terms of taking action on your financial behavior change SMART goal. Select a number from 1–10 that reflects your intent to change. Do *not* mark where you think you *should* be, where you think *others* think you should be, or even, where you would *like* to be. Place a mark where you are right now on the Readiness for Change Ruler.

What does your score mean? If you scored 3 or less, then this suggests that you are not ready to take action to achieve your financial behavior change goal. If you scored between 4–7, then you need to do some more "inner work" to identify more pros and fewer cons and also determine why you are seeking to make this financial behavior change. If this is the case, then please complete the Pro–Con Chart (under heading "Pro–Con Chart"). Lastly, if you scored 8 or higher, this suggests that you are ready to change your financial behavior and you should proceed to follow the TTM model step-by-step.

Pro–Con Chart

This tool is useful not only if you scored between 4 and 7 on the Readiness for Change Ruler, but also for those who scored 8 or higher. It can provide the latter with additional reasons for change. And if you scored between 1–3, completing this Pro–Con Chart may help you decide whether you need to leave this financial behavior change goal behind completely or just for now,

Table 10.1
Readiness for Change Ruler

1	2	3	4	5	6	7	8	9	10
Not ready				Thinking aboutt					Ready

given your total life picture. The Pro–Con Chart works by writing the advantages (pros) and disadvantages (cons) of embarking on a specific financial behavior change. This tool is not new. In fact, it dates back to Benjamin Franklin. In 1772, Benjamin Franklin wrote the following letter to his friend, Joseph Priestley.

To Joseph Priestley
London, September 19, 1772
Dear Sir,

In the Affair of so much Importance to you, wherein you ask my Advice, I cannot for want of sufficient Premises, advise you what to determine, but if you please I will tell you how. When these difficult Cases occur, they are difficult chiefly because while we have them under Consideration all the Reasons pro and con are not present to the Mind at the same time; but sometimes one Set present themselves, and at other times another, the first being out of Sight. Hence the various Purposes or Inclinations that alternately prevail, and the Uncertainty that perplexes us. To get over this, my Way is, to divide half a Sheet of Paper by a Line into two Columns, writing over the one Pro, and over the other Con. Then during three or four Days Consideration I put down under the different Heads short Hints of the different Motives that at different Times occur to me for or against the Measure. When I have thus got them all together in one View, I endeavour to estimate their respective Weights; and where I find two, one on each side, that seem equal, I strike them both out: If I find a Reason pro equal to some two Reasons con, I strike out the three. If I judge some two Reasons con equal to some three Reasons pro, I strike out the five; and thus proceeding I find at length where the Balance lies; and if after a Day or two of farther Consideration nothing new that is of Importance occurs on either side, I come to a Determination accordingly. And tho' the Weight of Reasons cannot be taken with the Precision of Algebraic Quantities, yet when each is thus considered separately and comparatively, and the whole lies before me, I think I can judge better, and am less likely to take a rash Step; and in fact I have found great Advantage from this kind of Equation, in what may be called Moral or Prudential Algebra. Wishing sincerely that you may determine for the best, I am ever, my dear Friend,

Yours most affectionately
B. Franklin (Labaree & Bell, 1956)

Benjamin Franklin in writing this letter to his dear friend Joseph Priestley offers several notable techniques, which we advocate when you are developing and/or using a Pro–Con Chart (see Table 10.2).

1. List your pros and cons over time. Do not rush through this identification process, but be deliberate and take time to reflect.
2. All pros and cons are not equal. As such, weigh them.
3. After weighing the pros and cons, step back and capture the big picture and determine whether the pros outweigh the cons. If so, then you know that you are (more than likely) ready for change regarding your financial behavior goal. If, on the other hand, the cons outweigh the pros, then it does not make sense right now to attempt to change. This does not mean that it will never make sense, but not right now. So, retreat, reflect, come back to the Pro–Con Chart again and see what you come up. Some even discover a new financial behavior change goal after engaging in reflection.

As you assess your readiness for change, there are some valuable lessons to be learned from physics and physicists, as discussed earlier but are worth repeating here. The famous physicist Sir Isaac Newton (1687) stated, "An object at rest stays at rest and an object in motion stays in motion with the same speed and in the same direction unless acted upon by an unbalanced force." This powerful statement recited and memorized in science and physics classes throughout the world is referred to as Newton's First Law of Motion. This is also often referred to as "inertia." This law also applies to human behavior change, including financial behavior change. Although discussed in detail in chapter 4 of this book, a review of how inertia works against us when making changes is worth the focus in part because of the importance of repetition, as captured in Malcolm Gladwell's book *The Tipping Point*.

To illustrate how inertia shows up in our financial life, picture yourself seeking to know how much money you have in your checking account to avoid paying overdraft fees at your bank. Your fallback or default position for many years has been to ignore your checking account balance hoping that

Table 10.2
Pro–Con Chart

Pros	Cons

you have enough and just pay the overdraft fee when forced to do so. You now realize that you are giving your bank your hard-earned money due to your lack of attention to your checking account balance and your spending habits. At this point, you have only been thinking about regularly checking your account balance and becoming more mindful of the how, when, what, and why of your spending but you have not actually modified any of your behaviors. Upon deeper reflection, you really do not want to invest the time, energy, and attention because you have never done it before, others you know don't do it, and you quite frankly don't need to focus on another behavior change in your life right now. As such, you say to yourself, "Leave well enough alone for now." This self-talk is not negative or positive but reflects your status quo bias or inertia. If you are experiencing inertia or the status quo bias about a particular financial behavior change goal, then you are not ready.

But once you are convinced you are ready to take on this change and feel confident of your success, or what psychologists refer to as having "high self-efficacy," then the time is right for you to read about how the TTM can help you achieve your financial behavior goals, which you have hopefully shared with others to build a wider circle of accountability.

THE TTM: A FIVE-STEP APPROACH TO FINANCIAL BEHAVIOR CHANGE

As you know, all behavior change, including financial behavior change, is rarely a discrete, single event. To change your financial behaviors, you move gradually from being uninterested (Stage 1: Precontemplation Stage), to considering a change in your financial behavior (Stage 2: Contemplation Stage), to getting ready for the change (Stage 3: Preparation Stage), to actually making the change (Stage 4: Action Stage), to turning that change into a new habit (Stage 5: Maintenance Stage).

The Model of Behavior Change, known as TTM, was created by James O. Prochaska and Carlo DiClemente (1983). Their theory represents the synthesis of over 300 behavior change theories used by psychotherapists. TTM was initially used to help individuals make health behavior changes, such as diet and exercise. Another way of looking at TTM is shown in the chart below, which uses an example of changing one financial behavior, that is, contributing to an employer-sponsored 401(k) plan or retirement plan.

Looking at this Sample TTM Chart (Table 10.3), you will note that it begins with shifting from not being aware (Precontemplation) of the need to contribute to your retirement plan to becoming aware (Contemplation). Then, as you move down the TTM Chart, after becoming aware, you can get ready (Preparation) to begin to make the behavior change. After you prepare, then you actually begin experimenting with the new behavior (Action), which in this example means contributing to your retirement plan.

Finally, after having some successes and learning from a few mistakes, you have developed a habit of contributing to your retirement account on a regular basis (Maintenance). It is almost as if saving for retirement is now an automatic behavior. How long will this take? Looking at the Sample TTM Chart, it can take about six months to start the new behavior and another six months before the behavior becomes a new habit.

Table 10.3
Sample Transtheoretical Theory Model Chart

Number	TTM stage of change	Another view of the change	Illustrative example	Time frame
1	Precontemplation	Awareness of problem or opportunity	Not aware of the costs or benefits of contributing to employer 401(k) plan	Not intending to take action within 6 months
2	Contemplation	Motivation to make a change	Becoming aware of costs and benefits of contributing to 401(k) plan with benefits outweighing costs	Intending to take action within the next 6 months
3	Preparation	Skill development to make a change	Participating in retirement seminars, readings books, and consulting advisors to learn how to make change	Intending to take action within the next 30 days
4	Action	Demonstration of change in actual behavior	Contributing a specified amount or percentage for each pay period	Took action and made changes within the last 6 months
5	Maintenance	Cultivation of a new habit integrated into one's life routines	Never considering ending the 401(k) plan contributions	Maintained changes for longer than 6 months

Stages of Change

This Sample TTM Chart shows you the five stages of change or the five steps to modifying your financial behavior. The five stages of change and the time frame, an important marker for setting realistic expectations and for measuring progress toward achieving your goal of changing a financial behavior, are both identified.

Reflecting back on the exercises that you have completed in this chapter, and for that matter the book, proceed to the next chart, which outlines the Stages of Change Five-Step Approach to Financial Behavioral Change. This chart looks just like the Sample TTM Chart except that it is blank. Based upon the financial behavior change goal that you have committed to making within the next 6 months, please complete the rest of this chart by answering these five questions:

1. *What* has to happen to bring me into awareness of the need to change?
2. *What* information, support, and resources are necessary to motivate me to make the change?
3. *What* skills, tools, and techniques do I need to learn how to make the change?
4. *What* will drive me to action and keep me moving toward my goal?
5. *How* will this new behavior become an old habit?

If you will carefully notice, none of these questions begin with *who* or *why*. The *who* is obvious. It's you. You are both responsible and accountable. The other obvious omission is *why*, because once you have deliberately set your goals or know that you are ready for change, then the *why* has been addressed.

More than that . . . you are the agent of the change because you are the captain of your ship. The famous British poet William Ernest Henley wrote the well-known poem "Invictus." In Latin, *invictus* means "invincible" or "unbeatable." The last stanza of this poem is quite appropriate for taking charge not only of your financial life in general but also financial behavior change goals:

> It matters not how strait the gate,
> How charged with punishments the scroll,
> I am the master of my fate:
> I am the captain of my soul.

Over the years, this stanza has brought me through dire, anxiety-provoking, and utterly depressing situations and circumstances, situations in which I could really only depend upon myself. Making changes of any type, but particularly financial behavior changes, is not easy. It is very challenging and can even be painful emotionally. Yet, even if it feels punishing, or you are punished by others for doing what you need to do for yourself, read this stanza as a source of inspiration, courage, and perseverance.

One of my clients struggled to withdraw as little as possible from her shrinking retirement account, recognizing that she had a fixed income, but her children manipulated her using guilt, pestering her, and whining for her to pay for this and that. It would not have been so bad, but her children were adults and financially independent, yet they still kept going back to momma for more money. I shared "Invictus" with this client and slowly she was able to accept the reality that she was the master of her fate and that she had to allow her children to be the masters of their own fates too. Are you the master of your fate? Are you the captain of your soul? (see Table 10.4).

Table 10.4
Stages of Change Five-Step Approach to Financial Behavioral Change

Number	TTM stage of change	Another view of the change	My financial behavior change goal	Time frame
1	Precontemplation	Awareness of problem or opportunity	What has to happen to bring me into awareness of the need to change?	Not intending to take action within 6 months
2	Contemplation	Motivation to make a change	What information, support, and resources are necessary to motivate me to make the change?	Intending to take action within the next 6 months
3	Preparation	Skill development to make a change	What skills, tools, and techniques do I need to learn how to make the change?	Intending to take action within the next 30 days
4	Action	Demonstration of change in actual behavior	What will drive me to action and keep me moving toward my goal?	Made changes within the last 6 months
5	Maintenance	Cultivation of a new habit integrated into one's life routines	How will this new behavior become an old habit?	Maintained changes for more than 6 months.

TTM has shown through 20 years of research that behavior change is a process, not an event. Although this stages of change model goes from step 1 to step 5, most individuals do not neatly and orderly proceed down from one to the next. In fact, many of us cycle back to a preceding stage, such as preparation, and a few of us get stuck in a certain stage, such as preparation. You are probably familiar with the classic weight loss and exercise story? It's one that has happened in my family.

Around New Year's Eve, a resolution is made to lose weight and exercise more. The local gym has a special deal on memberships and the local sports store is selling gym equipment at rock-bottom prices. We hop in our car, park as close to the door of the gym and sports store as possible, and sign up for a year to become members of the gym as we fantasize about how we're going to use that gym equipment every day before and after work and then we lug that heavy, bulky exercise equipment into our house or condo. We look at it in a strange kind of way and realize that we need a book, a MP3, a DVD, or a web-based tool to really learn how to work off those extra pounds. We look again at this equipment and we pass by the gym to and from work saying, "I'm too tired today . . . I'll go tomorrow" or "I'll go on the weekend when I have more time and energy" or "It's too crowded on the weekend, I'll go before work" or "I'd love to go before work, but I'll get sweaty and really don't like public showers" or "The best time is after work because I can get sweaty and go home and take a shower, but it is too late and I just want to relax not work out." Does this sound familiar . . . all too familiar? The moral of the story is that we may be aware of the need to change, we have convinced ourselves that this change is in our best long-term interest, we are all prepared, yet we never quite get to the action stage. Does this sound like Newton's First Law of Motion? A body at rest stays at rest. A body in motion stays in motion. If you ever wondered why cars and bikes have brakes, it is because once they get moving it takes a long time before they stop on their own. The same is true with us and changing our habits once we get going . . . really going.

How Do I Know Which Stage of Change I'm in Now?

Nine months after completing your Stages of Change Five-Step Approach to Financial Behavioral Change chart above, you may wonder if you have actually made progress and changed your financial behavior as planned. Prochaska and colleagues (1995) developed a simple way to assess behavioral change, and this simple assessment applies to financial behaviors too. This self-evaluation tool consists of the following four statements to which you reply *Yes* or *No*. Then there is a final step.

1. I changed my financial behavior *more than* 6 months ago.
2. I have taken action on my financial behavior *within the* past 6 months.
3. I am intending to take action on my financial behavior in the *next* 30 days.
4. I am intending to take action on my financial behavior in the *next* 6 months.

To determine which of the five stages you happen to be in now, follow the matrix in Table 10.5:

Table 10.5
Stages of Change Scoring Sheet

Precontemplators	Responded *No* to all four statements.
Contemplators	Responded *Yes* to statement #4 and *No* to #1-#3.
Preparers	Responded *Yes* to statement #3 and *No* to the rest.
Action takers	Responded *Yes* to statement #2 and *No* to the rest.
Maintainers	Responded *Yes* to statement #1 and *No* to the rest.

CULTIVATING NEW HABITS

Financial behavior change is not only about quitting habits that don't work well for us, but also about adopting new habits that do work well for us. The last step in Prochaska's TTM is *maintenance*. Maintenance is all about cultivating new habits. In the language of a famous social psychologist and thought leader in the area of change, Kurt Lewin, he would describe maintenance as "refreezing."

Kurt Lewin (1947), originally trained as a physicist, revolutionized the change management world by describing a three-stage model of change, beginning with unfreezing (breaking down business as usual), then movement (moving from the end of the old and embracing the new), and finally, refreezing (cultivating a new habit or maintenance). Refreezing is our focus here, because unfreezing and movement are captured in the Five-Step Approach to Financial Behavior Change, presented earlier in this chapter.

Refreezing seeks to make the new financial behaviors "stick" over time, in multiple situations and even under stress. A tool that Kurt Lewin developed that I use, both with individual clients and workshop participants, is a force field analysis. Assuming that you were an individual client or workshop participant, I would ask you to identify the facilitating and inhibiting forces for maintaining your new financial behavior or for cultivating your new financial habit.

Table 10.6
Financial Behavior Change Force Field Analysis

Desired financial behavior change: Write SMART goal here	
Facilitating factors	Inhibiting factors

There are four steps to completing this Financial Behavior Change Force Field Analysis.

1. Write down the SMART goal, which in the words of Kurt Lewin is the "desired state" (Table 10.6)
2. Write down all of the Facilitating Factors to achieving this desired change, such as telling others that you are going to make this change and thinking up ways to reward yourself as you pass through each of the five stages of the TTM model.
3. Write down all of the Inhibiting Factors that are barriers to achieving this desired change, such as not having enough time or energy or allowing other goals to overshadow this goal.
4. For each Inhibiting Factor identified, brainstorm and write down a way to prevent that Inhibiting Factor or barrier from keeping you from achieving the desired state.

By diligently going through the process of identifying the Facilitating and Inhibiting Factors, you are setting yourself up for success. Your success. What does it feel like when you achieve success?

MY NEW FINANCIAL LIFE: A CONSTELLATION OF HABITS

Individual stars make up a constellation. Individual behaviors make up ways of living. To begin your new financial life, focus on the individual stars, not upon the constellation. By focusing on one star at a time you will gradually reach the point where the constellation will look very different to you and others. As you design your new life or your new constellation, remember that everybody needs a North Star.

The North Star served as a guide for escaped slaves to break from the captivity of pain, suffering, and cruelty and then to arrive at a place where they were free and could live life more on their terms. Now it is time for you to put this book down knowing where to locate your North Star and live a life relatively free of financial thoughts and behaviors that are not working for you and the type of life that you desire and deserve to live.

REFERENCES

Fromm, E. (1973). *The Anatomy of Human Destructiveness.* New York: Holt: Rinehart and Winston.

Fromm, E. (1976). *To Have or To Be?* New York: Harper & Row.

Gladwell, M. (2002). *The Tipping Point: How Little Things Make a Big Difference.* New York: Back Bay Books.

Gladwell, M. (2008). *Outliers: The Story of Success.* New York: Little Brown and Company.

Labaree. L. W., & Bell, W. J., Jr. (Eds.). (1956). *Mr. Franklin: A Selection from His Personal Letters.* New Haven, CT: Yale University Press. http://www.questia. com/PM.qst?a=o&d=11628889

Lewin, K. (1947). Group decisions and social change. In T. M. Newcomb & E. L. Hartley (Eds.) *Reading in Social Psychology* Henry Holt, New York 459–473.

Newton, I. (1687). *Philosophiae Naturalis Principia Mathematica* (Mathematical Principles of Natural Philosophy). http://faithandheritage.com/2011/07/honoring-sir-isaac-newton/

Ozmete, E., &Hira, T. (2011). Conceptual analysis of behavioral theories/models: Application to financial behavior. *European Journal of Social Sciences, 18*(3), 386–404.

Pink, D. H. (2009). *Drive: The Surprising Truth of What Motivates Us.* New York: Riverhead.

Prochaska, J., & DiClemente, C. (1983). Stages and processes of self-change of smoking: Toward an integrative model of change. *Journal of Consulting and Clinical Psychology, 51*(3), 390–395.

Prochaska, J., Norcross, J. C. & DiClemente, C. C. (1995). *Changing for Good: A Revolutionary Six-Stage Program for Overcoming Bad Habits and Moving Your Life Positively Forward.* New York: Harper Collins.

Prochaska, J., & Velicer, W. (1997).The Transtheoretical Model of health behavior change. *American Journal of Health Promotion, 12*(1), 38–48.

Rohn, J. (n.d.) S.M.A.R.T. goals. http://www.appleseeds.org/rohn_smart-goals.htm

Ros, M., Schwartz, S., & Surkiss, S. (1999). Basic individual values, work values, and the meaning of work. *Applied Psychology, 48*(1), 49–71.

Ryan, R. M., & Kasser, T. (1993). A dark side of the American Dream: Correlates of financial success as a central life aspiration. *Journal of Personality and Social Psychology, 65*(2), 410–422.

Tills, T.S., Stach, D.J., Cross-Poline, G.N., Astroth, D.B., & Wolfe, P. (2003). The Transtheoretical Model applied to an oral self-care behavioral change: Development and testing of instruments for stages of change and decisional balance. *Journal of Dentist Hygiene, 77*(1):16–25.

Warren, R. (2002). *Purpose Driven Life.* Grand Rapids, MI: Zondervan.

Index

About the Author

DR. WM. MARTY MARTIN is a writer, speaker, and financial advisor/psychologist. He serves as a director and associate professor in the College of Commerce at DePaul University. He is also a financial advisor/psychologist at Aequus Wealth Management in Chicago, Illinois. As a member of the National Speaking Association, Marty speaks at conferences and training programs domestically and abroad, including Europe, the Middle East, and Asia.

Martin worked as an executive and manager in human resources management at the Johns Hopkins Hospital, Tulane Hospital and Clinics, and DePaul University. His employment experiences have enabled him to see first hand the psychological impact of money on employees, dependents, and retirees. He formerly served as an outplacement counselor and researcher at the National Institute for Occupational Safety & Health (NIOSH) as a visiting scholar in residence, where he studied the impact of downsizing on health and well-being of those laid off and the survivors.

He has written more than 50 articles for numerous publications both academic and professional. His work has appeared in the *Journal of Business Ethics*, the *Journal of Financial Planning*, and *Investments & Wealth Management*. His work has as a financial advisor/psychologist has been covered by the *Chicago Tribune*, *Kiplinger's*, and the *Wall Street Journal*.

Dr. Marty Martin is a graduate of Xavier University of Louisiana, where he earned his BS in biology with honors, and he earned his MA from Catholic University of America in psychology. He later earned a PsyD/MPH from Rutgers University, and shortly before beginning to work with clients on money issues, he completed his MS in Personal Financial Planning from the College for Financial Planning.

He enjoys spending time with his wife, Geral, and son, Armand, whether relaxing or taking an adventure to places such as New Zealand or Alaska for holidays. He is an avid roller skater and can be found skating indoors at some of Chicago's roller-skating rinks. He remarks, "Roller-skating forces you to respect balance."

For more information on the author, visit www.drmartymartin.com or e-mail him at drmartymartin@gmail.com.